EM

PARENTHOOD IN AMERICA

Parenthood in America

Undervalued, Underpaid, Under Siege

Edited by
Jack C. Westman

The University of Wisconsin Press

MT

The University of Wisconsin Press
2537 Daniels Street
Madison, Wisconsin 53718

3 Henrietta Street
London WC2E 8LU, England

5 4 3 2 1

Printed in the United States of America

In Chapter 2, material was adapted from "Culture and Human Development" by Patricia M. Greenfield and Lalita K. Suzuki in the *Handbook of Child Psychology, 5th Edition,* William Damon, editor-in-chief (copyright John Wiley & Sons, 1998) with the permission of John Wiley & Sons, Inc.
In Chapter 11, material was adapted from "Children of divorce: The psychological tasks of the child" as it appeared in the *American Journal of Orthopsychiatry* 53(2): 230–243. Copyright 1983 by the American Orthopsychiatric Association, Inc. Reproduced by permission.
In Chapter 16, material was adapted from *The Way We Never Were* (copyright Basic Books, 1992) by Stephanie Coontz with the permission of the Perseus Books Group for Basic Books.
The material in the epilog on the Family Resource Coalition of America was compiled with the assistance of Anthony Williams.

Library of Congress Cataloging-in-Publication Data
Parenthood in America : undervalued, underpaid, under siege /
edited by Jack C. Westman.
pp. cm.
Includes bibliographical references and index.
ISBN 0-299-17060-8 (hc : acid-free)
ISBN 0-299-17064-0 (pb : acid-free)
1. Parenting—United States. 2. Parent and child—United States. 3. Child rearing—United States. 4. Parenthood. I. Westman, Jack C. II. Title.
HQ755.8 .P377 2001
649′.1′0973—dc21 00-010976

Contents

Foreword

Families in the United States are under more stress than they can handle. In 1991, the National Commission on Children concluded in their report *Beyond Rhetoric: A New Agenda for Children and Families* that our society is not family or child oriented.

Parental stress is all too readily transmitted to children, who must learn to cope with too much stress early in their lives. One of the consequences of this stress is evident now in the increasing numbers of persons who do not have empathic consideration for others. Our society may well pay a terrible price in the future for this loss of capacity for empathy.

All parents, child-oriented professionals, and social policy makers should read this book, as it addresses the importance of support for families at all levels of our society. Its contributors are the best thinkers and researchers on parenthood. It is a milestone reference for all of us as to "where we are" and "where we would like to be." It can lead both parents and professionals toward a firm base for sharing their concerns about children.

This volume addresses ten parental stressors I have identified. These stressors have increased significantly since my children were raised in the 1950s and 1960s. They are:

- Isolation from extended families in communities where few people rely on each other. Rx: Parental peer groups focused on child development with the support of pediatricians, childcare providers, and parent organizations.
- Employment of both parents reduces time for each other, for families, and for assessing priorities. Rx: Place children and families first.
- Emotional and time split between careers and childrearing for mothers and fathers. Rx: Parental leave, family-friendly workplaces, decent childcare, and help for parents to face and resolve this dilemma.

- Lack of preventive medical care from pregnancy and infancy throughout childhood. Rx: Prevention outreach, pediatric care for all, emphasis on child development as well as physical health.
- Lack of optimal childcare and schools. Rx: Reach out to and include parents in childcaring and educational systems.
- Attraction of children to media and electronic game entertainment. Rx: Parental control of children's access to these diversions.
- Lack of family time. Rx: Assess parental priorities and set aside family times—breakfast, dinner, holidays, and weekends.
- Ethnic diversity treated as a deficit. Rx: Value diversity for the assets each culture brings to our society.
- Confusing advice from experts. Rx: Professionals value parents as experts for their own children.
- Lack of moral values. Rx: Change from valuing money, power, war, and aggression to religious and ethnic family values.

Can we generate enough commitment in this country to back up young parents as they face these stressors? In the 1980s, Bernice Weissbourd of Family Support America, Susie di Concini, wife of Senator di Concini, and I discovered how difficult this task is in the United States. We attempted to gather parent support for a national movement "Parent Action."

Although parents were touched and excited by the idea of "Parent Action," there was little effort on their part to join our coalition. We promised that they would not be asked to do more than lend their names and their backing for national and state reforms. But parents were "too tired." They did not feel the pressure that we did to engender support for themselves. Or, perhaps, they felt that public family support might lead to invading family privacy. At any rate, our effort to generate a movement to define and advocate for families' needs did not succeed.

As a nation, we are beginning to attend to two of the issues faced by the parents of young children: preventive health care to optimize child development and better childcare (more than half of the young children in the United States are in childcare that you or I would not trust—nor do their besieged parents).

Over the years, I have focused on shifting the professional paradigm of child development from identifying failures in parenting to an emphasis on parenting strengths. By placing strengths first, powerful opportunities develop for relationships with professionals in which parents can share their stresses and questions. These relationships can foster a parent's and, consequently, a child's development. From a transactional viewpoint, a child's development and temperament provide a shared language for parents and professionals.

Suppose that each visit to a medical person included an opportunity for parents to share their concerns about child developmental issues. Suppose that childcare also meant support for parents. We know that adults who care about the same child are bound to feel competitive. But, if we could turn this competitive passion around to give parents a feeling of support for their expertise, we might well find that their improved sense of competence will balance their stress. In turn, their improved self-esteem would be conveyed to their children. As children's self-esteem improves, their ability to master their environments, to face their learning tasks, and even their ability to care about others around them will be strengthened.

Parents are starving for information and the opportunity to share it with providers. In response to this need, multidisciplinary outreach programs based on my concept of "touchpoints" as opportunities for supporting parents in optimizing their children's development have been instituted in thirty sites. "Touchpoints" are predictable times in child development when a child regresses to gather steam for the next step in motor, cognitive, or social development. When a child regresses, parents often feel a sense of failure and regress with her or him. If a supportive medical or childcare provider can offer insight into this regression as a positive time for reorganization, a parent's vulnerability can be converted to a sense of competence.

We have found entire communities can become involved where "touchpoint" programs focus on strengths and use a child's development as a shared language. Childcare workers and parents form teams. Everyone feels the success of shared relationships. This approach especially offers the potential to help hard-to-reach, vulnerable parents.

We can turn our parenting failures around. We can and must build communities that care about besieged parents and that demonstrate their caring through action. Then more parents will be able to provide a secure base for their children. We know what to do. Will we do it?

T. Berry Brazelton

Preface

> Each of our children represents either a potential addition to the productive capacity and the enlightened citizenship of the nation, or, if allowed to suffer from neglect, a potential addition to the destructive forces of the community.
>
> President Theodore Roosevelt, Special Message to Congress February 15, 1909

The inspiration for this book was captured in a conversation I had with my eleven-year-old grandson, Matthew, and my eight-year-old granddaughter, Carly. I asked them what was the most important thing in their lives. Both answered without hesitation: "my mom and my dad."

Although most children are raised by the parents who conceived or adopted them and who live in committed relationships with their children, an increasing number are not. Too many children are unable to say with confidence that their parents are the most important factors in their lives. Too many do not know their fathers, or their mothers. The aim of this book is to bring out the unfortunate consequences for these children, for their parents, and for society—and what you and I can do about these consequences.

As we enter the twenty-first century, we are developing the capacity to think about the future outcomes of our present actions or inactions. We can readily envision the comforts and pleasures that money can buy, but we are only beginning to think about the kind of citizens we need in our society. We are faced with deciding whether or not we seek thoughtful, moral persons, capable of rearing their children and contributing to their communities. This is a crucial issue because of the current trend toward a self-centered, amoral, and exploitative citizenry.

At the core of the hostility, loneliness, and unhappiness that lie beneath the surface of our society is an inability to form and sustain intimate relationships, even during relatively favorable economic times. We no longer can afford to focus only on the socioeconomic and cultural factors that contribute to our social problems. Inadequate, disrupted, and strained parent-child relationships are more important. Donald Winnicott, a British pediatrician, pointed out long ago that "goodenough" parenting prevents social problems and that parenting that is not "goodenough" contributes to our social problems. We must recognize these facts and act accordingly to strengthen families. We must focus on parenthood in America with its multicultural roots.

If we do decide to aspire to a competent, moral citizenry, we need a paradigm shift from emphasizing material wealth to emphasizing the quality of our lives. Inherent in that shift is valuing the things that contribute to personal fulfillment in life. At the core of personal fulfillment is the capacity to form and sustain intimate relationships—to care about other people. That capacity is formed in the parent-child relationship in early life.

The purpose of this book is to identify the parent-child relationship—parenthood—as the fundamental institution in our society. It is part of an effort to use quality of life, rather than material achievement, as the central measure of success in life.

This book is an outgrowth of the Parenthood in America Conference held at the University of Wisconsin in April of 1998. Unlike other writings on parenting and the family, it does more than report the state of affairs. It brings the insights of research to bear on the practical aspects of childrearing and on policies that influence the context in which parenting occurs. It offers a vision for the future.

We deliberately chose *parenthood* rather than *parenting* as the theme of this book. *Parenting* refers to a set of nurturing, protective, and advocacy functions each of which can be delegated to others, as with childcare. Parenting functions also can be, and too often are, pieced together around children in foster homes and institutions without providing those children with parents.

In contrast *parenthood* is a way of life—a career. It is a role in life along with adult companionship and remunerated careers. It is "hands on" developmental work in which parents and children are bonded to each other and in which parents grow with their children. The responsibilities for managing other persons and for decision making qualify parenthood as a managerial position in business-world terms.

We need to clarify our understanding of parenthood because we live with dramatic and rapid changes. These changes lead to confusion about family and employment roles; about mothering and fathering; about love and sex; and about authority in homes, schools, and communities. Many adults and youth are drawn to exciting activities and seek freedom from responsibilities.

Many parents fear that frustrating children through setting limits on their speech and behavior will damage their self-esteem. These adults then reap the harvest of living with demanding, undisciplined children. In the past some parents tyrannized children. Now some children tyrannize their parents. Some adults seem to prefer to act like children rather than care for children. Because they have been traumatized in their past families, many persons experience anxiety in their present families and tend to avoid intimate relationships or to disrupt them.

Compounding all of this is the tendency of the generous side of our society to turn to childcaring institutions, schools, professionals, and volunteers to fill in when parents fail. There is a strong tendency to avoid holding parents as responsible for their actions with their own children as they are for their actions with persons outside of the family. This tendency reflects the persistent belief that children are the property of their parents.

Although the pressures of change have negative effects, they also provide opportunities for constructive developments. Many fathers now participate more significantly in their children's lives than in the past. Many women and men choose to give their careers as parents as much priority as their remunerated work, or more. Many foundering parents are receiving education and support. There is a significant trend toward shifting the helping focus from children and their families as freestanding units to children and parents as vital members of neighborhoods and communities.

Part 1 of this book deals with parenthood in the home. It portrays parenthood as a developmental experience influenced by cultural values and traditions. It describes the variety of parenting styles, mothering and fathering, and the importance of individual differences in children and parents with a particular emphasis on adolescence.

Part 2 places parenthood in the context of the community and the workplace. The importance of grandparents as principal members of extended families and the impact of the lifestyle of divorce on parents and children are addressed. The challenges confronting parents in the realms of school, health care, and childcare are outlined.

Part 3 views parenthood in the context of our society. It is devoted to identifying the difficulties parents face in a society that does not provide an adequate voice for their concerns. It offers suggestions about what can be done to create a social and physical environment that supports the rearing of our nation's children.

Double words that are frequently used together eventually become single words through common usage. In this text, *childcare* appears as one word in the same sense that *caregiving, childbearing,* and *childrearing* have become single words to indicate their acceptance as integrated concepts.

I encourage you to envision what our society would be like in the twenty-first century if every child had an effective parent and if parents felt supported by their families, neighborhoods, and communities . . . to envision what our society would be like if parenthood were a valued and supported career. This paradigm shift from society valuing only remunerated work to valuing parenthood as well would produce dramatic reductions in our social problems and dramatic improvements in personal well-being for everyone. It would make it possible for every child, when asked what the most important thing in his or her life is, to answer: "my mom and my dad."

JACK C. WESTMAN

Part I

Parenthood in the Home

When seen only as presiding over a child's growth, parenting can be frustrating and burdensome. However, when seen as an opportunity for personal growth for parents, parenthood is one of the most creative and affirming experiences that life offers. Although peers, adults outside of the home, and the media usually are more important than parents in influencing children's fashions, friendships, interests, and aspirations, parents are the most important influences on the development of their children's characters and values. Parents also determine the resources available to their children.

The parent-child relationship is the crucible in which a child grows and develops. Marc Bornstein focuses on the behavioral side of parenthood by defining parenting functions that depend upon the expectations parents hold for their children. These expectations vary from one culture and from one family to another. Still, there are fundamental parenting functions based on the universal needs of children. The first set consists of *material* functions that involve providing food, clothing, and shelter for children and advocating the fulfillment of the educational, health care, childcare, recreational, and organizational needs of children within their communities. The second set of *nurturant* functions meets the biological, physical, and health requirements of children. The third set enhances the *social development* of children in the form of affection, restraint, and modeling coping skills and values. The fourth *didactic* set consists of introducing, teaching, describing, and demonstrating ways of learning about life and the world.

Patricia Greenfield and Lalita Suzuki show how culture and child development are inextricably intertwined. From a child's perspective, acquiring cultural knowledge is an important aspect of development. From society's perspective, from birth children are exposed to a cultural surround that spans everything from sleeping arrangements and feeding practices to the child's eventual value systems, school experiences, and interpersonal interactions. In the United States, cultural diversity is such that parent-child relations are not limited to a single dominant model. Because the weaknesses of one model are the strengths of another, cross-cultural exchange can help to solve some common childrearing problems in our multicultural society.

The latest research on brain development undergirds Jack Westman's discussion of child development. Childrearing is a mutual growth process for both parents and children. For parents, it is balancing their needs and wishes with the needs and wishes of their children. Genetic factors play key roles in intelligence and temperament; peer influences are important in shaping children's interests and fashions; and parents shape the characters of their children and determine the resources available to them. Children need to learn that being responsible for themselves and for others is the source of meaning and purpose that brings fulfillment in life. Helping them do so is the satisfaction that parents gain from growing with their children.

Bernice Weissbourd notes that motherhood is a more clearly defined role than fatherhood in our society. Past roles are changing so that both mothers and fathers now are nurturers and providers. But mothering still tends to be viewed as synonymous with homemaking. For most mothers today, daily life is a balancing act between the demands of employment and family, between being nurturing and being efficient, and between feeling competent and feeling overwhelmed. Families, friends, and strong communities serve to lessen the pressures. Equally important, mothers deserve, starting from pregnancy, to have supportive policies and programs in order to meet the needs of their children—needs they know so well and often find difficult to fulfill. Daughters and sons also have different kinds of relationships with their mothers and their fathers. We are moving toward a time in which motherhood and fatherhood will be seen as distinct from homemaking and vocations, so we will be able to understand more clearly the unique offerings that mothers and fathers have for their children.

Roger Williams points out that the world of fathering is becoming more divided. On the one hand, there are growing numbers of men who view fatherhood as their first priority in life. They invest time in their family and demonstrate in words and deeds that they love, value, and appreciate their children. On the other hand, there are millions of fathers who opt out of fathering responsibilities. Boys and girls experience "father hunger" when they grow up with fathers physically or emotionally absent from their lives. Williams describes the variety of movements that are attempting to help fathers reconnect with their families, to place their wives and children first, and to hold fathers to higher levels of accountability for their family lives. Efforts also are being made to help adolescent boys transition into responsible and caring men.

When parenthood is seen as a mutual growth process, family life becomes an exchange of ideas, emotions, and power as children and parents learn how to respect and influence each other. Jack Westman describes how children become mature persons in their families by learning how to be responsible for themselves and for their actions, by learning how to tolerate frustration, by learning how to postpone gratification, by learning how to control their impulses, and by learning how to solve problems. Children develop self-esteem by being realistically affirmed as competent, unique individuals in an atmosphere of mutual trust and respect. The vital issues in family life revolve around intimacy, identification, influence, irrationality, and industry. In symbolic terms, the expression of these qualities of individual persons' "I's" makes it possible to fulfill the "we" of family life.

Robert Larzelere notes the distinctions between authoritarian, authoritative, and permissive parenting styles first described by Diana Baumrind. He calls attention to the contradictions inherent in the conclusions of cognitive developmental and clinical behavioral researchers, who mirror the swing back and forth between permissive and punitive societal attitudes. The cognitive view focuses on reasoning, and the behavioral view focuses on rewards and punishment. Neither takes into account the possibility that a combination of the two approaches might be advantageous. Larzelere presents evidence that a combination of love and limits in the authoritative parenting style offers advantages to both children and parents. He describes a *conditional sequence model* that incorporates degrees of intervention in the context of affection and limits.

David Popenoe shows that modeling is the most important way in which parents influence the moral development of their children. He calls attention to the fact that children are being thrust into our adult culture at an early age, just as they were during preindustrial times. He cites evidence that two-biological-parent families that regularly share activities, routines, and traditions are the most successful families in instilling moral values in their children. In spite of the inherent difficulties in doing so, he suggests, our society needs to revitalize marriage and reorganize employment so that committed relationships will be encouraged and so that parents will have more time to spend with their children.

Richard Lerner and his colleagues address the parenting of adolescents and adolescents as parents. They describe adolescence as a confusing time for both parents and adolescents. They view parenthood in the context of interpersonal relationships, the home, the neighborhood, the workplace, and society. They review the research that indicates that warmth, nonhostility, and closeness in parent-adolescent interactions are associated with positive outcomes among youth. Factors that are associated with negative outcomes are parent-adolescent conflicts, parental personal problems, divorce, and lack of supervision after school. Although family influences are not the only sources of problems, or solutions, for adolescents, they interact with other sources in both causing and protecting youth from problem behaviors. The authors also review the research on adolescent parenthood and call attention to the some $25 billion in federal funds spent annually to provide social, welfare, and health services to families begun by teenagers.

1

Refocusing on Parenthood

MARC H. BORNSTEIN

Each day more than three quarters of a million adults around the world experience the challenges and rewards of becoming new parents. Indeed, most adults are parents and certainly everyone has or has had parents. *Parenting* is a subject about which almost everyone has opinions, but about which few agree.

Many factors influence the development of children, but parenthood is the "final common pathway" to childrearing. Childhood is the time when the sheer amount of interaction between parent and child is the greatest, and when human beings are particularly susceptible and responsive to external experiences.[1]

Yet parenthood is under "friendly fire" today on account of strong secular and historical trends operating in modern society. Industrialization, urbanization, poverty, increasing population growth and density, and especially widespread dual parental employment constitute centrifugal forces on parenthood and on families. Society at large also is witnessing the emergence of striking permutations in family structures, notably in the rise of single-parent-headed households, divorced and blended families, and teenage first-time mothers and fathers.[2]

The family generally, and parenthood specifically, are in agitated states of question, flux, and redefinition. Because of these society-wide changes, organizations at all levels of society increasingly feel the need to intercede in childrearing and right some of society's ills vis-à-vis childrearing. This trend leads away from a focus on *parents* as the proximal protectors, providers, and proponents of their own progeny.

Yet parents are children's primary advocates. Parents are the corps available in the greatest numbers to lobby and labor for children. Few parents *want* to abrogate their childrearing responsibilities. Quite the opposite, virtually all parents *want only the best* for their children. Insofar as parents can be enlisted and empowered to provide children with environments and experiences that optimize children's development, society can obviate after-the-fact remediation. In the United States, about eleven thousand babies are born every day—a number equivalent to the population of a small town. Every one is unique and dear and special. Because we are all concerned about how these children grow and develop, we need to *refocus on parenthood.*

This chapter asks and answers questions about the benefits of parenthood for parents, the responsibilities of parenthood, who parents, influences on parenthood, the tools parents need, and how parents are faring today.

WHAT IS IN PARENTHOOD FOR PARENTS?

First, it is important to stress that parenthood has its own intrinsic pleasures, privileges, and profits. Parenting is not all giving.

According to a recent nationwide survey by *Zero-to-Three,* a publication of the National Center for Infants, Toddlers, and Families, more than 90 percent of parents say that when they had their first child, they not only felt "in love" with their baby but were personally happier than ever before in their lives.[3] Parents can derive considerable and continuing pleasure from their relationships and activities with their children.

Parenthood can enhance one's psychological development, self-confidence, and sense of well-being. Parenting children augments one's self-esteem and sense of fulfillment. Parenthood also gives adults ample opportunity to confront new challenges and to test and display diverse competencies.

In essence, parents receive a great deal "in kind" for their hard work and commitment. They are often recipients of unconditional love, they acquire skills, they gain an enhanced sense of self, and they even achieve immortality through their children.

WHAT ARE PARENTS' RESPONSIBILITIES?

From the start, parenthood is a twenty-four-hour-a-day job. Young children are totally dependent on parents for survival. Childhood is the time when we first make sense of and understand objects in the world, forge our first social bonds, and first learn how to express and read basic human emotions. Parents escort their children through all these dramatic "firsts."[4]

Children do not—and cannot—grow up as solitary individuals; parenthood is the immediate ecology of a child's development. Mothers and fathers, as well as siblings, other family members, and even children's nonfamilial daycare providers, guide the development of children via many direct and indirect means. *Direct effects* are of two kinds: genetic and experiential. Biological parents endow their children with a significant and pervasive *genetic makeup* that has beneficial or other consequences for children's proclivities and abilities.

Beyond parents' genes, all prominent theories of human development put *experience* in the world as either the principal source of individual growth or a major contributing component. Parents directly influence their children's development both by the beliefs they hold and by the behaviors they exhibit.

Parenting beliefs include *perceptions* about, *attitudes* toward, and *knowledge* of all aspects of parenting and childhood.[5] Parents who believe that they can or cannot affect their children's temperament, intelligence, or personality often modify their parenting accordingly. For example, parents who regard their children as being difficult are less likely to pay attention or respond to their children's overtures.[6] In this way, parental beliefs can foster further temperamental difficulties, because they can lead adults to treat children more negatively. It is important to remember in this connection that parents in different cultures or subcultures hold different understandings about the meaning and significance of their parenting beliefs and behaviors, as well as the development of their children.[7]

Perhaps more salient are parents' *behaviors,* the tangible experiences parents provide children. A few central domains of parental caregiving (referred to elsewhere in this book as parenting functions) have been identified as a "core" in the childcare repertoire:[8]

1. *Nurturant caregiving* meets the biological, physical, and health requirements of children.
2. *Social caregiving* includes helping children to regulate their own affect and emotions, and influencing the communication styles and interpersonal repertoires that children use to form meaningful and sustained relationships with others. Through positive feedback, openness and negotiation, listening, and emotional closeness, parents can make their children feel valued, accepted, and approved of.
3. *Didactic caregiving* consists of the variety of strategies parents use to stimulate children to engage and understand the environment and to enter the world of learning. Didactic caregiving means introducing, mediating, and interpreting the external world. It means teaching, describing, and demonstrating as well as provoking or providing opportunities to observe, to imitate, and to learn.

4. *Material caregiving* includes the ways in which parents provision, organize, and arrange the child's physical world, including home and local environments.

These caregiving beliefs and behaviors are *direct* effects of parenting. *Indirect effects* are more subtle and less noticeable than direct effects, but perhaps no less meaningful. Parents indirectly influence their children by virtue of their influence on each other, for example, by marital support and communication.[9] Parents' attitudes about their spouses and their marriages can modify the quality of their interactions with their children and, in turn, their children's adjustment and development. Intimate support from husbands enhances maternal competence, family dynamics, and child outcomes. Women who report having supportive relationships with husbands (or lovers or grandparents) are more attentive and sensitively responsive to their children.

In contrast, quarreling parents are likely to convey confusing messages to their children, have less time for and become less involved in their children's lives, and engage in more hostile relationships with their children. In short, parents who feel negatively about their marriages (like those who feel negatively about themselves) tend to act with their children in negative, inattentive, and nonresponsive ways.

Successful parenting entails affective components (in terms of commitment, empathy, and positive regard for children, for example) as well as cognitive components (the how, what, and why of caring for children). Moreover, the path to achieving satisfaction and success in parenting is not linear or incremental but tends to be cyclic. Different tasks are more or less salient and challenging at different times in the course of childrearing.

Parenthood is a process that formally begins during or before pregnancy and continues through the balance of one's life span: practically speaking, *once a parent, always a parent.* It is obvious to say that parenthood is central to childhood, to child development, and to society's long-term investment in children. But parenthood also is a critical component of adulthood.

WHO ARE PARENTS?

In the minds of many, the role of *mother* is unique, universal, and unequivocally primary in the development of young children.[10] Cross-cultural surveys attest to the primacy of biological mothers in all forms of caregiving. Theorists, researchers, and clinicians have in the past typically concerned themselves with motherhood, rather than parenthood, in recognition of this fact, even if historically fathers' social and legal claims and responsibilities on children were preeminent.[11]

The recent *Zero-to-Three* survey found that, although the days when most women "stay home" with children are in the past, fully 65 percent of America's mothers—whether working outside the home or not—continue to bear the largest part of the day-to-day responsibilities of childrearing; only 25 percent say that the mother and father share these duties equally, and a meager 10 percent indicate that fathers do most of the basic caregiving each day.[12]

Western industrialized nations have witnessed some increases in the amount of time fathers spend with their children.[13] But in everyday life, fathers still assume relatively little responsibility for childcare and childrearing. That said, research suggests that mothers and fathers tend to interact with, and care for, their children in complementary ways; that is, they divide and share the labors of caregiving and engage children by taking responsibility for different types of interactions. For example, mothers are more likely to kiss, hug, talk to, smile at, and hold babies, whereas fathers are more likely to engage in physical playful interactions.[14] Various constraints and differences in interests and abilities no doubt cause mothers and fathers to devote different amounts of time and resources to their children in different domains, such as school, sports, or the household.

Beyond mother and father, pluralistic caregiving arrangements are common and, as we know, significant in the lives of today's children. Hillary Clinton includes a variety of caring adults in the "village" of critical persons responsible for and responsive to children.[15] Of children under age three, 60 percent are cared for on a regular basis by someone other than their parents; 80 percent have had at least one nonparental careprovider; and 50 percent have had two or more.[16] Thus, many individuals "parent" young children.[17]

Sources of nonparental childcare divide roughly into four types. The first (and unfortunately not infrequent) childcare arrangement used throughout the world—in spite of the hazards involved—is *nonexistent childcare.* Children are simply left unattended while their mothers and fathers are otherwise occupied. Second is childcare provided by other members of the parents' *household* or *kin group,* including siblings, grandparents, aunts, and the like. The third source of nonparental care involves reciprocal exchanges of childcare among members of a *residential group* (usually without any financial compensation). The fourth type is a combination of *formal and informal childcare services:* childcare is provided for a fee at home (either the home of the child or the provider) or in an institutional setting. The implications of these increasingly common and diverse patterns of early "parenting" relationships for children's development are still unclear.

WHAT FACTORS INFLUENCE PARENTING?

The origins of maternal and paternal beliefs and behaviors are extremely complex, but certain factors seem to be of paramount importance.[18]

First, some aspects of parenting appear initially to arise out of *biological processes* associated with pregnancy and parturition.[19] Pregnancy in human beings causes the release of certain hormones thought to be involved in the development and expression of protective, nurturant, and responsive feelings toward offspring. Prenatal biological events—age, diet, and stress, as well as other factors, such as disease, exposure to environmental toxins, and even birth anesthetics—all affect postnatal parenting as well as child development.[20]

Some characteristics of parenting may be "wired" into our biological makeup.[21] The ethologist Konrad Lorenz contended that structural characteristics of the very young, such as facial features, excite feelings of affection and solicitude in mature members of different species. Parents commonly speak to babies even though they know that babies cannot understand language and will not respond, and parents and nonparents alike even speak to babies in a special voice register, which is specifically geared to promote language learning and understanding.[22]

Second, parenting calls upon enduring *personality* and *associated characteristics,* including intelligence, traits and attitudes, motivation to become involved with children, and childcare knowledge and skills. Some characteristics that favor good parenting include general well-being, empathic awareness, predictability, responsiveness, and emotional availability. More educated parents tend to engage in the authoritative style of childrearing (see chapter 7).[23]

On the other hand, negative characteristics of personality, such as self-centeredness and depression, whether transient or permanent, typically affect parenting adversely.[24] Mothers with elevated depression are more likely to ignore, protest, or verbally attack their children in problem-solving situations, and even subclinical depression is negatively related to mothers' communication of nurturance and trust. Mothers who are depressed generally have a difficult time providing nurturant care to children and become frustrated and raise their voices more.

Third, *characteristics of children* influence parenting and, in turn, children's own development. These characteristics may be more obvious ones, like age, gender, or physical appearance, or they may be more subtle ones, like temperament and other individual differences. Children's temperaments affect parents' confidence, management styles, levels of involvement, and control strategies.[25]

Fourth, *contextual factors* motivate and help to define parental beliefs and behaviors.[26] Family configuration, social support, economic class, and cultural worldview encourage divergent patterns of parenting perceptions and practices.[27] The family life of a later-born child is not the same as that of the firstborn, for example, for many reasons including parents' changing experiences and the new family constellation.[28]

Mothers of different socioeconomic status (SES) groups might behave similarly in certain parenting domains; however, SES, through environment or education, also orders home circumstances and multiple attitudes and actions of parents toward children.[29] Higher-compared to lower-SES parents typically provide children with more opportunities for variety in daily stimulation, more appropriate play materials, and more language. The *Zero-to-Three* survey confirms that young, low-income, and single parents feel relatively *un*prepared for their daunting new roles as caregivers.[30]

Furthermore, virtually all aspects of parenting children, whether beliefs or behaviors, are shaped by cultural traditions.[31] Generational, social, and media images of parenting, children, and family life, handed-down or ready-made, play significant roles in helping people form their parenting beliefs and guide their parenting behaviors. Parents from different cultures vary in the ages at which they expect children will reach different milestones or acquire different competencies, and they differ in their opinions about the significance of certain competencies for children's success and adjustment.

WHAT TOOLS DO PARENTS NEED?

The *family* is the principal source of care and development of the child,[32] and we need to refocus on parents in this practical regard. Contemporary parenting programs are often guided by three assumptions: (1) Parents are usually the most consistent and caring people in the lives of their children; (2) if parents are provided with knowledge, skills, and supports, they can respond more positively and effectively to their children; and (3) parents' own emotional and physical needs must be met if they are to respond to their children. The following tools can help to address these parenting requirements:

Tool 1: Parents benefit from knowledge of the normative patterns and stages of children's physical, verbal, cognitive, emotional, and social development, as well as their nutrition and health. Concretely, parents' understanding the patterns and processes of their children's growth helps them to develop more realistic expectations of the stages of child development and the requisite skills for children achieving more mature competencies.

Tool 2: Parents need to know how to observe young children. Child watching helps us to understand a child's level of development in relation to what we want our children to learn or to accomplish. Parents need information *and* observation skills to help them discover the match between their child's ability or readiness and ways and means to help their child achieve developmental goals. Observing also allows parents to spot potential trouble early and may help parents handle a child's daily frustrations more skillfully.

Tool 3: Parents need all manner of insights for managing their children's behaviors. Knowledge and skills regarding alternative methods of discipline and problem avoidance are basic. Parents' knowing how to implement a variety of positive rewards can help their children more fully enjoy and appreciate the exploration and struggles required in mastering new skills.

Tool 4: Knowing how to take advantage of settings, routines, and activities to create learning and problem-solving opportunities enhances parenthood and childhood. Parents generally realize that they exercise important influences on their children's development but often do not fully appreciate how their day-to-day interactions affect their children. They need to understand the impact they have on their children's lives through the simplest things: their attention, expressed pleasure, listening, and interest. These activities nourish a child's growing sense of self, just as food nourishes a child's growing body.

Tool 5: Parents need patience, flexibility, and to be goal-oriented, and they must command an ability to extract pleasure from their encounters with children. We do not remind ourselves of those parental positives often enough, so refocusing on parenting promises to be useful in practice and policy arenas.

Tool 6: Parents need to use formal and informal support systems, extended families, community ties with friends and neighbors, work sites, and social, educational, and medical institutions, as well as participating in their cultural traditions and rituals.

Beyond the nucleus, all families are also embedded in, influence, and are themselves affected by larger social systems.[33] To fathom the nature of parenthood and parent-child relationships within families requires a *multivariate* and *dynamic* stance.

It is only through the *multivariate* approach that multiple circumstances can be taken into consideration simultaneously so that we can appreciate individual-, dyadic-, and family-level aspects within the family and accurately reflect the embeddedness of the family within its many relevant extrafamilial systems as well.

The *dynamic* approach involves the different developmental trajectories of individuals in the family. Parenting a child is akin to trying to "hit a moving target," the ever-changing child developing in fits and starts at his or her own pace. Parents and children stimulate and provide feedback to one another. In order to maintain appropriate influence and guidance, parents must effectively adjust their interactions, cognitions, emotions, affections, and strategies for exerting influence to the age-graded activities, abilities, and experiences of children.

HOW ARE PARENTS FARING?

In everyday life, parenting children does not always go well. Infanticide was practiced historically, and although it is rare today, it occurs. But, short of that extreme, too many children live in poverty, are the common victims of abuse and neglect, are born drug addicted, or are never immunized. For these and other reasons, contemporary parenting has witnessed an explosive growth in information and support programs.[34]

As a consequence of contemporary social and cultural changes, most notably dual-parent employment,[35] a demand for high-quality community-based childcare services has burgeoned,[36] and nonfamilial caregivers in these settings have assumed responsibility for meeting children's developmental need—essentially for preparing children for their future in society.

Parenthood is our least expensive and best resource for ensuring viable children and a viable future for our children. This is not to trivialize the daunting problems that parents face: In the 1940s and 1950s chewing gum and talking out of turn were the classroom problems listed by teachers as most prominent; today drug abuse and violence—as extreme as the shootings at Pearl, Paducah, Jonesboro, Springfield, and Littleton—top their list.

Almost two in five parents (37 percent in the *Zero-to-Three* survey) say that they do not spend as much quality time with their children as they would like to.[37] Parents typically complain that they have too many balls in the air: working, errands, multiple commitments.

The costs of inadequate parenting and failures to address problems in family life are high. Children lacking appropriate care are exposed more frequently to illness, poor nutrition, stress, and unstimulating environments. Children need to receive deep psychological messages about how special and precious they are. Just feeding and clothing a child will not produce the kind of person who will be nurturant in the next generation. The long-term costs can be measured in terms of school dropouts, unemployment, delinquency, and the intergenerational perpetuation of poverty and low self-esteem.

CONCLUSION

Parents hope for much in their interactions with their children. They promote their children's mental development through the structures they create and the meanings they place on those structures. They foster their children's emotional regulation, verbal competence, development of self, social sensitivities, and participation in meaningful relationships and experiences outside of the family through the models they portray and the values they display. As children move out of the nest, parenthood ultimately means having facilitated a child's self-confidence, capacity for intimacy, achievement motivation, pleasure in play and work, friendships with peers, and continuing academic success and fulfillment.

Family experiences are thought to exercise a major impact during the early years of life. The parent-child relationship constitutes the crucible in which children initially grow and develop. A full understanding of what it means to parent a child, however, depends on the ecology in which that parenting takes place. Family constitution, context, social class, and cultural variation also affect patterns of childrearing and exert salient influences on the ways in which young children are reared and what is expected of them as they grow. These early relationships all ensure that the "parenting" which children experience is rich and appropriate.

Parenthood requires immense amounts of time-consuming effort. In parenting, we sometimes do not know what to do, but we can find out; sometimes, we do know what to do but still do not get into the trenches and do it. Of course, human development is too subtle, dynamic, and intricate for us to assert that parenthood *alone* determines the course and outcome of ontogeny; stature in adulthood is shaped by genetic endowment, the actions of individuals themselves, peer influences, and experiences that take place after childhood. Parenthood does not fix the route or terminus of a child's development. But it makes sense that effects have causes—and that the start exerts an impact on the end. There are compelling reasons to *refocus on parenthood.*

NOTES

This chapter summarizes selected aspects of my research, and portions of the text have appeared in my previous scientific publications. I thank B. Wright for assistance.

1. Bornstein, M. H., & Lamb, M. E. (1992) *Development in infancy: An introduction* (3e). New York: McGraw-Hill.

2. Brooks-Gunn, J., & Chase-Lansdale, P. L. (1995) Adolescent parenthood. In M. H. Bornstein (ed.), *Handbook of parenting*. Mahwah, N.J.: Erlbaum, vol. 3, pp. 113–149; Hetherington, E. M., & Arasteh, J. D. (eds.) (1988) *Impact of divorce, single parenting, and stepparenting of children*. Hillsdale, N.J.: Erlbaum; Hetherington, E. M., & Stanley-Hagan, M. M. (1995) Parenting in divorced and remarried families. In M. H. Bornstein (ed.), *Handbook of parenting*. Mahwah, N.J.: Erlbaum, vol. 3, pp. 233–254; Patterson, C. J. (1995) Lesbian and gay parenthood. In M. H. Bornstein (ed.), *Handbook of parenting*. Mahwah, N.J.: Erlbaum, vol. 3, pp. 255–274; and Weinraub, M., & Gringlas, M. B. (1995) Single parenthood. In M. H. Bornstein (ed.), *Handbook of parenting*. Mahwah, N.J.: Erlbaum, vol. 3, pp. 255–274.

3. *Zero-to-Three* (1997) Key findings for a nationwide survey among parents of zero-to-three-year-olds. Conducted by Peter D. Hart Research Associates. Baltimore, Md.: National Center for Infants, Toddlers and Families.

4. Bornstein, M. H. (1995) Parenting infants. In M. H. Bornstein (ed.), *Handbook of parenting*. Mahwah, N.J.: Erlbaum, vol. 1, pp. 3–39.

5. Goodnow, J. J. (1995) Parents' knowledge and expectations. In M. H. Bornstein (ed.), *Handbook of parenting*. Mahwah, N.J.: Erlbaum, vol. 3, pp. 305–332; Holden, G. W. (1995) Parental attitudes toward childrearing. In M. H. Bornstein (ed.), *Handbook of parenting*. Mahwah, N.J.: Erlbaum, vol. 3, pp. 359–392; and McGillicuddy–De Lisi, A. V., & Sigel, I. E. (1995) Parental beliefs. In M. H. Bornstein (ed.), *Handbook of parenting*. Mahwah, N.J.: Erlbaum, vol. 3, pp. 333–358.

6. Sanson, A., & Rothbart, M. K. (1995) Child temperament and parenting. In M. H. Bornstein (ed.), *Handbook of parenting*. Mahwah, N.J.: Erlbaum, vol. 4, pp. 299–321.

7. Most contemporary research about parenthood is Western in origin. Some of the following observations apply outside of that context, but the limitations of projecting ideas onto behaviors and experiences in other societies should be kept in mind. Bornstein, M. H. (1995) Parenting infants. In M. H. Bornstein (ed.), *Handbook of parenting*. Mahwah, N.J.: Erlbaum, vol. 1, pp. 3–39; Greenfield, P. M., & Suzuki, L. K. (1998) Culture and human development: Implications for parenting, education, pediatrics, and mental health. In I. E. Sigel & K. A. Renninger (eds.), W. Damon (series ed.), *Handbook of child psychology: Vol. 4. Child psychology in practice* (5e). New York: Wiley, pp. 1059–1109; Harkness, S., & Super, C. M. (1995) Culture and parenting. In M. H. Bornstein (ed.), *Handbook of parenting*. Mahwah, N.J.: Erlbaum, vol. 2, pp. 211–234; Kagitcibasi, C. (1996) *Family and human development across culture: A view from the other side*. Mahwah, N.J.: Erlbaum; Leiderman, P. H., Tulkin, S. R., & Rosenfield, A. (eds.) (1977) *Culture and infancy: Variations in human experience*. New York: Academic Press; and McLoyd, V. C. (1998) Children in poverty: Development, public policy, and practice. In I. E. Sigel & K. A. Renninger (eds.), W. Damon (series ed.), *Handbook of child psychology: Vol. 4. Child psychology in practice* (5e). New York: Wiley, pp. 135–208.

8. Bornstein, M. H. (1995) Parenting infants. In M. H. Bornstein (ed.), *Handbook of parenting*. Mahwah, N.J.: Erlbaum, vol. 1, pp. 3–39.

9. Wilson, B. J., & Gottman, J. M. (1995) Marital interaction and parenting. In M. H. Bornstein (ed.), *Handbook of parenting*. Mahwah, N.J.: Erlbaum, vol. 4, pp. 33–55; and Fincham, F. D. (1998) Child development and marital relations. *Child Development* 69: 543–574.

10. Barnard, K. E., & Martell, L. K. (1995) Mothering. In M. H. Bornstein (ed.), *Handbook of parenting*. Mahwah, N.J.: Erlbaum, vol. 3, pp. 3–26; Brody, S. (1956) *Patterns of mothering: Maternal influence during infancy*. New York: International Universities Press; Leiderman, P. H., Tulkin, S. R., & Rosenfield, A. (eds.) (1977) *Culture and infancy: Variations in human experience*. New York: Academic Press; Ruddick, S. (1989) *Maternal thinking: Toward a politics of peace*. New York: Ballantine Press; and Sears, R. R., Maccoby, E. E., & Levin, H. (1957) *Patterns of child rearing*. White Plains, N.Y.: Row, Peterson.

11. French, V. (1995) History of parenting: The ancient Mediterranean world. In M. H. Bornstein (ed.), *Handbook of parenting*. Mahwah, N.J.: Erlbaum, vol. 2, pp. 263–284; Parke, R. D. (1995) Fathers and families. In M. H. Bornstein (ed.), *Handbook of parenting*. Mahwah, N.J.: Erlbaum, vol. 3, pp. 27–63; and UNICEF (1990) *Convention of the rights of the child*. New York: United Nations Children's Fund.

12. *Zero to Three* (1997) Key findings for a nationwide survey among parents of zero-to-three-year-olds. Conducted by Peter D. Hart Research Associates. Baltimore, Md.: National Center for Infants, Toddlers and Families.

13. Berman, P. W., & Pedersen, F. A. (eds.) (1987) *Men's transitions to parenthood: Longitudinal studies of early family experience*. Hillsdale, N.J.: Erlbaum; Parke, R. D. (1995) Fathers and families. In M. H. Bornstein (ed.), *Handbook of parenting*. Mahwah, N.J.: Erlbaum, vol. 3, pp. 27–63; and Russell, A., & Saebel, J. (1997) Mother-son, mother-daughter, father-son, and father-daughter: Are they distinct relationships? *Developmental Review* 17: 111–147.

14. Barnard, K. E., & Martell, L. K. (1995) Mothering. In M. H. Bornstein (ed.) *Handbook of parenting*. Mahwah, N.J.: Erlbaum, vol. 3, pp. 3–26; and Parke, R. D. (1995) Fathers and families. In M. H. Bornstein (ed.), *Handbook of parenting*. Mahwah, N.J.: Erlbaum, vol. 3, pp. 27–63.

15. Clinton, H. R. (1996) *It takes a village and other lessons children teach us*. New York: Simon & Schuster.

16. Clarke-Stewart, K. A., Allhusen, V. D., & Clements, D.C. (1995) Nonparental caregiving. In M. H. Bornstein (ed.), *Handbook of parenting*. Mahwah, N.J.: Erlbaum, vol. 3, pp. 151–176; Honig, A. S. (1995) Choosing childcare for young children. In M. H. Bornstein (ed.), *Handbook of parenting*. Mahwah, N.J.: Erlbaum, vol. 4, pp. 411–435; and Lamb, M. E. (1998) Nonparental childcare: Context, quality, correlates, and consequences. In I. E. Sigel & K. A. Renninger (eds.), W. Damon (series ed.), *Handbook of child psychology: Vol. 4. Child psychology in practice* (5e). New York: Wiley, pp. 73–133.

17. Honig, A. S. (1995) Choosing childcare for young children. In M. H. Bornstein (ed.), *Handbook of parenting*. Mahwah, N.J.: Erlbaum, vol. 4, pp. 411–435; Lamb, M. E. (1998) Nonparental childcare: Context, quality, correlates, and consequences. In I. E. Sigel & K. A. Renninger (eds.), W. Damon (series

ed.), *Handbook of child psychology: Vol. 4. Child psychology in practice* (5e). New York: Wiley, pp. 73–133; Zukow, P. G. (ed.) (1989) *Sibling interaction across cultures: Theoretical and methodological issues.* New York: Springer-Verlag; and Zukow-Goldring, P. (1995) Sibling caregiving. In M. H. Bornstein (ed.), *Handbook of parenting.* Mahwah, N.J.: Erlbaum, vol. 3, pp. 177–208.

18. Bornstein, M. H. (ed.) (1995) *Handbook of parenting* (vols. 1–4). Mahwah, N.J.: Erlbaum; Demick, J., Bursik, K., & Dibiase, R. (eds.) (1993) *Parental development.* Hillsdale, N.J.: Erlbaum; and Martin, C. A., & Colbert, K. K. (1997) *Parenting: A life span perspective.* New York: McGraw-Hill.

19. Corter, C. M., & Fleming, A. S. (1995) Psychobiology of maternal behavior in human beings. In M. H. Bornstein (ed.), *Handbook of parenting.* Mahwah, N.J.: Erlbaum, vol. 2, pp. 87–116; Krasnegor, N. A., & Bridges, R. S. (eds.) (1990) *Mammalian parenting: Biochemical, neurobiological, and behavioral determinants.* New York: Oxford University Press; and Rosenblatt, J. S. (1995) Hormonal basis of parenting in mammals. In M. H. Bornstein (ed.), *Handbook of parenting.* Mahwah, N.J.: Erlbaum, vol. 2, pp. 3–25.

20. Vorhees, C. V., & Mollnow, E. (1987) Behavioral teratogenesis: Long-term influences on behavior from early exposure to environmental agents. In J. D. Osofsky (ed.), *Handbook of infant development* (2e). New York: Wiley, pp. 913–971.

21. Bard, K. A. (1995) Parenting in primates. In M. H. Bornstein (ed.), *Handbook of parenting.* Mahwah, N.J.: Erlbaum, vol. 2, pp. 27–58; and Papousek, H., & Papousek, M. (1995) Intuitive parenting. In M. H. Bornstein (ed.), *Handbook of parenting.* Mahwah, N.J.: Erlbaum, vol. 2, pp. 117–136.

22. Papousek, M., Papousek, H., & Bornstein, M. H. (1985) The naturalistic vocal environment of young infants: On the significance of homogeneity and variability in parental speech. In T. M. Field & N. Fox (eds.), *Social perception in infants.* Norwood, N.J.: Ablex, pp. 269–297.

23. Luster, T., & Okagaki, L. (eds.) (1993) *Parenting: An ecological perspective.* Hillsdale, N.J.: Erlbaum.

24. Field, T. (1995) Psychologically depressed parents. In M. H. Bornstein (ed.), *Handbook of parenting.* Mahwah, N.J.: Erlbaum, vol. 4, pp. 85–99.

25. Ruddick, S. (1989) *Maternal thinking: Toward a politics of peace.* New York: Ballantine Press; and Sanson, A., & Rothbart, M. K. (1995) Child temperament and parenting. In M. H. Bornstein (ed.), *Handbook of parenting.* Mahwah, N.J.: Erlbaum, vol. 4, pp. 299–321.

26. Sameroff, A. J. (1983) Developmental systems: Contexts and evolution. In W. Kessen (ed.), P. H. Mussen (series ed.) *Handbook of child psychology: Vol. 1. History, theory, and methods.* New York: Wiley, pp. 237–294.

27. Bornstein, M. H. (ed.) (1991) *Cultural approaches to parenting.* Hillsdale, N.J.: Erlbaum; Bornstein, M. H. (1995) Form and function: Implications for studies of culture and human development. *Culture & Psychology* 1: 123–137; Bradley, R. H. (1995) Environment and parenting. In M. H. Bornstein (ed.), *Handbook of parenting.* Mahwah, N.J.: Erlbaum, vol. 2, pp. 235–261; Bronfenbrenner, U., & Crouter, A. C. (1983) The evolution of environmental models in

developmental research. In W. Kessen (ed.), P. H. Mussen (series ed.), *Handbook of child psychology: Vol. 1. History, theory, and methods*. New York: Wiley, pp. 357–414; Bronfenbrenner, U., & Morris, P. A. (1998) The ecology of developmental processes. In R. M. Lerner (ed.), W. Damon (series ed.), *Handbook of child psychology: Vol. 1. Theoretical models of human development* (5e). New York: Wiley, pp. 993–1028; Cochran, M., & Niego, S. (1995) Parenting and social networks. In M. H. Bornstein (ed.), *Handbook of parenting*. Mahwah, N.J.: Erlbaum, vol. 3, pp. 393–418; Hernandez, D. J. (1993) *America's children: Resources from family, government, and the economy*. New York: Russell Sage Foundation; and Luster, T., & Okagaki, L. (eds.) (1993) *Parenting: An ecological perspective*. Hillsdale, N.J.: Erlbaum.

28. Dunn, J., & Plomin, R. (1990) *Separate lives: Why siblings are so different*. New York: Basic Books.

29. Hoff-Ginsberg, E., & Tardif, T. (1995) Socioeconomic status and parenting. In M. H. Bornstein (ed.), *Handbook of parenting*. Mahwah, N.J.: Erlbaum, vol. 2, pp. 161–188; and Wachs, T. D. (1992) *The nature of nurture*. Newbury Park, Calif.: Sage Publications.

30. *Zero-to-Three* (1997) Key findings for a nationwide survey among parents of zero-to-three-year-olds. Conducted by Peter D. Hart Research Associates. Baltimore, Md.: National Center for Infants, Toddlers and Families.

31. Bornstein, M. H. (ed.) (1991) *Cultural approaches to parenting*. Hillsdale, N.J.: Erlbaum; Bornstein, M H. (1995) Form and function: Implications for studies of culture and human development. *Culture & Psychology* 1: 123–137; Goodnow, J. J. (1995) Parents' knowledge and expectations. In M. H. Bornstein (ed.), *Handbook of parenting*. Mahwah, N.J.: Erlbaum, vol. 3, pp. 305–332; and Harkness, S., & Super, C. M. (1995) Culture and parenting. In M. H. Bornstein (ed.), *Handbook of parenting*. Mahwah, N.J.: Erlbaum, vol. 2, pp. 211–234.

32. McHale, J. P., & Cowan, P. A. (eds.) (1996) Understanding how family-level dynamics affect children's development: Studies of two-parent families. *New Directions for Child Development* 74. San Francisco: Jossey-Bass; Patterson, G. R. (1975) *Families: Applications of social learning to family life*. Champaign, Ill.: Research Press.

33. Bronfenbrenner, U., & Crouter, A. C. (1983) The evolution of environmental models in developmental research. In W. Kessen (ed.), P. H. Mussen (series ed., *Handbook of child psychology: Vol. 1. History, theory, and methods*. New York: Wiley, pp. 357–414; and Bronfenbrenner, U., & Morris, P. A. (1998) The ecology of developmental processes. In R. M. Lerner (ed.), W. Damon (series ed.), *Handbook of child psychology: Vol. 1. Theoretical models of human development* (5e). New York: Wiley, pp. 993–1028.

34. Alexander, J. F., & Malouf, R. E. (1983) Intervention with children experiencing problems in personality and social development. In E. M. Hetherington (ed.), P. H. Mussen (series ed.), *Handbook of child psychology: Vol. 4. Socialization, personality, and social development*. New York: Wiley, pp. 913–981; Chamberlain, P., & Patterson, G. R. (1995) Discipline and child compliance in parenting. In M. H. Bornstein (ed.), *Handbook of parenting*. Mahwah, N.J.: Erlbaum,

vol. 4, pp. 205–225; Cowan, P. A., Powell, D., & Cowan, C. P. (1998) Parenting interventions: A family systems perspective. In I. E. Sigel & K. A. Renninger (eds.), W. Damon (series ed., *Handbook of child psychology: Vol. 4. Child psychology in practice* (5e). New York: Wiley, pp. 3–72; Crnic, K., & Acevedo, M. (1995) Everyday stresses and parenting. In M. H. Bornstein (ed.), *Handbook of parenting*. Mahwah, N.J.: Erlbaum, vol. 4, pp. 277–297; Garbarino, J., & Kostelny, K. (1995) Parenting and public policy. In M. H. Bornstein (ed.), *Handbook of parenting*. Mahwah, N.J.: Erlbaum, vol. 3, pp. 419–436; and Goodman, G. S., Emery, R. E., & Haugaard, J. J. (1998) Developmental psychology and law: Divorce, child maltreatment, foster care, and adoption. In I. E. Sigel & K. A. Renninger (eds.), W. Damon (series ed.), *Handbook of child psychology: Vol. 4. Child psychology in practice* (5e). New York: Wiley, pp. 775–874.

35. Gottfried, A. E., Gottfried, A. W., & Bathurst, K. (1995) Maternal and dual-earner employment status and parenting. In M. H. Bornstein (ed.), *Handbook of parenting*. Mahwah, N.J.: Erlbaum, vol. 2, pp. 139–159.

36. Clarke-Stewart, K. A., Allhusen, V. D., & Clements, D.C. (1995) Nonparental caregiving. In M. H. Bornstein (ed.), *Handbook of parenting*. Mahwah, N.J.: Erlbaum, vol. 3, pp. 151–176; Lamb, M. E. (1998) Nonparental childcare: Context, quality, correlates, and consequences. In I. E. Sigel & K. A. Renninger (eds.), W. Damon (series ed.), *Handbook of child psychology: Vol. 4. Child psychology in practice* (5e). New York: Wiley, pp. 73–133.

37. *Zero-to-Three* (1997) Key findings for a nationwide survey among parents of zero-to-three-year-olds. Conducted by Peter D. Hart Research Associates. Baltimore, Md.: National Center for Infants, Toddlers and Families.

2

Culture and Parenthood

PATRICIA M. GREENFIELD
and LALITA K. SUZUKI

This chapter shows how culture and child development are inextricably intertwined. From a child's perspective, acquiring cultural knowledge is a vital aspect of development. Each child is exposed to a cultural surround that spans everything from sleeping arrangements and feeding practices to the child's value systems, school experiences, and interpersonal interactions.

In multicultural societies, the cultural surround in which a child develops can be divided into two broad categories, *home culture* and *societal culture*. Home culture refers to the values, practices, and cultural background of a child's immediate family. Societal culture refers to a child's interactions with schools, peers, community, and media from which the child learns the cultural values communicated by the dominant society.

The contrasting cultural models of *collectivism* (focusing on group harmony) and *individualism* (focusing on individual rights) provide a framework to account for cultural diversity in the United States.[1] Many immigrant and other minority groups bring a collectivistic frame of reference from their ancestral cultures when they enter the United States, which is built on individualistic principles. This produces a dialectical process between the collectivistic goals of a child's home culture and the individualistic goals of the societal culture.

CULTURAL VARIATIONS IN DEVELOPMENTAL GOALS

The collectivistic and individualistic cultural models generate specific cross-cultural differences in parenting practices. These models come into contact and influence each other. However, without considering each model separately, we cannot adequately understand cross-cultural variations in parental behaviors and parent-child relations.

In general, parents' goals for their children across cultures include the following: child survival and health, the acquisition of economic capabilities, and the attainment of culturally appropriate values.[2] However, cultural differences do exist.

In the collectivistic model, children are viewed as starting life as asocial creatures and as achieving increasing social responsibility and interdependence as they grow older.[3] In this model, infants are often indulged, whereas older children are socialized to comprehend, follow, and internalize directives from elders, particularly parents. In the individualistic model, infants and young children are viewed as dependent on their parents and as achieving increasing independence from their parents as they grow older. The developmental outcome of the collectivistic model is the interdependent self; the developmental outcome of the individualistic model is the independent, individuated self.[4]

In the United States, guiding children to learn to make their own decisions and establish their separate individual existences is one of the most important parental goals; parents want their children to grow up to be independent and individuated adults.[5] U.S. mothers tend to value skills in their children's behaviors that relate to matters of individual action, such as self-assertion and standing up for one's rights.[6] These goals reflect the cultural model of individualism.

In contrast, parents in Japan "want their children to develop a sense of what can be loosely translated as dependence from the very beginning."[7] Japanese mothers contrast with U.S. mothers in their greater concern about issues of self-control, compliance with adult authority, and social interaction in child development.[8] These contrasting models of child development characterize other countries and other cultures as well.

CULTURAL VARIATIONS IN CHILDREARING PRACTICES

Within every culture, there are important individual variations around each cultural norm. Cultural typologies do not eradicate or minimize individual differences; they simply point to the norms around which those differences range. The following examples of childrearing practices illustrate contrasting cultural norms.

Sleeping Arrangements

In considering sleeping arrangements in the United States, parents and pediatricians alike are concerned about a child's physical well-being (e.g., reducing the risk of SIDS), emotional well-being (e.g., nighttime comforting), parental sleep patterns (e.g., parental privacy, nighttime feeding issues), practical constraints (e.g., housing situation), family ecology (e.g., single parenthood versus married parents), adult needs (e.g., for autonomy), and cultural goals (e.g., independence versus interdependence).

In the United States, most infants sleep alone in a separate crib, most often in a separate room from their parents.[9] In many cultures (particularly non-Western cultures), however, cosleeping is the predominant sleeping arrangement.[10] In fact, mothers in approximately two thirds of the world's cultures sleep with their infants in their beds, and this portion is much higher if mothers sleeping with their babies in the same room are included.[11] Examples of cosleeping cultures include Japan, where children typically sleep with their parents until five or six years of age.[12] This cosleeping is often referred to as *kawa,* or river, in which the parents form the symbolic riverbanks for the children who sleep in their own futons between them.[13] Whereas the norm in the United States is adaptive for the childrearing goal of independence, the Japanese norm is adaptive for the childrearing goal of interdependence.

Although the dominant culture in the United States adheres to separate sleeping practices, many minority and immigrant groups still hold on to cosleeping practices from their ancestral cultures. For example, 20 percent of Hispanic American families slept with their children at least three times a week in contrast to 6 percent of European American families.[14] In a similar pattern, more African American than European American infants and toddlers regularly coslept with their parent or parents.[15]

From the perspective of a neurologist, Richard Restak's research shows that "physical holding and carrying of the infant turns out to be the most important factor responsible for the infant's normal mental and social development."[16] However, infants in the United States are not held during bedtime hours. Hence, we must strongly consider the possibility that sleep problems are a major cultural problem in infant care in the United States precisely because the professional advice of pediatricians and the culturally dominant practice are fighting the biology of the human infant that has evolved over hundreds of thousands of years.[17]

Sleeping arrangements are an integral part of whole systems of cultural meaning and ecological constraints. Cosleeping of mother and infant is part of a meaning system that emphasizes interdependence, whereas separate sleeping in a crib or another room is part of a meaning system that emphasizes independence as a developmental goal.

On the one hand, a cross-cultural look at these practices opens up new options for potential cross-cultural exchange. However, to borrow one part of a cultural system and insert it into a totally different system often brings on problems in itself. For example, T. Berry Brazelton warns parents from the dominant U.S. culture who "sleep with a small infant and a toddler but then become desperate to assign the child to a separate room and bed and may desert the child by letting him or her 'scream it out.'"[18] Perhaps this outcome stems from a mismatch between the child's socialized dependence on cosleeping and the parents' own culturally shaped needs for independence. But, whatever the reason, Brazelton notes, "This anger and desertion are not deserved, and leaving the child to cry it out only blames the victim." Hence, the long-term and systemic implications of cross-cultural borrowing must always be taken into account.

Attachment Behavior

Closely related to cross-cultural variations in infant sleeping practices is cross-cultural variation in attachment behaviors. Both domains reflect cross-cultural differences in parental goals.

Cultural variation in parents' perceptions of attachment behavior was studied by Robin Harwood.[19] She compared European American and Puerto Rican parental reactions to separation situations and their relationship to parental goals for their children. European American mothers focused on issues of individual autonomy for their children in the context of their attachment behaviors; they wanted a balance between autonomy and relatedness.[20] Puerto Rican mothers, on the other hand, placed a greater emphasis on their child's ability to maintain "proper demeanor" in a social context, even when the child is separated from the parent; they wanted a balance between respect and caring.

Each cultural model has its own set of benefits and costs in the attachment domain.[21] These can still be seen in adulthood, the endpoint of development. For example, the mother-child bond remains strong throughout life in Japan, but the husband-wife tie is of a less romantic and close nature than in the United States.[22] By the same token, while European American mothers generally subscribe to the benefits of autonomy as a developmental goal, its cost to them could be seen as the "empty nest" syndrome.

Parent-Child Communication Behaviors

Parental goals for child development also are reflected in the communication patterns of parents toward their infants. For example, the European-based way of socializing children can be seen as geared to the goal of technological intelligence, and the African way can be seen as geared to the goal of social intelligence.[23] The early socialization of technological intelligence focuses on objects and their manipulation with an emphasis on cognitive development in isolation from social development. In contrast, the early socialization of social intelligence focuses on interpersonal relationships, including triadic or group relationships. These different emphases are expressed in the communication patterns used in parent-infant interaction within each culture.

The African emphasis on social intelligence is seen in research on the !Kung hunter-gatherers in Botswana.[24] In !Kung society, no toys are made for infants. Instead, natural objects, such as twigs, grass, stones, and nutshells, are always available, along with cooking implements. However, adults do not encourage babies to play with these objects. Adults are unlikely to interact with infants while they are exploring objects independently. For example, they are not concerned about labeling objects and their functions. Thus, technological intelligence for its own sake is not actively encouraged. It is only when a baby offers an object to another person that adults become highly responsive, encouraging and vocalizing much more than at other times. For example, when babies are between six and twelve months old, !Kung grandmothers start to train them in the importance of giving to others by guiding them to hand beads to relatives. Thus, the !Kung cultural emphasis on the interpersonal rather than the physical aspects of existence is reflected in how adults communicate the importance of objects as social mediators in their interactions with the very youngest members of their community.

In another study, Jacqueline Rabain found that West Africans in Africa and West African immigrants in Paris respond more to child-initiated social activity than French mothers, who focus more on their infants' technological competence, i.e., object manipulation.[25] Compared with the African mothers, they respond more frequently to child-initiated object manipulation. In these ways, French mothers display a heavier emphasis on technological than on social intelligence.

Japanese mothers also display a preference for social intelligence by talking gently and using sounds that the infant can easily imitate.[26] Japanese mothers are less interested in object labeling. Instead, they focus more attention on acting out polite verbal exchanges. The following example also involves objects used in the social context of giving: "Here! It's a vroom vroom. I give it to you. Now give it to me. Give me. Yes! Thank you." Japanese mothers also are more likely to engage in routines that arouse empathy with the object, encouraging positive feelings toward the toy by saying things like, "Here. It's a doggy. Give it love. Love, love, love," while patting the toy. As in Africa, social intelligence seems to be a developmental goal in Japanese mothers' communication pattern.

Later in development, Japanese mothers (and nursery school teachers) rely more on empathy and nonverbal communication, whereas mothers in the United States rely more on verbal communication with their children.[27] The physical closeness of the Japanese mother-child pair in infancy may well be connected to the development of empathy as a mode of communication in later years. Verbalization is necessary when there is greater physical and psychological distance between parent and child. Empathy as a mode of parent-child communication may be linked to social intelligence as a developmental priority. Emphasis on verbal communication may, in contrast, serve the developmental goal of technological intelligence.

Parenting styles also may be related to priorities in social versus technological intelligence.

Parenting Styles

Although not generally acknowledged in the developmental literature, Diana Baumrind's typology of permissive, authoritarian, and authoritative parenting is closely tied to the normative goals for child development in North America.[28] Authoritative parenting is considered to be the most adaptive style because it is associated with children who are "self-reliant, self-controlled, explorative, and content." These are the qualities of the independent individual valued in the cultural model of individualism in countries such as the United States.

Different ethnic groups within the United States and many Eastern and developing countries have been found to utilize an authoritarian parenting style to a greater degree than do middle-class European American parents in the United States. Authoritarian parenting is common in East Asia,[29] Africa,[30] and Mexico,[31] as well as in ethnic groups derived from these ancestral cultures: Asian Americans,[32] African Americans,[33] and Mexican Americans.[34]

Under Confucianism, standards that may be viewed as authoritarian are used, not to dominate the child, but rather to preserve the integrity of the family unit and to ensure harmonious relationships with others.[35] The Chinese version also emphasizes high concern and care for the children. Thus the goals and behaviors behind this form of authoritarian parenting are quite different from those originally posited by Baumrind.

Even Baumrind found that, in lower-middle-class African American families, authoritarian parenting seemed to produce different effects on child development than in European American families.[36] Rather than resulting in negative outcomes, authoritarian parenting by African Americans was associated with self-assertive, independent behavior in preschool girls.

One possibility is that African American parents use so-called authoritarian means because, through the retention of some African values at an implicit level, they are more interested in instilling respect and obedience than are parents in the dominant North American culture.[37] From the socialization perspective, an emphasis on obedience and respect is achieved by strictness and the use of parental commands as a communication strategy.[38] Such a socialization pattern would fit Baumrind's authoritarian parenting. Similarly, immigrant Latino families bring from Mexico and Central America the developmental goal of respect and the socialization mode of authoritarian parenting to achieve respect for parents.[39]

Authoritarian parenting, as seen in Africa,[40] Mexico,[41] and Latino populations in the United States,[42] has an associated style of parent-child communication. Directives and imperatives are frequent, along with encouragement of the social values of obedience and respect. The imperative style elicits action (e.g., carrying out chores) rather than verbalization from the child.

On the other hand, authoritative parenting brings with it a communication style that encourages verbal self-expression and autonomy in the child. This parenting style often features a high rate of questions from the parent, particularly "test questions," in which the answer is already known to the parent,[43] as well as parent-child negotiation.[44] Child-initiated questions are also encouraged and accepted. This style is intrinsic to the process of formal education in which the teacher asks questions to which he or she already knows the answer and tests children on their verbal expression. An important aspect of the interrogative style is that it elicits verbalization from the child. Such verbal expression is an important part of becoming a formally educated person and is particularly functional and common in commercial and technological societies where academic achievement, autonomy, and creativity are important child development goals. This style is the cultural norm in North America and northern Europe.

CHILDREN'S BEHAVIOR TOWARD PARENTS

Children's behavior toward their parents is an important reflection of the way in which their social development is influenced by their cultures.

Asian American students, particularly those close to Asian culture in their acculturation levels, are significantly more likely than European American students to sacrifice certain personal goals for their parents. This finding reflects the collectivistic emphasis on filial piety and respect for parents found in the Confucian worldview of East Asia.[45] The Confucian value of filial piety deeply influences the desired behavior of children toward their parents. "[Confucius] viewed the parent-child relationship as the foundation from which interpersonal love and trust would grow, and thus interpreted filial piety as the virtue for every person to follow."[46] This multidimensional concept of filial piety is believed to be a virtue that everyone must practice, since "the love and affection of a child for his or her parents . . . is the prototype of goodness in interpersonal relationships."[47]

On the other hand, the behavior of European American children seems to reflect the importance of individual goals and personal property prominent in the dominant North American worldview. Implicit in the response is a certain personal distance between parent and child; this is consonant with a view of human development that emphasizes the achievement of autonomy by late adolescence.

IMPLICATIONS FOR PROFESSIONALS

Differing patterns of costs and benefits provide opportunities for useful cross-cultural exchange. From the perspective of both insider and outsider, each cultural model has its strengths and weaknesses, its costs and benefits, and its pathological extremes. For this reason, cross-cultural exchange of values and practices can sometimes serve as a corrective force to counteract the weaknesses, costs, and pathologies of any given cultural system. For example, cosleeping is a practice that many immigrants have brought with them from Mexico and Central America. Current experimental research documents the potential physiological benefits of cosleeping to prevent sudden infant death syndrome (SIDS) in a society (the United States) with a relatively high rate of SIDS.[48] The findings therefore have direct relevance to pediatric advice on sleeping arrangements.

Brazelton suggests that practitioners should reevaluate their stance toward children's sleep.[49] Pediatricians have traditionally concluded that infant-parent cosleeping is a risk factor for healthy development. However, they should be cautious before imposing judgments about the childrearing practices of persons with whom they do not share a common culture and should consider infant sleeping arrangements from all of the relevant angles: physiological, psychological, and cultural.

Teachers and childcare workers also should be aware of differences in infant-rearing practices. For example, crying or lack thereof when children are dropped off at daycare in the morning may be partially attributable to cultural differences in familiarity with separation. Through a better understanding of these differences, childcare professionals can become more understanding and helpful to the child's transition between home and daycare.

In the United States, where the learning of object names is culturally important, mothers spend a good deal of time labeling objects in their communicative interactions with their young children. Although this tendency seems perfectly reasonable in this cultural context, it would be important to understand that other parents may have other cultural goals for their children. Teachers and childcare workers should be sensitive to the value of developing children's social intelligence, not merely their knowledge of the physical world, and of developing social skills for communicating with groups, not only with dyads. Through cross-cultural exchange, both styles of communication could be used to socialize children for both technological and social intelligence.

A lack of cultural understanding can also lead to misinterpretations by social workers.[50] Negative judgments by social workers of cultural practices they do not understand, using criteria from their own culture, can lead to tragedy. For instance, social workers can misinterpret sibling care (a practice utilized in many cultures worldwide) as child neglect, leading to children being taken away from loving parents who may have been following a different cultural model of competent parenting and child development. One can imagine other situations in which cultural practices may be misinterpreted as abuse. Cosleeping or cobathing practices acceptable in many cultures may be misinterpreted as sexual in nature. Social workers and other clinicians should be trained to recognize differences between cultural variations in practice and truly abusive situations.

Multicultural understanding has direct implications for clinical work with families. Consider the following case:[51] A child in an African American family is punished when a younger sibling, under her care, falls off the bed. The older child feels as though the punishment is unfair and complains of holding too much responsibility in the family. The family seeks family therapy for these issues. In this case, armed with unconscious cultural assumptions about the developmental goal and value of independence, the first reaction of the therapist is to blame the parents for "parentifying" the older child; in this framework parentification is considered pathological. Parentification of a child compromises the autonomy and opportunities for self-actualization that are implicit developmental goals in psychotherapy, itself an outgrowth of an individualistic framework. However, task assignment to older children is a component of a more authoritarian parent-child relationship featuring parental directives and child obedience. Assigning childcare to an older sibling is also a natural and important aspect of developing a sense of social responsibility.

Conversely, one cause of impulsiveness and immaturity may be an excess of family democracy in which all chores and tasks are either a matter of discussion and negotiation between parent and child or are simply left up to the child. Eleanor Maccoby notes that adolescent impulsiveness occurs when parents have not assigned tasks to their children.[52] Clinicians could make parents aware of household chores as a potential tool to prevent child and adolescent problems in this area. Clinicians from ethnic groups in which chore assignment is already used can lead the way.

On the other hand, a disinclination to ask questions and assert opinions is a detriment to the school achievement of certain ethnic groups in the United States, such as Latino immigrant children.[53] Soliciting children's views, a component of the authoritative parenting style favored in the dominant U.S. culture, can enhance school achievement. By confining such routines to school-related activities such as reading, immigrant Latino families can strike a bicultural pose that enhances children's school achievement while maintaining the value of respect in other family situations.[54]

IMPLICATIONS FOR RESEARCHERS

The same behavior may have a different meaning and therefore a different outcome in other cultures. For this reason, assessments and measures must be used with caution in making cross-cultural comparisons. This is especially true when looking at the styles of parental interaction and discipline used by different cultural groups. For example, using a measure of authoritarian parenting developed in the United States to study parenting styles in China would provide an inaccurate and incomplete perspective on parenting practices there.[55] It is important to adapt methods of research to the cultural ideas and values of people native to the society under study.

CONCLUSION

Because parents often acculturate slowly to a host culture, there is a great potential for parent-child conflict when families immigrate from a collectivistic to an individualistic society. Parents may expect respect, but the dominant culture may encourage their children to argue and negotiate.[56] Those parents may see strictness as a sign of caring, but their adolescent children may see it as robbing them of autonomy and self-direction.[57]

Because multicultural societies, such as the United States, contain many ethnic groups with varied childrearing practices, parents deviating from the dominant norm should not be made to feel they are doing something harmful to their child. Understanding that practices such as sleeping alone and cosleeping are two different cultural modes, each with its own set of risks and benefits, can lead to pride in rather than shame for diverse cultural heritages. For members of the dominant majority, such understanding leads to respect for rather than denigration of ethnic minorities. Similarly, understanding the reasons behind alternative practices can help immigrants understand norms in their new cultural surround.

In the United States, cultural diversity is such that parent-child relations are not limited to one model. Because the weaknesses of one model may well be the strengths of another, cross-ethnic exchange can help to solve some common childrearing problems in our multicultural society.

NOTES

1. Greenfield, P. M., & Cocking, R. R. (1994) *Cross-cultural roots of minority child development*. Hillsdale, N.J.: Erlbaum.

2. LeVine, R. A. (1988) Human and parental care: Universal goals, cultural strategies, individual behavior. In R. A. Levine, P. A. Miller, & M. M. West (eds.), *Parental behavior in diverse societies. New Directions for Child and Adolescent Development*. San Francisco: Jossey-Bass, vol. 40, pp. 3–12.

3. Greenfield, P. M. (1994) Independence and dependence as developmental scripts. In P. M. Greenfield & R. R. Cocking (eds.), *Cross-cultural roots of minority child development*. Hillsdale, N.J.: Erlbaum, pp. 1–40.

4. Markus, H., & Kitayama, S. (1991) Culture and the self. *Psychological Review* 98(2): 224–253.

5. Richman, A. L., Miller, P. M., & Johnson Solomon, M. (1988) The socialization of infants in suburban Boston. In R. A. Levine, P. M. Miller, & M. West (eds.), *Parental behavior in diverse societies. New Directions for Child and Adolescent Development*. San Francisco: Jossey-Bass, vol. 40, pp. 65–74.

6. Hess, R. D., Kashiwagi, K., Azuma, H., Price, G. G., & Dickson, W. P. (1980) Maternal expectation of mastery of developmental tasks in Japan and the United States. *International Journal of Psychology* 15: 259–271.

7. Nugent, J. K. (1994) Cross-cultural studies of child development: Implications for clinicians. *Zero to Three* 15(2): 1, 3–8. Quoted, p. 6.

8. Hess, R. D., Kashiwagi, K., Azuma, H., Price, G. G., & Dickson, W. P. (1980) Maternal expectation of mastery of developmental tasks in Japan and the United States. *International Journal of Psychology* 15: 259–271.

9. Morelli, O. A., Rogoff, B., Oppenheim, D., & Goldsmith, D. (1992) Cultural variation in infants' sleeping arrangements: Questions of independence. *Developmental Psychology* 28(4): 604–613.

10. Konner, M. J., & Worthman, C. (1980) Nursing frequency, gonadal function and birth-spacing among !Kung hunters and gatherers. *Science* 207: 788–791.

11. Barry, H., III, & Paxson, L. M. (1971) Infancy and early child-hood: Cross-cultural codes: 2. *Ethology* 10: 466–508; and Burton, R. V., & Whiting, J.W.M. (1961) The absent father and cross-sex identity. *Merrill-Palmer Quarterly* 7: 85–95.

12. Caudill, W., & Plath, D. (1966) Who sleeps by whom? Parent-child involvement in urban Japanese families. *Psychiatry* 29: 344–366.

13. Brazelton, T. B. (1990) Commentary: Parent-infant co-sleeping revisited. *Ab Initio* 2(1): 1–7.

14. Schachter, F. F., Fuchs, M. L., Bijur, P. E., & Stone, R. (1989) Co-sleeping

and sleep problems in Hispanic-American urban young children. *Pediatrics* 84: 522–530.

15. Lozoff, B., Wolf, A., & Davis, N. (1984) Cosleeping in urban families with young children in the United States. *Pediatrics* 74(2): 171–182.

16. Restak, R. (1979) *The brain.* New York: Doubleday. Quoted, p. 122.

17. Konner, M. (1982) *The tangled wing: Biological constraints on the human spirit.* New York: Holt, Rinehart and Winston.

18. Brazelton, T. B. (1990) Commentary: Parent-infant co-sleeping revisited. *Ab Initio* 2(1): 1–7. Quoted, p. 7 and p. 5.

19. Harwood, R. (1992) The influence of culturally derived values on Anglo and Puerto Rican mothers' perceptions of attachment behavior. *Child Development* 63: 822–839.

20. Harwood, R., Miller, J., & Lucca Irizarry, N. (1995) *Culture and attachment: Perceptions of the child in context.* New York: Guilford Press.

21. LeVine, R. A. (1994, July) Culture and infant-mother attachment. Paper presented at the meeting of the International Society for the Study of Behavioral Development, Amsterdam, Netherlands.

22. Lebra, T. S. (1994) Mother and child in Japanese socialization: A Japan–U.S. comparison. In P. M. Greenfield & R. R. Cocking (eds.), *Cross-cultural roots of minority child development.* Hillsdale, N.J.: Erlbaum, pp. 259–274.

23. Mundy-Castle, A. C. (1974) Social and technological intelligence in Western and non-Western cultures. *Universitas* 4: 46–52.

24. Bakeman, R., Adamson, L. B., Konner, M., & Barr, R. G. (1990) !Kung infancy: The social context of object exploration. *Child Development* 61: 794–809.

25. Rabain, J. (1979) *L'enfant du lignage.* Paris: Payot; Rabain-Jamain, J. (1994) Language and socialization of the child in African families living in France. In P. M. Greenfield & R. R. Cocking (eds.), *Cross-cultural roots of minority child development.* Hillsdale, N.J.: Erlbaum, pp. 147–166; and Zempleni-Rabain, J. (1973) Food and the strategy involved in learning fraternal exchange among Wolof children. In P. Alexandre (ed.), *French perspectives in African studies.* London: Oxford University Press.

26. Clancy, P. M. (1986) The acquisition of communicative style in Japanese. In B. B. Schieffelin & E. Ochs (eds.), *Language socialization across cultures.* Cambridge: Cambridge University Press. Quoted (twice), p. 653; and Fernald, A., & Morikawa, H. (1993) Common themes and cultural variation in Japanese and American mothers' speech to infants. *Child Development* 64: 637–656. Quoted, p. 653.

27. Azuma, H. (1994) Two modes of cognitive socialization in Japan and the United States. In P. M. Greenfield & R. R. Cocking (eds.), *Cross-cultural roots of minority child development.* Hillsdale, N.J.: Erlbaum.

28. Baumrind, D. (1983) Socialization and instrumental competence in young children. In W. Damon (ed.), *Social and personality development: Essays on the growth of the child.* New York: Norton. Quoted, p. 121.

29. Chao, R. (1994) Beyond parental control and authoritarian parenting style: Understanding Chinese parenting through the cultural notion of training. *Child Development* 65: 1111–1119.

30. Harkness, S., & Super, C. (1982) Why African children are so hard to test. In L. L. Adler (ed.), *Cross-cultural research at issue.* New York: Academic Press, pp. 145–152.

31. Tapia Uribe, F., LeVine, R. A., & Levine, S. E. (1994) Maternal behavior in a Mexican community: The changing environment of children. In P. M. Greenfield & R. R. Cocking (eds.), *Cross-cultural roots of minority child development.* Hillsdale, N.J.: Erlbaum, pp. 41–54.

32. Ho, D.Y.F. (1994) Cognitive socialization in Confucian heritage cultures. In P. M. Greenfield & R. R. Cocking (eds.), *Cross-cultural roots of minority child development.* Hillsdale, N.J.: Erlbaum, pp. 285–313.

33. Baumrind, D. (1972) An exploratory study of socialization effects on black children: Some black-white comparisons. *Child Development* 43: 261–267.

34. Delgado-Gaitan, C. (1994) Socializing young children in Mexican-American families: An intergenerational perspective. In P. M. Greenfield & R. R. Cocking (eds.), *Cross-cultural roots of minority child development.* Hillsdale, N.J.: Erlbaum, pp. 55–86.

35. Ho, D.Y.F. (1994) Cognitive socialization in Confucian heritage cultures. In P. M. Greenfield & R. R. Cocking (eds.), *Cross-cultural roots of minority child development.* Hillsdale, N.J.: Erlbaum, pp. 285–313; and Kim, U., & Choi, S. H. (1994) Individualism, collectivism, and child development. In P. M. Greenfield & R. R. Cocking (eds.), *Cross-cultural roots of minority child development.* Hillsdale, N.J.: Erlbaum, pp. 227–258.

36. Baumrind, D. (1972) An exploratory study of socialization effects on black children: Some black-white comparisons. *Child Development* 43: 261–267.

37. Sudarkasa, N. (1988) Interpreting the African heritage in Afro-American family organization. In H. P. McAdoo (ed.), *Black families* (2e). Newbury Park, Calif.: Sage.

38. Nsamenang, A. B., & Lamb, M. E. (1994) Socialization of Nso children in the Bamenda grassfields of Northwest Cameroon. In P. M. Greenfield & R. R. Cocking (eds.), *Cross-cultural roots of minority child development.* Hillsdale, N.J.: Erlbaum, pp. 133–146; and LeVine, R. A., Dixon, S., LeVine, S., Richman, A., Leiderman, P., Keefer, C., & Brazelton, T. (1994) *Child care and culture. Lessons from Africa.* Cambridge: Cambridge University Press.

39. Delgado-Gaitan, C. (1994) Socializing young children in Mexican-American families: An intergenerational perspective. In P. M. Greenfield & R. R. Cocking (eds.), *Cross-cultural roots of minority child development.* Hillsdale, N.J.: Erlbaum, pp. 55–86.

40. Harkness, S., & Super, C. (1982) Why African children are so hard to test. In L. L. Adler (ed.), *Cross-cultural research at issue.* New York: Academic Press, pp. 145–152.

41. Tapia Uribe, F., LeVine, R. A., & Levine, S. E. (1994) Maternal behavior in a Mexican community: The changing environment of children. In P. M. Greenfield & R. R. Cocking (eds.), *Cross-cultural roots of minority child development.* Hillsdale, N.J.: Erlbaum, pp. 41–54.

42. Delgado-Gaitan, C. (1994) Socializing young children in Mexican-American families: An intergenerational perspective. In P. M. Greenfield & R. R.

Cocking (eds.), *Cross-cultural roots of minority child development.* Hillsdale, N.J.: Erlbaum, pp. 55–86.

43. Duranti, A., & Ochs, E. (1986) Literacy instruction in a Samoan village. In B. B. Schieffelin & P. Gilmore (eds.), Acquisition of literacy: Ethnographic perspectives. Norwood, N.J.: Ablex, pp. 213–232.

44. Delgado-Gaitan, C. (1994) Socializing young children in Mexican-American families: An intergenerational perspective. In P. M. Greenfield & R. R. Cocking (eds.), *Cross-cultural roots of minority child development.* Hillsdale, N.J.: Erlbaum, pp. 55–86.

45. Suzuki, L. K., & Greenfield, P. M. The construction of everyday sacrifice in Asian-American and Euro-American college students: The role of ethnicity and acculturation. Manuscript submitted for publication.

46. Tseng, W. S. (1973) The concept of personality in Confucian thought. *Psychiatry* 36: 191–202. Quoted, p. 199.

47. Tseng, W. S. Ibid. Quoted, p. 195.

48. McKenna, J. J., & Mosko, S. S. (1994) Sleep and arousal, synchrony and independence, among mothers and infants sleeping apart and together (same bed): An experiment in evolutionary medicine. *Acta Paediatric Supplement* 397: 94–102.

49. Brazelton, T. B. (1990) Commentary: Parent-infant co-sleeping revisited. *Ab Initio* 2: 1–7.

50. Schroen, C. (1995, May) Is it child abuse? Toward a multi-cultural field guide for social workers. Paper presented at the University of California Undergraduate Psychology Conference, Los Angeles.

51. Carolyn McCarty (1996, June) Personal communication.

52. Maccoby, E. E. (1980) *Social development: Psychological growth and the parent-child relationship.* New York: Harcourt Brace Jovanovich.

53. Greenfield, P. M., Raeff, C., & Quiroz, B. (1995) Cultural values in learning and education. In B. Williams (ed.), *Closing the achievement gap: A vision for changing beliefs and practices.* Alexandria, Va.: Association for Supervision and Curriculum Development, pp. 37–55.

54. Delgado-Gaitan, C. (1994) Socializing young children in Mexican-American families: An intergenerational perspective. In P. M. Greenfield & R. R. Cocking (eds.), *Cross-cultural roots of minority child development.* Hillsdale, N.J.: Erlbaum, pp. 55–86.

55. Chao, R. (1994) Beyond parental control and authoritarian parenting style: Understanding Chinese parenting through the cultural notion of training. *Child Development* 65: 1111–1119.

56. Delgado-Gaitan, C. (1994) Socializing young children in Mexican-American families: An intergenerational perspective. In P. M. Greenfield & R. R. Cocking (eds.), *Cross-cultural roots of minority child development.* Hillsdale, N.J.: Erlbaum, pp. 55–86.

57. Rohner, R. P., & Pettengill, S. M. (1985) Perceived parental acceptance-rejection and parental control among Korean adolescents [Special Issue]. *Child Development* 56: 524–528.

3

Growing Together

Parenthood as a Developmental Experience

JACK C. WESTMAN

If a child lives with criticism,
    She learns to condemn.
If a child lives with hostility,
    He learns to fight.
If a child lives with ridicule,
    She learns to be shy.
If a child lives with shame,
    He learns to feel guilty.
If a child lives with tolerance,
    She learns to be patient.
If a child lives with encouragement,
    He learns confidence.
If a child lives with praise,
    She learns to appreciate.
If a child lives with fairness,
    He learns justice.
If a child lives with security,
    She learns to have faith.
If a child lives with approval,
    He learns to like himself.
If a child lives with acceptance and friendship,
    She learns to find love in the world.

Anonymous

When seen only as presiding over a child's growth, parenting can be frustrating and burdensome. However, when seen as an opportunity for personal growth, parenthood is one of the most creative and affirming experiences life offers.

Parenthood is a career that deserves as much planning and diligence as does a remunerated career. Individuals grow as much, or more, in their careers as parents as in their vocations. Parenthood offers opportunities to broaden personal horizons when parents try to model the qualities they would like to see in their own children. For some parents, rearing their own children offers an opportunity for them to become the parents they wish they had.

The parent-child relationship begins before conception in a parent's dreams and expectations about having a child. The relationship extends throughout life with a sequence of phases, sometimes reversing parenting roles in later life. Erik Erikson eloquently described the themes of the stages beyond adolescence as growing in intimacy, generativity, and integrity.[1]

The emphasis of this chapter is on the developmental stages of childhood and the adult developmental stage of generativity. I will focus on parenthood as a growth process, commonly accepted principles of childrearing, individual differences in children and parents, and the integration of parenthood and the developmental stages of childhood.

PARENTHOOD AS A GROWTH PROCESS

Parenthood necessitates sacrificing personal interests, particularly those related to careers, entertainment, and recreation. It means the loss of privacy, time, and personal freedom. It entails emotional, physical, and financial burdens, not the least of which are worries about the health, behavior, and achievement of one's children. It means coping with annoying behavior, noise, and distractions. For women, there are health and physical consequences of pregnancy and childbirth.

With all of these disadvantages, one wonders why parenthood is attractive to anyone. But for most persons both childbirth and childrearing are eminently creative processes that fulfill their biological capacities to reproduce and to nurture. Biological and adopted children provide for parents such growth opportunities as reliving their own childhoods and being nurturing adults. When it is a mutual growth process, childrearing becomes an exchange of ideas, emotions, and power as children and parents learn how to respect, love, and influence each other.

PRINCIPLES OF CHILDREARING

Nature provides instincts that underlie both mothering and fathering, but throughout history parents have relied upon advice from their extended families and support from their communities. Today parents turn to experts for advice with and without the support of their extended families and communities.

There is a body of knowledge about child development of value to parents. However, it is important to use that knowledge without reinforcing the inclination of parents to desire and seek perfection in themselves and in their children.

Some commonly agreed-upon principles of childrearing are:

- Childrearing is guiding your child from self-centeredness to contributing citizenship.
- Sacrificial parenthood means adjusting your lifestyle to childrearing. It does not mean permitting your life to be dominated by your child. Find time for yourself and your other vital relationships.
- Physical expressions of love are essential from birth on, diminishing in openness and frequency as they become awkward for your child.
- The amount of time you spend with your child is more important than the amount of money you spend on him or her.
- Provide a limited number of toys and games that have lasting value for your child. Cups and blocks are just as much fun as expensive toys for young children.
- Talking, singing, reading, and playing are important ways to get to know your child.
- Identify and encourage your child's interests.
- Maintain your legitimate authority. You are needed more as a parent than as a pal.
- Build your child's self-esteem through realistic accomplishments, not unearned praise.
- Your self-esteem as a parent comes from your attachment bond with your child, not from your child's expressed gratitude, which will come later.
- Just as you internalized parts of own parents and find yourself acting and speaking like them, your child is internalizing parts of you.
- Take care to avoid treating your child as a possession or as an extension of yourself.
- Do not be seduced by the convenience of an "independent child" and encourage your child to grow up too fast too soon.[2]

INDIVIDUAL DIFFERENCES

Individual differences in appearance, skills, and behavior are essential for successful group living. They are most apparent in early and late life, but they tend to be regarded as personal foibles in adults and as problems in children, who usually are expected to fit a standard pattern.

Whether these individual differences are due to nature or nurture is endlessly debated. When we are unhappy with our offspring, we are likely to stress the nature side. When we are proud of them, of course, we are more likely to stress nurture. In fact, both nature and nurture interact in determining human behavior. However, it is possible to sort out the percentage of the variance in individual traits and behavior that is influenced by genetic or environmental factors.

Genetic influences on development generally become more evident as children grow older and even continue to manifest themselves in adulthood. About 50 percent of the variance between individuals in intelligence as measured by IQ tests and temperament (emotionality, activity, and sociability) can be accounted for by genetic factors.[3] Genetic factors also play an important role in the rates in which various parts of the brain mature. For example, some children are not ready to read words fluently until the age of seven.[4]

The behavior of parents toward their children also is influenced by genes. Individual parents differ in the levels of warmth they display toward their children, depending on their genetically influenced temperaments. In contrast, the level of parental protectiveness and authoritarianism is determined by family and cultural backgrounds. At the same time, the temperaments of children do influence levels of parental protectiveness and authoritarianism.[5]

The temperaments of children color parent-child interactions. When they cause interpersonal conflicts or disappointments, they contribute to unwarranted parental frustration and guilt. This is especially true when parents and others expect all children to have the same temperament—the "easy" type as originally described by the child psychiatrists Stella Chess and Alexander Thomas.[6]

The "easy" temperament is characterized by regularity in biological functioning, positive responses to new stimuli, easy adaptability to change, a preponderance of positive mood, and mild to moderate emotional reactions. The "easy" child develops regular sleep and feeding schedules easily, takes to new foods readily, smiles at strangers, adapts quickly to a new school, accepts frustrations with a minimum of fuss, and learns and accepts new rules quickly. An occasional parent worries that such a child is "too easygoing" or a "pushover."

In stark contrast, a child with a "difficult" temperament shows irregularity in biological functioning, predominately negative responses to new stimuli, slow adaptability to change, frequent negative moods, and emotional responses of high intensity. This child is not easy to feed, put to sleep, bathe, or dress. New places, new activities, and strange faces may produce initial responses of protest or crying. Frustration often results in a tantrum. Because brain development ultimately catches up, these children finally adapt and often function easily, consistently, and even ebulliently. While their final adaptations may be excellent, how their parents react to their "difficult" temperament is crucial in determining whether they move toward adaptive or maladaptive interactions with people.

The "slow-to-warm-up" child combines quiet withdrawal from the unfamiliar with slow adaptability to new situations. The child does not exhibit the intense reactions, negative mood, and irregular biological functioning of the "difficult" child. When first given a new food, the "slow-to-warm-up" baby turns away quietly. Later, when first put in a tub, the child lies quietly and fusses mildly. When introduced to a stranger, the child clings to the mother. Parents need to learn to know when to shield such children from anxiety-producing experiences and when and how often to provide those exposures so that such children have opportunities to become comfortable in new situations.

It is helpful for parents to recognize their personal qualities that reflect their own temperaments. Parents and children who share "difficult" and "slow-to-warm-up" temperaments are prone to conflicts.

PARENTHOOD AND THE STAGES OF CHILD DEVELOPMENT

When entered by choice in adulthood, after one has passed through the developmental stages of childhood and adolescence, parenthood is an expression of the Eriksonian generative stage in the life cycle. This stage builds on a balance of interpersonal dependence and interdependence so that a person can sustain loving relationships with others. Achieving the generative stage of adult development is signaled by a person's capacity to care for others based on a reasonably solid sense of one's own identity as a worthwhile person.

As an expression of generativity, parenthood involves growing with a child through the child's unfolding stages of development. In this way parent and child are intertwined in a process of mutual growth. The baby's compelling needs initially set the agenda as the baby stimulates responses from a parent. In turn the parent's responses stimulate the baby, who responds to those stimuli in an evolving synergistic circle.

Child development has recently been popularized as brain development. As is true of all popular fashions in child development theories, this trend runs the risk of increasing the fear of some parents that they will permanently damage their children's brains. For this reason, it is important to know that the newly developed brain-imaging techniques simply affirm the well-established fact that human interactions are vital to the healthy development of children. Their main value is providing indisputable evidence that can be used to shape public policies about childrearing.

The early years of life are vital to success in later life because the brain is not fully developed at birth, just as the rest of the body is not. During the early years, brain cells form connections that are strengthened or weeded out by the presence or lack of stimuli from other people and objects in a child's environment and by a child's own activities. A child's play shapes brain development, as does human interaction.

The brain requires modulated levels of activation in order to grow and to develop its functions properly. Just as the body will not grow without the input of food, the brain will not grow without the input of human interactions and environmental experiences. Furthermore, physical and emotional abuse can cause damage to the vulnerable developing brain. Fortunately, the brain continues to grow throughout life so that the effects of early life experiences can be modified.

Because all children's brains develop at different rates, the times of developmental stages that reflect breakthroughs in brain development are only approximations. The stages of development shift back and forth between a child's dependent and independent yearnings. After each stage a new person—a new self—emerges.

Pregnancy and Birth

For a mother, three babies come together at the moment of birth: the imagined baby prior to pregnancy; the developing fetus; and the actual newborn baby who can be seen, heard, and finally held.[7]

When the time of delivery arrives, the mother must be ready to create a new bond with the baby. There is an abrupt ending of the sense of fusion with the fetus fostered by pregnancy. She must adapt to a new being who evokes feelings of strangeness, mourn the loss of the imaginary baby and the fetus in her body, cope with fears of harming the helpless baby, and learn to tolerate and enjoy the enormous demands made on her by the total dependency of the baby.

The Infant

Dependence is obvious during the first eighteen months while children create body images—the foundation of the self—from interacting with their own bodies, other people, and their physical environments. A baby and parent begin an intertwined, mutually rewarding relationship that is most intense at the beginning of the child's life and gradually matures to an adult level of independence and appropriate interdependence.

The first three months are exciting for parents because new capacities become evident every week. Newborns are ready to express their needs and experience the world through sight, sound, taste, touch, and smell. They form internal images of the physical features of the mother's face.

They reach out to the world by taking objects and their perceptions of other persons into themselves. In the same way, a baby becomes a part of the parent through mutually rewarding smiling, cooing, and cuddling. These internalized images of their bodies and behaviors are the building blocks for emotional attachment bonds with each other.

After birth the parent needs to adapt to the baby's rhythms and learn the baby's "language," such as what the baby's fussing and crying mean. Newborns need help in developing their attention spans through eye contact with parents. Through their intimate interaction, both baby and parent learn to anticipate each other's responses and become a single unit. This process strengthens the baby's internal controls so that the baby becomes more and more capable of self-regulation. The baby's brain development is stimulated by these interactions.

From three to six months, babies begin to develop muscle control so that they learn to roll over and sit up. They begin to interact with things in the environment and with other people through their hands and mouths. A baby's senses of touch, taste, and smell are important ways of relating to the human and material environment. Parents need to follow their urges to caress, cuddle, and kiss their babies.

From six to twelve months, babies can distinguish between family members and strangers. "Stranger anxiety" appears, indicating that the child has achieved enough self-awareness to recognize dependency on familiar persons. During this period children begin vocal communication. Babbling turns into simple sounds with meaning.

Although currently out of vogue, well-stocked playpens provide all the exploratory opportunities that mobile babies need, relieve parents of constant supervision, and offer safe time-out places later on.

During the first year, babies set the agenda, so parents need not be concerned about "spoiling" them.

The Toddler

Independence begins to emerge between twelve months and three and a half years, a time of testing limits and taking risks. The first part of the self—self-awareness—emerges as children use *I* to express their wishes and needs. They seek independence from others though oppositional behavior and words, especially *no*. Because self-awareness is embedded in a child's wishes, the frustration of a child's impulsive wishes is tantamount to the temporary loss of the self, as seen in the catastrophic reaction of a temper tantrum (in the words of one child, "my brain flew out").

From twelve to eighteen months, toddlers are in perpetual motion, both walking and talking. They seek new activities, take things apart and put them back together. They use words for self-expression, often two-word combinations. They are possessive of their toys and belongings.

Two-year-olds insist on a degree of independence that makes them difficult to manage. At the same time, they become attached to security objects, such as blankets, stuffed animals, and dolls. They expand their motor skills and their vocabularies and increase their attention spans. Their play becomes more creative.

Life is much easier for parents who show their children that they mean *no* by using their feet instead of their voices in enforcing limits. A parent's *no* must supersede a child's *no* if the child is to learn how to tolerate frustration and postpone gratification. The failure to set and enforce reasonable limits from this stage on can "spoil" a child.

The Young Child

Independence clearly is the theme between three and a half and six years, when children begin to be aware of their attributes and when their actions test the limits of their power. Children feel manipulated by others and want to control them, leading to a clash of wills. This stage of self-development has been aptly called the "Imperial Stage" by Robert Kegan.[8]

Three-year-olds may be well-developed young people, who lead a life full of contrasts from running fast to sitting quietly and from enjoying the playground to concentrating on a puzzle.[9] Sometimes they express themselves with grown-up words and phrases, using proper grammar. Some will be able to tell stories and play games. They know the difference between "good" and "bad" behavior but need firm guidance to be able to control themselves. They can learn rules and understand instructions in cooperative play. When they are so inclined, they can follow the example of older children and adults and learn to use the toilet.

Four-year-olds continue to become more independent. They can learn to skip, jump, throw, kick, and turn somersaults. At the same time, they are achieving fine motor skills like cutting and drawing. They begin to understand concepts in greater depth. They can understand directions that have more than one step and stories with details. Some begin writing their names and recognize letters and words. They enjoy having their ideas written down for them by adults. They have inquiring minds and can solve simple problems. They like sorting and sequencing and can learn to have a positive attitude toward cleaning up and doing chores. "Why" and "how" questions are prevalent and provide many opportunities for learning facts. They understand gender differences but usually do not prefer to play with either boys or girls.

Three-and four-year-olds rapidly build their vocabularies and can benefit from having things explained to them. This period is a critical time for learning language. Never again will the child have the ability to learn language-related activities with such ease. Reading aloud exposes a child to the delights and pleasures of reading.

Everyone has the potential for being creative. This is the time for parents to begin to stimulate creativity by setting up situations and allowing children to complete them; by giving children materials and allowing them to put together a product; and by stressing *doing* an activity over the end result. Parents can be models of creative acts and attitudes and can provide access to and become involved in preschool and kindergarten programs.

The Older Child

Dependence reappears between the ages of six and twelve when children become more sensitive to the evaluations of others and are able to make judgments about themselves. They gradually come to rely more on knowledge than action. They are able to relate to and identify with their teachers, to delay gratification, to pay attention, to persist in activities, and to enjoy mastering challenges. The self becomes more distinctly defined in terms of what one can and cannot do and what one does or does not know in comparison to others. Children tend toward conformity and are sensitive to embarrassment during this stage.

The involvement of parents in their school activities and homework plays an essential role in children's success in school. Parents need to help their children deal with the negative things they see at school, in their communities, and in the media. Parents can help their children learn how to forgive others and themselves, especially by modeling forgiveness in their own behavior.

The Early Adolescent

Independence begins to dominate again between twelve and fifteen when adolescents are able to theorize about themselves and to conceive of themselves as separate independent persons composed of many parts. One's self-evaluation is based on the fashions and behaviors of peers and adulated adults. This is expressed through the tendency of the young person to create an "imaginary audience" before which one continually performs, as described by David Elkind.[10] At the same time, defining oneself occurs through contrasting oneself with parents and other adults, often with accurate criticisms and oppositional behavior.

Early adolescents are preoccupied with accommodating bodily changes and learning how to cope with newly acquired sensations and skills. They turn to others for mirroring and acceptance that provides them with self-validation. They are highly sensitive to criticism and to enticements that foster risk-taking behavior. This is the time for parents to encourage sensitivity to the needs and viewpoints of others through opportunities to help others in their communities.

When adolescents become parents, they must simultaneously deal with the responsibilities of childrearing and their own physical, emotional, psychological, educational, and social developmental issues. They continue to need parenting themselves.

The Middle Adolescent

During middle adolescence from fifteen to seventeen, young persons are preoccupied with exploring intimate relationships with other people. At the same time, instinctual activity encouraged by contemporary social values thrusts boys and girls into sexual encounters before they have had the opportunity to become fully familiar with their own bodies, feelings, and cultural values. As a result many assume pseudo-adult facades and engage in adult behaviors in efforts to quickly shed the trappings of adolescence. They are vulnerable to seduction, exploitation, and betrayal. This is especially the case for those who are temperamentally inclined to form intense relationships.

The availability and interest of parents in the background is reassuring to middle adolescents, who still need to talk with their parents about important issues. Scheduling meals together is a way of setting aside time for conversation.

The Late Adolescent

Late adolescence flowers during the senior year of high school and a variable number of succeeding years. The central issue is settling on one's identity in realistic social roles and choosing a lifestyle and career. During this time access to education or employment is vital.

Erik Erikson identified the need for a "psychosocial moratorium" after high school—a period to take time off from preparing for later life and to actively explore the world.[11] The military service and youth service programs can fill this important developmental need for many young people.

The Adult

Both independence and dependence are reconciled during adulthood as an interdependent self emerges when one fits self-concepts into an expanding number of social roles. This stage has sufficient autonomy to permit intimacy with others so that one can be both independent of and dependent upon others.

UNREALISTIC PARENT-CHILD INTERACTIONS

The child psychoanalyst Selma Fraiberg pointed out the presence of "ghosts in the nursery." She called them visitors from the pasts of the parents.[12] Such an intrusive ghost can hamper a loving engagement with a child when a parent reacts to imagined characteristics of a child rather than to the real child.

All parents must adjust to their children's imperfections, just as spouses must do after marriage. But the physicians Berry Brazelton and Bertrand Cramer describe a number of ways in which realistic interaction between a parent and child can be derailed.[13] A parent may react to a child as if the child is someone from the parent's past and endow the child with features of that person. For example, unreasonable fears that a child might die can be seen with the "replacement child" after the death of a sibling.

Babies can be so idealized that parents are disappointed with reality. This can occur with any child but is more likely to occur with a child who has a birth defect or a disorder. It also is more likely to occur with adolescent parents.

A child may be expected to be a source of love for a parent who did not experience sufficient love in the past. Such a parent may demand that a small baby show overt signs of affection. Parents who felt deprived by their own parents may expect their children to become loving mother figures to them. The parent interprets a baby's smiles as expressions of love and crying as expressions of dislike of the parent. A parent also may experience a child as a judgmental parent and interpret the behavior of an unhappy infant as criticism or rejection.

A child may be experienced as a sibling of a parent. Such a parent resents the affection and gratification that the child receives from others because of revived jealousy of a sibling. A child may be experienced as a tyrant who rules the parent, like an older sibling did in the past. Or a child may be experienced as a vulnerable sibling and be overprotected.

When a parent unconsciously views a child as a feared or hated person from the past, the parent may avoid or lash out at the child. When parents have unrealistic avoidant, hostile, or other inappropriate interactions with their children, the possibility of a "ghost in the nursery" merits consideration.

Besides projecting images of past persons or ways of relating onto others, parents tend to project parts of themselves on their children. While most parents tend to see ideal, highly cherished qualities in their children, especially babies, others project their own "bad" characteristics onto children. It is literally true that the qualities we like least in other persons are our own. When aspects of a child's behavior seem to match an equivalent tendency that the parents despise in themselves, a vicious circle of condemnation and self-fulfilling prophecy may prevail. Parents then overreact to and discourage or inhibit the corresponding behavior in a child. For example, a passive infant may be seen as lazy. A baby's stubborn feeding behavior may reflect a hidden feeding preference of the parents. A parent may complain about clinging, dependent behavior in a child when it is the parent who fears separation.

CONCLUSION

Childrearing is a mutual growth process for both parents and children. For parents, it is balancing their needs and wishes with the needs and wishes of their children.

The early years of life are vital to success in later life because the brain, just as the rest of the body, is not fully developed at birth. A baby and parent begin an intertwined, mutually rewarding relationship that is most intense at the beginning of the child's life and gradually matures to an adult level of independence and appropriate interdependence. The stages of development shift back and forth between dependent and independent yearnings. After each stage a new person—a new self—emerges.

Whether individual differences in appearance, skills, and behavior are due to nature or nurture is endlessly debated. In fact, both nature and nurture interact in determining human behavior. It is helpful for parents to recognize their children's temperamental patterns and their own personal qualities that reflect their own temperaments.

Children need to learn that being responsible for themselves and for others is the source of meaning and purpose that brings fulfillment in life. Helping them do so is the satisfaction that parents gain from growing with their children.

NOTES

1. Erikson, E. (1959) *Identity and the life cycle: Selected papers.* New York: International Universities Press.
2. Elkind, D. (1981) *The hurried child: Growing up too fast too soon.* Reading, Mass.: Addison-Wesley.
3. Plomin, R., et al. (1997) *Behavioral genetics* (3e). New York: W. H. Freeman.

4. Westman, J. C. (1990) *Handbook of learning disabilities: A multisystem approach*. Boston: Allyn and Bacon, p. 332.

5. Kendler, K. S. (1996) Parenting: A genetic-epidemiologic perspective. *American Journal of Psychiatry* 153 (1): 11–20.

6. Chess, S., & Thomas, A. (1977) *Temperament and development*. New York: Bruner/Mazel.

7. Brazelton, T. B., & Cramer, B. G. (1990) *The earliest relationship: Parents, infants, and the drama of early attachment*. Reading, Mass.: Addison-Wesley, p. 3.

8. Kegan, R. (1982) *The evolving self*. Cambridge: Harvard University Press.

9. Goldberg, S. (1997) *Parent involvement begins at birth*. Boston: Allyn and Bacon, pp. 112–114.

10. Elkind, D. (1968) Cognitive development in adolescence. In J. F. Adams (ed.), *Understanding adolescence: Current developments in adolescent psychology*. Boston: Allyn and Bacon.

11. Erikson, E. H. (1968) *Identity: Youth and crisis*. New York: Norton.

12. Fraiberg, S. (1980) *Clinical studies in infant mental health: The first year of life*. New York: Basic Books.

13. Brazelton, T. B., & Cramer, B. G. (1990) *The earliest relationship: Parents, infants, and the drama of early attachment*. Reading, Mass.: Addison-Wesley, pp. 139–161.

4

Motherhood

BERNICE WEISSBOURD

> Mother cradles the baby in her arms. Father takes the baby up to the mountain top to view the world.
>
> Mayan proverb

This Mayan proverb beautifully expresses the unique roles of both mothers and fathers in children's lives.

This chapter will address the things children need from their parents, the idealization of motherhood, the "motherly attitude," "second shift mothers," the "time crunch," "mommy wars," mothers-in-law, and how society can support motherhood.

WHAT CHILDREN NEED FROM THEIR PARENTS

Any discussion of motherhood and fatherhood raises the question of what children need from their parents in order to grow up to be healthy, productive citizens.

All children benefit from environments that provide some order and that meet their basic physical and material needs for food, shelter, and clothing. All children need a continuous relationship with a consistently attentive and caring adult—someone unconditionally in love with them who stimulates, nurtures, and treats them as special. All children need adults who provide limits, appropriate responsibilities, and challenges and who pass on important social and moral expectations. All children need freedom from exploitation and discrimination, opportunities for constructive achievement in their schools and communities, and friendships with adults. And all children should have a sense of justice in their world.

When their developmental needs are fulfilled, children are likely, as are adults, to trust themselves and the environment in which they live. In a nation searching for answers to childhood violence, that perpetrated by children as well as by adults on children, we must apply our knowledge of what children need.

Ideally, children thrive when they have both a mother and a father who care deeply about them and about each other, who are attentive to their signals, and who guide them appropriately. Children who have both mothers and fathers actively involved in their lives are fortunate. Many children grow up to be healthy adults who have single (whether divorced or never married) mothers or fathers, blended families, extended families, multigenerational families, and adoptive families. Although there are different family structures, the functions of parents remain the same.

Stereotyped parental roles have changed dramatically. Both mothers and fathers can be and are nurturers. Both mothers and fathers can be and are providers. This change in attitude toward motherhood was seen in a national survey that asked, "Do you agree or disagree that it is much better for everyone involved if the man is the achiever outside the home and the woman takes care of the home and family?" Sixty-six percent of adults agreed in 1977. By 1996, only 38 percent did so.[1]

THE IDEALIZATION OF MOTHERHOOD

The image of a mother has changed from a saintly, adored woman tirelessly and lovingly caring for her brood of children, as in the poem of Alfred Lord Tennyson, "Mother is the name for God in the lives and hearts of little children," or Victor Hugo's "Mother's arms are made of tenderness—and sweet sleep blesses the child who lies therein." Today the image of motherhood is a woman devoted not only to her children but also to her career (which may be childrearing) and to her personal interests.

While both mothers and fathers struggle with stereotypes, mothers are especially prone to disillusionment.[2] This is in part because the needs of young children are increasingly at variance with our society's way of life. When things go wrong with children, mothers often are blamed, either for leaving home to work and neglecting their children or for staying at home and overprotecting them. This situation reflects our society's simultaneous idealization and disparagement of motherhood.

Most of this century has been dominated by an idealization of motherhood in the popular emphasis on the irreplaceable nature of mother love and mother-infant attachment bonding.[3] In spite of this idealization, mothers actually have been subjected to social pressures that disparage mothering as a rewarding and important career. For example, mothers receive little help in adapting their places of employment to their family lives.

Because of this polarized idealization and disparagement, a historical perspective on motherhood is needed.[4] Most people do not realize that for the first time in history the majority of mothers in the United States brought up their children virtually alone during the middle of the last century. Their husbands were away at work all day, and they had little help at home. There was little or no community or neighborhood life and little or no contact with their own families. Coming from small families themselves, they had limited previous experience with young children. Experts told them that children needed their continuous and exclusive presence and that separating mothers and children was psychologically damaging to the children. That era of mothers and children segregated from the mainstream of society was a historically new phenomenon that ultimately broke down when most mothers became employed away from their homes.

Motherhood today has a new face. Since women have fewer children and live longer than in previous generations, the period with children at home is a much smaller percentage of a women's total lifetime. It also is obvious that casting blame on mothers who go to work is no longer an option; both liberals and conservatives recognize that this phenomenon is here to stay. At the same time, we must not undervalue the mother who stays at home and the uniqueness of motherhood.

THE "MOTHERLY ATTITUDE"

Because women give birth to children, motherhood is a much more clearly defined social role than fatherhood. Deeply ingrained biological, cultural, and social forces drive women toward maternal and men toward paternal role distinctions.

"Motherliness" is a nurturant human quality that is not confined to women. Many men have motherly qualities, and more would develop them if society or circumstances permitted them to do so.[5] However, the psychologist Carol Gilligan points out that in our society the "ideal" person has not been "motherly."[6] Based on the masculine model, the ideal person is commonly imagined to be independent and capable of distancing oneself from one's own emotions. Motivated by fierce individualism, the ideal person neither asks for nor gives quarter, as in competitive athletics or business.

In contrast with the masculine stereotypical emphasis on one's image in the eyes of others, Gilligan describes a "motherly attitude" as one of caring for others. Rather than using visual imagery to depict the self, she employs the metaphor of the voice. For her, it is not by looking that the self develops but by talking and listening. Through dialogue with others and sharing their concerns and desires, we come to understand ourselves and our responsibilities in the world. In this image, the self gains strength by becoming part of a network of relationships, not by wielding power over others.

Sara Ruddick proposed that, in a societal sense, the "motherly attitude" is an excellent foundation for world peace, not because mothers are adept at love in a sentimental way but because their parenting work is so embedded in the actual potential for small-scale violence in parent-child interactions that they have had to work out strategies for daily nonviolence.[7] Ruddick suggests that resolving the temptations to assault, abandon, and seek vengeance is inherent in women's relationships with children and with their husbands. This quality is important because violent tendencies are inherent in childhood and in family life. A nonviolent attitude can evolve from daily encounters with resolving conflicts between children and between children and parents.

For most women motherhood is the most satisfying experience of their lives despite its stresses. Unfortunately, for some it may be the only satisfying experience they have known. Those mothers encounter difficulty when the active phase of mothering is over, especially if they have made no preparations for the postchildrearing years of their lives.

"SECOND SHIFT MOTHERS"

A new phrase aptly describes how employment away from home affects a mother's daily life: "second shift mothers." The old expression "a woman's work is never done," which referred to the endless chores of shopping, cooking, laundry, and housekeeping, has given way to "second shift." After working away from home during the day, the woman assumes her second job—that of caring for house and children.

In 1950, only 25 percent of all wives were in the paid labor force, and just 16 percent of children had mothers who worked outside the home. By 1998, of the mothers with children under the age of six 44 percent were in the labor force full-time and 20 percent part-time.[8]

Although fathers are increasingly committed to sharing responsibilities in their homes, research indicates that over the period of a year women spend a full month of twenty-four-hour days more than their husbands on childcare and housework. In fact, the way survey questions are asked reflects prevailing attitudes: "Does your husband *help* with the house and with the children?" The assumption persists that the responsibility is the mother's, while fathers have the choice of whether or not to give assistance. In some instances, a woman taking on the roles of both nurturing mother and breadwinner has created a situation in which the father feels he is not needed or cannot find a place in the family constellation. An awareness on the part of mothers that they may cause the father's alienation might be a first step in alleviating it.

These factors contribute to making the roles of mothers today exceedingly stressful. Mothers start early in the morning with getting one child ready for daycare, another for school, leaving a note for the cleaner, and figuring out what to have for dinner, and end the day with the precious few minutes of reading a bedtime story to a child who wants more and more. It is difficult for the middle-class mother, especially the single mother. For the poor mother who may also be single, it can be overwhelming. In addition to routine daily tasks, poor mothers are expected to work efficiently through the complicated systems of welfare, health, jobs, and social services.

Stress results not only from efforts to balance employment and family responsibilities but from problems within one realm or the other. Demands on the job may be unreasonable or the employer inflexible, often not allowing phone calls home or time off to attend a child's school performance. Being primarily responsible for what goes on at home while having little or no control of the job situation is a breeding ground for tension. Conversely, tension at home affects performance in the place of employment.

In addition, family-unfriendly communities are major factors in making life more difficult for parents. If mothers do not feel that it is safe for their children to walk to the bus and must arrange for transportation—worse yet, if there is no adequate public transportation—managing each day becomes increasingly complicated. The lack of after-school care or early morning care forces many mothers to resort to "latchkeys" for their children.

THE TIME CRUNCH

Parents are experiencing a time crunch. One of the most serious pressures on mothers is the lack of time they have with their children. It takes time to provide what children need, time to listen to their concerns, and time for children and mothers to enjoy each other.

The phrase *quality time* is misleading, because it implies that it is what you do with time with your children that is important, not the amount of time. If, for example, you have twenty minutes to spend and want to have a serious talk with your child about her day, but she happens to be deeply immersed in a book she's reading, should you expect her to stop and talk to you? Whose quality time is it? Being there when your child has questions or wants to tell you something is important—and being there takes time. A recent survey of teenagers surprised many when the question "What do you think would make your life better?" prompted a majority of teens to respond: "more time with my parents—doing things together—not cars, fine homes, or televisions."

Such pressures take their toll. Of special concern for our nation is the increasing rate of depression in mothers.[9] Between 20 and 25 percent of mothers between twenty-five and forty years of age experience a major depression. And minor depressions characterized by chronic feelings of helplessness, worthlessness, and lack of any hope are experienced by 30 to 50 percent of mothers of young school-age children; this figure goes up to 70 percent among families living in poor neighborhoods. If we are concerned with motherhood in the context of children's needs, we must translate those figures into what they mean for children's lives. Children of depressed mothers are four times as likely as other children to be depressed themselves and five times as likely to abuse drugs.

"MOMMY WARS"

Stay-at-home mothers and employed mothers are not enemies, as implied in the unfortunate phrase "mommy wars." In the interests of their children, they each need support in the choices they make.

The answer to the stresses of mothering is not simply for mothers to stay at home, which for some employed mothers would be financially impossible. Besides, for many mothers, a fulfilling career enhances their ability to be good mothers and to build positive relationships with their children.[10] We say that children must have at least one person unconditionally in love with them and totally involved with them. If a child's mother is told her place is at home with the children, but she resents very much being at home, how can she build a good relationship with her child? On the other hand, if she has to work and wants to be home with her child, but cannot be, how does that affect her feelings about being a mother and her relationship with her child? In both cases, the mothers' feelings inevitably spill over into their parenting interactions.

MOTHERS-IN-LAW

The mother-in-law role deserves special mention because it is so vulnerable to misunderstandings and conflicts. Successful navigation of this role involves being willing to let go of the relationship with one's son or daughter and being willing to cultivate a new relationship with the son- or daughter-in-law.

The first principle is to accept and honor your son's or daughter's choice of a spouse. Hopefully it will be easy; however, there are times when it is not. Once your son or daughter decides to marry someone, being critical, angry, or judgmental is unlikely to change the situation. If you continue to harbor a negative attitude, you most likely will drive a wedge between you and your child, and you will be the loser.

On the other hand, extending acceptance and unconditional love can positively influence your own and the lives of others. Being careful about criticizing your son- or daughter-in-law directly or indirectly is an important policy. Even if your children are making obvious mistakes in your view, patience will be more successful than intervening, unless there are extreme problems, such as child abuse or destructive addictions.

HOW SOCIETY CAN SUPPORT MOTHERHOOD

The changed roles of mothers necessitate changing the way our society works for children and families. Although there is general consensus on what children need, less has been written on what parents need. Just as it is difficult for hungry children to learn in school, it is difficult for hungry parents to learn in parent education classes. Parents need economic security. They need to know where the next meal is coming from, that there is money to pay the rent, and that there are jobs where they can make a decent living. Social networks are essential to provide emotional and concrete support for parents. Isolation is an important cause of depression and of violence in families.

Underlying the need for a societal commitment to families is the fact that no family can raise children alone. We are all, regardless of economic status, dependent on the quality and availability of necessary resources—good schools, parks, libraries, family resource centers, childcare programs, and adequate health care. Families thrive when they are part of a community in which they participate and contribute. And parents and children need time to spend together in family activities. The valid, though perhaps overused, expression "it takes a village to raise a child" embraces the notion that families need each other to provide a healthy environment for the community's children. We need a U.S. Declaration of *Interdependence.*

What can we do as a society to reorient our systems of employment for mothers and fathers? We can focus on making society family-friendly:

- Our workplaces must provide part-time work, flexible working hours, easily available, high-quality childcare, and/or work at home for mothers who are employed, and assured maternity leave for at least six months, including a plan for salary provisions.
- Our tax structure must recognize the financial value of parenthood in our economy by varied forms of deductions and allowances.
- Our health care systems must deliver high-quality medical care from the prenatal period forward and a program for home visitors after childbirth.
- Our communities must maintain excellent public schools, provide after-school programs, offer a rich array of community activities, and provide family resource centers where parents can obtain information and form friendships necessary to reduce their isolation.

Creating a society in which the above mentioned systems are working for families is not an idealist's dream. In our wealthy nation it is not even out of reach. In fact, it is more fiscally responsible than our usual pattern of waiting for crises to occur before providing services.

Along with our expanding knowledge of programs that work is burgeoning research on the early years of a child's life and the importance of giving children a "right start." This information often creates anxiety in mothers whose stressful lives leave little time for providing what their infants and toddlers require. The cost of providing parental leave could prove to be less than the cost of providing quality childcare for infants and toddlers and be far better for the emotional health of both baby and mother. Presently, our parental leave policies are woefully inadequate, though they mark what could be the first steps in formulating public policy consistent with current information on infant development.

Some encouraging things are happening. Increasingly, states are changing their systems to work for families, and more communities are coming together to plan for their children. Childcare has moved to the top of our domestic agenda. We know the programs necessary to alleviate the stresses on mothers, starting with good prenatal care, and we also know that 80 percent of the mothers suffering from depression can move to recovery with a combination of antidepressants, therapy, and ongoing family support.[11]

Urie Brofenbrenner emphasizes the importance of one indispensable loving person in a child's life. He uses scientific language to describe this simple concept as a proximal process—active participation in progressively complex reciprocal interactions with persons, objects, symbols—on a regular basis over extended periods of time. We know what polices could create an environment in which children were able to have these necessary experiences.[12]

There is a strange contradiction in our society: we demand that mothers on welfare go into the workforce at the same time that we want tax relief to allow middle-class mothers to stay at home. Should mothers of all classes who prefer to be at home with their children in the early years be able to, and should mothers of all classes who prefer to work be assured of good-quality childcare? The fact is, most parents need help with the increasing financial demands of raising children today. This is reflected in the striking expansion in the number of childcare proposals: subsidies for the working poor, tax credits for the middle class, expansion of Head Start and Early Head Start, and funds for after-school programs.

CONCLUSION

Motherhood is a more clearly defined role than fatherhood in our society. As a result the age-old tensions between motherhood and other social roles have intensified in recent decades. Mothering still tends to be viewed as synonymous with homemaking.

The giving, caring, and doing that women provide in the ordinary course of day-to-day mothering often goes unnoticed by men, by women who are not mothers, and by society in general. This is a dire oversight. Not only are mothers essential for the future of society, but to be a mother is to give of oneself in a way unique in human experience.

Still mothers continue to be discriminated against in their unfair treatment by fathers who shun domestic and childrearing responsibilities, by divorce laws that reduce their standard of living and opportunities for advancement, by single-parent situations that hold some in a life of poverty, and by the failure of workplaces to accommodate the needs of families. At the same time, the growing influences of motherliness on social values is seen in a gradual shift of the image of the ideal person from a purely individualistic, competitive image to a more caring, conflict-resolving, and cooperative image.

For most mothers today, daily life is a balancing act between the demands of work and family, between being nurturing and being efficient, and between feeling competent and feeling overwhelmed. Families, friends, and strong communities serve to lessen the pressures. Equally important, mothers deserve, starting from pregnancy, to have supportive policies and programs in order to meet the needs of their children—needs they know so well and often find difficult to fulfill.

NOTES

1. Cherlin, A. (1998) By the numbers. *New York Times Magazine,* April 5.

2. Dally, A. (1983) *Inventing motherhood: The consequences of an ideal.* New York: Schocken, p. 18.

3. Ibid, p. 92.

4. DeVault, M. L. (1991) *Feeding the family: The social organization of caring as gendered work.* Chicago: University of Chicago Press.

5. Dally, A. (1983) *Inventing motherhood: The consequences of an ideal.* New York: Schocken, p. 200.

6. Gilligan, C., Ward, J. V., & Taylor, J. McL. (1989) *Mapping the moral domain: A contribution to women's thinking to psychological theory and education.* Cambridge: Harvard University Press.

7. Ruddick, S. (1989) *Maternal thinking: Toward a politics of peace.* Boston: Beacon Press, p. xxvi.

8. Bureau of Labor Statistics (1998) *Marital and family characteristics of the labor force from the March 1998 current population survey.* Washington, D.C.: U.S. Department of Labor.

9. Weissbourd, R. (1998) The impact of parental depression on children. Unpublished paper. Kennedy School of Government, Graduate School of Education, Harvard University.

10. Shreve, A. (1987) *Remaking motherhood: How working mothers are shaping our children's future.* New York: Viking Press, p. 205.

11. Weissbourd, R. (1998) The impact of parental depression on children. Unpublished paper. Kennedy School of Government, Graduate School of Education, Harvard University.

12. Bronfenbrenner, U. (2000) Growing chaos in the lives of children, youth, and families: How can we turn it around? In J. C. Westman (ed.), *Parenthood in America.* Madison: University of Wisconsin Press.

5

Fatherhood

ROGER T. WILLIAMS

One night, when I tucked my then seven-year-old son in bed, I said my usual "good night" and told him I loved him. He looked up at me and said, "Dad, why do you keep telling me you love me? You've probably told me that a zillion times!" His comment took me by surprise, and I could not respond for several seconds. Then, my response came from deep inside of me: "Landon, I guess it's because when I was a kid I never heard my Dad say he loved me. I want you to know that I love you. I don't want you to ever have to wonder about that. And I want you to know that I will love you always, no matter what happens." Landon looked up at me and said, "Thanks, Dad—I love you too!"

This event brought me face-to-face with the fact that my fathering style represents a 180-degree shift from my father's. My dad could never really find the words to say he loved me. I have come to understand that it was not his fault: he was parenting the way his parents did, and they parented the way previous generations of Welsh parents did. It has taken time, but I have come to forgive him.

This story highlights the importance of making a conscious decision about how to father. The one rock-solid gift we can give our sons and daughters is our unconditional love and support. A child's knowledge that he or she is loved, valued, and appreciated is the basic building block of a strong self-concept. If we do not make this basic decision, then we are likely to father the way our fathers did, and that is likely to be the way their father's fathered them.

In *The Five Key Habits of Smart Dads,* Paul Lewis emphasizes there are five tasks in making a conscious choice as to what kind of a father one wants to be: (1) grasping your significance as a father, (2) acting intentionally, (3) using your social networks, (4) communicating life skills and principles, and (5) maximizing your fathering moments. Lewis argues that a father's job is to raise a child "to function maturely and productively in society." The imprint a father leaves "is largely shaped by the kind of life skills and principles you select, and affected by whether these are communicated with love, affection and consistency."[1]

This chapter explores several issues: the divided world of fathering, disabled dads, father hunger, fatherhood initiatives, and boys-to-men initiatives.

THE DIVIDED WORLD OF FATHERING

The world of fathering is becoming more divided between the growing numbers of men who view fatherhood as their first priority in life and the millions of fathers who opt out of their fathering responsibilities.

Fathers who invest time in their families demonstrate in words and deeds that they love, value, and appreciate their children. These fathers are supported by a rapidly growing literature on fathering, including books on African American fathering, such as *Becoming Dad: Black Men and the Journey to Fatherhood* by Leonard Pitts, Jr.[2] and *Faith of Our Fathers: African American Men Reflect on Fatherhood* edited by Andre C. Willis.[3]

One of these books, *The Sixty-Minute Father* by Rob Parsons, argues that the first goal of fatherhood should be to "seize the day."[4] Parsons quotes Vincent Foster, deputy counsel to the president of the United States, as he addressed the graduating class of the University of Arkansas School of Law: "Balance wisely your professional life and your family life. If you are fortunate to have children, your parents will warn you that they will grow up and be gone before you know it. I can testify that it is true. God only allows us so many opportunities with our children to read a story, go fishing, play catch, and say our prayers together. Try not to miss one of them. The office can wait. It will still be there after your children are gone."

A growing number of fathers view fatherhood as a very important responsibility. Twenty-five percent of families now report that the father and mother share parenting responsibilities equally, while 10 percent report that the father is the primary caregiver, and 65 percent report that the mother is the primary caregiver.[5] These fathers are supported in their efforts by a growing number of fatherhood initiatives as well as courses specifically targeted to their needs. Several states have launched fatherhood initiatives, and community-based family resource centers increasingly sponsor courses specifically geared to fathers of children who utilize their services.

While millions of fathers are becoming more involved with their families and children, millions are opting out of their responsibility as fathers. They may be fathers of children born out of wedlock who do not wish to own up to their fatherhood. Or they may have experienced nasty divorces and been embittered by a legal process that leaves them out of the loop. Regardless of the cause, there are staggering numbers of children who do not have meaningful relationships with their fathers. Approximately half a million children are born out of wedlock each year, and 50 percent of marriages end in divorce. Thus, the harsh reality is that more than 60 percent of American children will live in a single-parent family sometime during their childhood years and more than 75 percent of children who live in single-parent, mother-headed families will have little or no contact with their biological fathers during that time.[6]

In *Fatherless in America* David Blankenhorn, president of the Institute for American Values, argues that the fatherless family in America "is a radical departure from virtually all of human history and experience." He goes on to say: "Fatherlessness is the most harmful demographic trend of this generation. It is the leading cause of declining child well-being in our society. It also is the engine driving our most urgent social problems, from crime to adolescent pregnancy to child sexual abuse to domestic violence against women. Yet, despite its scale and social consequences, fatherlessness is a problem that is frequently ignored or denied."[7]

Sociologist David Popenoe in *Life without Father* shares Blankenhorn's dismay over fatherless families: "In just three decades, from 1960 to 1990, the percentage of children living apart from their biological fathers more than doubled, from 17 percent to 36 percent."[8] He goes on to identify the negative outcomes associated with fatherless families: crime and delinquency; premature sexuality and out-of-wedlock teen births; deteriorating educational achievement; depression, substance abuse, and alienation among teenagers; and the growing number of women and children in poverty.

DISABLED DADS

Sylvia Ann Hewlett and Cornel West, authors of *The War against Parents,* believe "a major national objective should be to increase the proportion of children who live with and are nurtured by their fathers."[9] If this objective is to be met, we need to understand why men opt out of their responsibility as fathers. Hewlett and West provide powerful insights into this issue. They argue that we have disabled dads in three ways.

- Devalued in the workplace: Real wages have fallen over the past twenty-five years, and the rate of decline has been more rapid for men than for women, down 25 percent for men twenty-five to thirty-four years of age. Hewlett and West argue that a third of all men in that age group now earn less than the amount necessary to keep a family of four above the poverty line. In addition, thousands of men have been affected by corporate downsizing. Health insurance, pensions, and seniority have been eliminated in many work settings. For men who link manhood with being the family provider, these changes have had a negative effect on their actual and perceived ability to serve as providers for their families.

- Abandoned by government: There is virtually no safety net for men who have lost jobs or security in the workplace, since the social welfare system in our country is focused largely on the needs of women and children. In recent years, significant attention has been paid to the issue of "deadbeat dads" who are not contributing to the well-being of their families. Yet much of the resistance to making child support payments is tied to the fact that large numbers of fathers are not granted custody or visitation privileges with their children. Recent measures to deal with "deadbeat dads" exacerbate the situation. Fathers who make payments to the government, rather than to their families, feel even more alienated since they do not see any direct link between these payments and the well-being of their children.
- Demoralized by the media: The media and popular culture increasingly portray men and fathers as redundant, superfluous, and expendable. Television sitcoms and movies like *Thelma and Louise, Boys on the Side,* and *Waiting to Exhale* show strong, vital women in solidarity with each other and living without men who are portrayed as inadequate and unappealing. Murphy Brown, in a famous episode of that situation comedy, joyously chose single motherhood and in doing so granted legitimacy to the notion of fatherless, single-parent families. This attitude has made it difficult for men to experience the dignity, respect, and self-confidence needed to fulfill the roles of husband and father in our society.

FATHER HUNGER

A vast array of literature related to men's issues and the psychology of men has emerged over the past ten years. *Father hunger* is a term that consistently comes through in this literature. It was coined by Sam Osherson in a book entitled *Finding Our Fathers* and has been echoed by many other authors in recent years. Father hunger has come to mean "the gnawing hunger that males feel if they are not able to link with their fathers due to the physical or emotional absence of a father in the family."[10]

The emphasis is on males because most of these authors believe that a father is the best bridge to help adolescent boys cross into responsible and caring adult manhood. Yet girls and women also can experience father hunger if they grow up with a father physically or emotionally absent from their lives.

In a haunting video entitled *Show Your Love* by Sam Kauffmann, several adolescent boys and girls describe what life without a father is like.[11] The father hunger and sense of abandonment come through in a powerful way. A twelve-year-old boy, when asked how he felt about not having his father around, responded by saying, "It sucks—I'd like to be able to spend time with him." When this same boy was asked how he would be as a father, he said, "I'd be doing stuff with him. I would never leave him." In responding to the question "If you could say one thing to all fathers, what would that be?" a twelve-year-old boy said, "Don't screw around with other women. Be loyal to your wife." A sixteen-year-old boy said, "Anybody can make a baby, but it takes a man to be a father." And a sixteen-year-old girl replied, "Show your love to your kids. Let them know how much you care."

It isn't just adolescents who hunger for father contact. A recent article by Andy Hall in the *Wisconsin State Journal* documented the search of a fifty-three-year-old man whose father was killed in a military plane accident as World War II was coming to a close.[12] All Bruce Smith had were a few snapshots of his father, who was killed when Smith was ten months old. Smith knew his time was running out since all of the men who would have served with his father in the Army Air Corps were in their seventies. By displaying one of the photos at an airfield in Madison, Wisconsin, he was eventually able to find more than ten veterans who had served with his father in the war. Smith learned from these veterans that his father tinkered with cars, was fun to be around, could be depended on by his buddies, and was buried with full military honors. After fifty-plus years, the gaping hole left by his father's sudden death was being filled.

Is it just males who benefit from the presence of a father in their lives? Clearly not. Leslie Grendahl shared her account of a National Organization of Women (NOW) meeting.[13] Several of the original founders of NOW—Kathryn Clarenbach, Gene Boyer, and others—were informally exploring what all of these strong, pioneering women had in common. There were very few commonalties, yet one came through clearly: they all had fathers who had faith in them and thought they could do what they wanted to do and be. This faith and encouragement had been a key factor in their success as professional women.

The conclusion is inescapable. Fathers who are physically and emotionally present in the lives of their children, who accept them, nurture them, support them, and encourage them, make a powerful difference. When fathers are absent from their families—physically, emotionally, or economically—they leave their children with a gnawing "father hunger" that is difficult to satisfy.

FATHERHOOD INITIATIVES

How do we go about empowering disabled dads? Several initiatives under way do just that. Two of the most visible movements are the Promise Keepers and the Million Man March. Both are religious movements—the first Christian, attracting primarily Caucasian men, and the second Nation of Islam, aimed at African American men. Both have been criticized for reasserting a male-dominant model of parenting into family life.

Participants maintain that each of these faith-based movements has helped them to reconnect with their families, to place their wives and children first, and to hold themselves to higher levels of accountability for their family lives. They also say they have gained faith-based support groups that help them establish a sense of pride in their manhood and help them deal with the problems and conflicted feelings associated with contemporary family life.

In response to the critique about male dominance, both groups emphasize that the focus is on leading and serving the family, not on dominating others in the family. While this criticism is not likely to go away, there are thousands—perhaps even millions—of men who have become more involved in their families through these two faith-based movements.

There are other fathering initiatives as well. The National Center on Fathering is a nonprofit organization founded in 1990 that focuses on research and education related to fathering.[14] The organization offers seminars, books, and a Web site, publishes a newsletter entitled *Today's Fathers,* and sponsors a biannual Father of the Year essay contest. There is a strong emphasis on instructing fathers in fathering skills and on "turning the hearts of fathers back to their children."

The National Fatherhood Initiative, founded in 1994, is another nonprofit organization aimed at improving children's lives by getting fathers to commit to their families.[15] This initiative sponsors a clearinghouse and resource center, includes over two thousand groups across the country in its resource directory, is actively involved in starting state chapters, and offers a newsletter entitled *Fatherhood Today.* The organization sponsors an annual conference and has initiated an advertising campaign focusing on the importance of fathering in our society.

The Center on Fathers, Families and Public Policy is a training, technical assistance, and public education organization aimed at helping create a society in which parents—both mothers and fathers—can support their children physically, emotionally, and financially.[16] The organization challenges the negative public perception of low-income fathers, who "have much to contribute to their children in the way of emotional and developmental support." There is a strong emphasis on child welfare issues; the organization sees paternity and child support enforcement as central issues for involving men in the lives of their children. The organization also publishes materials, including a newsletter entitled *Issues and Insights*.

Wisconsin is one of the first states to create a statewide fathering initiative: the Wisconsin Fatherhood Initiative.[17] The focus is on an advertising campaign aimed at getting fathers to commit or recommit to carrying out their parenting responsibilities. Small grants are available as incentives for communities to launch their own public awareness campaigns aimed at responsible fatherhood. The initiative includes an executive order from the governor mandating that each state agency examine the father-friendliness of its policies and involve service and religious groups as well as state and local agencies in making fathers more important in the lives of their children.

Also in Wisconsin, the Children's Trust Fund has developed a Positive Fathering initiative. A video created by the fund, showing fathers in positive interactions with their children, has been distributed through family resource centers and other agencies throughout the state, along with a study guide.[18] Beyond developing this video, the Children's Trust Fund helps family resource centers throughout the state conduct workshops and establish libraries on fathering.

BOYS-TO-MEN INITIATIVES

Finally, we come to the thorny issue of how to help adolescent boys evolve into responsible and caring men. School shooting sprees by adolescent boys are dramatic reminders that our society does a poor job of helping adolescent boys transform into manhood. Horrendous damage can be inflicted on our society when immature boys, who lack judgment and impulse control, deal with their frustrations through violence and other irresponsible behavior.

Many adolescent boys are confused about what it means to be a man in our society. Some associate manhood with violence, some with alcohol or other drug abuse, some with sexual prowess, some with a fierce sense of competition, and some with a detached isolationism. Substance abuse, adolescent pregnancy, juvenile delinquency, gang involvement, dropping out of school, teen homicide, and teen suicide are likely outcomes when boys are confused about their male identity.

Several authors in the rapidly evolving field of men's psychology—Robert Bly, Sam Keen, Aaron Kipniss, Michael Meade, Robert Moore, and Sam Osherson—agree that adult males need to guide the transformation from boyhood into manhood. If fathers or other adult males are not present in the family, this function needs to be fulfilled by other adult males in the community.

Michael Meade and Robert Moore point to the critical importance of men initiating boys into manhood. Meade puts it this way:[19] "In many tribal cultures, it was said that if the boys were not initiated into manhood, if they were not shaped by the skills and love of elders, then they would destroy the culture. If the fires that innately burn inside youth are not intentionally and lovingly added to the hearth of community, they will burn down the structures of culture, just to feel the warmth." Robert Moore argues that our society does not provide initiation activities powerful enough to transform boys into responsible and caring men.[20] In his words, "A man who 'cannot get it together' is a man who has probably not had the opportunity to undergo ritual initiation into the deep structures of manhood. He remains a boy, not because he wants to, but because no one has shown him the way to transform his boy energies into man energies."

Initiation processes can be a key component in transforming boys into responsible and caring men. In the last few years, leaders within the African American community and the Native American community have recreated initiation or rites-of-passage activities powerful enough to transition boys into manhood. The Young Warrior Initiation was developed by Chuck Skelton, a Native American of Blackfoot heritage.[21] It is an intense experience, for all boys between thirteen and sixteen, that blends traditional tribal customs with modern male psychology to bring boys face-to-face with what it means to be men, to be responsible and accountable, and to care for themselves and their people. The process is based on the four traditional stages of initiation: the Call, the Separation, the Ordeal, and the Blessing. The final Blessing welcomes adolescents into the community of men; they then choose mentors who will be available for support and guidance during the next year.

The Rites-of-Passage Initiation was developed by Dr. Anthony Mense, based on the West African traditions of his forefathers. This process builds on the traditional stages of initiation, includes the seven principles of Nguzo Saba (unity, self-determination, collective responsibility, cooperative economics, purpose, creativity, and faith), and ends with a celebration experience.[22] Over the course of the initiation, the boy is encouraged to connect with his spiritual calling as a man. He also is brought face-to-face with the heritage of his people and is encouraged to take pride in that heritage. The process can also be used with adults, recognizing that many adults have not experienced the benefits of an initiatory experience.

Beyond initiation, another key component in transforming boys into manhood is the process of mentoring. Emmy Werner conducted longitudinal research on children growing up with persistent poverty and high incidences of alcoholism and mental illness on Hawaii's sugar plantations.[23] She concluded: "Research on resilient children has shown repeatedly that, if a parent is incapacitated or unavailable, other significant people in a young child's life can play an enabling role."

Marc Freedman, in *The Kindness of Strangers,* highlights the growing body of research showing that mentoring relationships with caring adults "can make an important difference in the lives of vulnerable youth as they navigate their way toward adulthood."[24] Freedman examined a variety of different mentoring programs and summarized the benefits of such linkages in the lives of youth:

- Supplying information and opportunities: Mentors can act as a bridge to the outside world, linking youth with social and cultural experiences, college education, and the world of work. Mentors can also serve as advocates for their mentees, making sure they get the kind of treatment in school and community settings that they deserve.
- Providing nurturance and support: Mentors can provide sympathetic ears—caring adults who will listen, offer advice, and help solve problems—in addition to providing a source of affiliation and security for youth. This support is especially important in times of crisis, which can lead to a downward spiral of behavior.
- Preparing youth for adulthood: Mentors can help young people grow up, think through important career decisions, and accept responsibility for their decisions and actions. Mentors can help youth make these difficult decisions in ways that build self-esteem and social competence.

This growing body of research on the importance of mentors in the lives of resilient youth led Colin Powell to sponsor a national summit meeting and launch a nationwide mentoring initiative. This national effort spawned a number of statewide mentoring projects. Among them is the Wisconsin Promise, a partnership between the Alliance for Wisconsin Youth and the Wisconsin National and Community Services Board, which fosters community-based programming based on the five fundamental resources of the initiative: mentoring, nurturing, protecting, teaching, and engaging underserved youth in service.

The Department of Professional Development and Applied Studies at the University of Wisconsin is launching a Boys To Men Project. The overall goal of the project is to engage adult males throughout Wisconsin in mentoring and initiation activities that will help them become responsible and caring men. The project is unique in four ways: (1) it builds on a learning from men's psychology that adult males are a critical factor in guiding boys into manhood; (2) it is a cross-cultural project, drawing on the best traditions in the Native American, African American, Hispanic, and Anglo cultures; (3) it is aimed at preventing a range of problems, including substance abuse, adolescent pregnancy, school dropout, juvenile delinquency, gang involvement, teen homicide, and teen suicide; and (4) it is a statewide effort that establishes local projects in communities across the state and builds on existing programs, such as Big Brothers/Big Sisters, 4-H, and Scouts.

A CLOSING STORY

I began with a story involving my son when he was seven years old. I will close with a recent story about my daughter at the age of nineteen. Stephanie was a sophomore at a small liberal arts college in Wisconsin. Her mother, Kristi, and I were invited to share our experiences with the college at a meeting of prospective students' parents. We arrived at the hall where the meeting was to take place, expecting to meet Stephanie *after* the meeting for a leisurely dinner. She arrived a few minutes *before* the meeting, and I gave her a big welcoming hug. But she continued to hang on long after our initial hug. I asked her what was wrong, and she sobbed, "I'm just stressed out . . . I have so much to do. I didn't do well on a test I had this week, and I have another big test coming up next Wednesday."

Stephanie was taking organic chemistry, calculus, English literature, Buddhism, and chorus and was involved in a leadership role in Girls and Women in Science, Model UN, Gold Key (hosting prospective students on campus), and water aerobics. She was carrying a heavy load, but she had developed an amazing ability to balance multiple tasks. I had never seen her that stressed out before. We talked her through the situation before our meeting and again later while we were having dinner. After arriving home, I sent her a card with this message: "Dear Stephanie, Just a quick note to wish you the best with your exam on Wednesday and with all the other stresses in your life right now. Your mother and I have a lot of faith in you and we love you very much. We are thinking of you and praying for you. Just do the best you can! With much love, Dad and Mom." Enclosed with the card, I enclosed a copy of Virginia Satir's *Rules for Being Human.*[25] The next time we talked she was in good spirits, she had gotten an A on her exam, and she was thankful for our support.

In short, fatherhood is about "being there" for our kids, whether they are seven or nineteen or thirty-three. It is about loving, nurturing, supporting, sharing, and guiding our children. But most of all, it is about having faith in them even when they have lost faith in themselves.

Rob Parsons reminds us that "if we are going to make a difference as fathers, we need to do it now . . . and it has to do with carving those times out of busy lives—today." Carpe diem . . . seize the day!

NOTES

1. Lewis, P. (1996) *The five key habits of smart dads: A powerful strategy for successful fathering.* Grand Rapids, Mich.: Zondervan.
2. Pitts, L., Jr. (1999) *Becoming dad: Black men and the journey to fatherhood.* Atlanta: Longstreet Press.
3. Willis, A. C. (ed.) (1996) *Faith of our fathers: African American men reflect on fatherhood.* New York: Penguin Books.
4. Parsons, R. (1996) *The sixty-minute father: How time well spent can change your child's life.* Nashville: Broadman & Holman.
5. *Zero to Three* (1997) Key findings from a nationwide survey among parents of zero- to three-year-olds. Conducted by Peter D. Hart Research Associates. Baltimore, Md.: National Center for Infants, Toddlers and Families.
6. Phares, V. (1992) Where's Poppa? *American Psychologist,* May.
7. Blankenhorn, D. (1995) *Fatherless America: Confronting our most urgent social problem.* New York: Harper Collins.
8. Popenoe, D. (1996) *Life without father: Compelling new evidence that fatherhood and marriage are indispensable for the good of children and society.* New York: Free Press.
9. Hewlett, S. A., & West, C. (1998) *The war against parents: What we can do for America's beleaguered moms and dads.* New York: Houghton Mifflin.
10. Osherson, S. (1987) *Finding our fathers: How a man's life is shaped by his relationship with his father.* New York: Fawcett Books.
11. Kauffmann, S. (1994) *Show your love.* Video produced at the Boston University College of Communication.
12. Hall, A. (1998) How a long-dead veteran came to life. *Wisconsin State Journal,* November 11.
13. Grendahl, L. (1998) Personal communication, November 19.
14. National Center on Fathering (1998) Information packet. Shawnee Mission, Kansas.
15. National Fatherhood Initiative (1998) Information packet. Gaithersburg, Maryland.
16. Center on Fathers, Families and Public Policy (1998) Information packet. Chicago, Illinois.
17. Wisconsin Fatherhood Initiative (1999) Information packet. Madison, Wisconsin.

18. Children's Trust Fund of Wisconsin (1996) *Positive parenting: Tips on fathering*. Video and study guide. Madison, Wisconsin.

19. Meade, M. (1993) *Men and the water of life: Initiation and the tempering of men*. New York: Harper Collins.

20. Moore, R., & Gillette, D. (1990) *King, warrior, magician, lover: Rediscovering the archetypes of the mature masculine*. New York: Harper Collins.

21. Bear Spirit Medicine Lodge (1998) Informational brochure on the Young Warrior Initiation. Evanston, Illinois.

22. Fields, D. (1999) Personal communication. April 5.

23. Werner, E. E., & Smith, R. S. (1982) *Vulnerable but invincible: A study of resilient children*. New York: McGraw-Hill.

24. Freedman, M. (1993) *The kindness of strangers: Adult mentors, urban youth and the new volunteerism*. San Francisco: Jossey-Bass.

25. Satir, V. (1986) Sixth International Summer Training Institute. Crested Butte, Colo., July/August.

6

Family Life

JACK C. WESTMAN

You are the bows from which your children as living
arrows are sent forth.
The archer sees the mark upon the path of the infinite, and He
bends you with his might that his arrows may go swift and far.
Let your bending in the archer's hand be for gladness;
For even as He loves the arrow that flies, so he loves also the bow
that is stable.

Kahlil Gibran, *The Prophet*

Parenthood often is not seen as an opportunity for growth and personal discovery. Consequently, many parents live in households that are little more than way stations for family members who lead separate lives. As the seductions of materialism and individualism encourage the pursuit of personal excellence and purchasing things, many parents and children do not draw upon each other as sources of pleasure and affirmation. Those parents do not fulfill their potentials for growth in family life.

This chapter focuses on the major issues that deserve consideration in efforts to enhance the quality of family life: parental authority, setting family priorities, the practice of morality, mutual affirmation, and the family's participation in its community and society.

WHAT IS A STRONG FAMILY?

More research has been conducted with troubled and disrupted families than with strong families. However, significant studies demonstrate that competent parenting is both a protective factor that prevents social problems and a positive factor in promoting an individual's successful life course.[1]

The developmental psychologists Hamilton McCubbin and Charles

Figley reported a study of competent parenting in "strong families."[2] They found that a strong family was one in which there was mutual respect between family members who had coherent, positive views of life expressed through overt displays of affection and open communication. In these families individuals were valued explicitly for what they are rather than for their achievements. Realistic expectations were held of family members, so that children learned what is acceptable and what is unacceptable with opportunities for both parents and children to correct their errors. The parents gave clear directions and enforce reasonable limits by emphasizing the positives rather than the negatives.

In strong families, family life is a mutual growth experience for both parents and children. Parents are not totally enmeshed in their children's lives. They have clear moral senses that are demonstrated through their words and actions. They have a sense of meaning and purpose in life, often related to a spiritual orientation with a trusting, optimistic outlook on life. They treat their children courteously and with respect. Through tolerating irrationality family members can relax, "let their hair down," and refuel for meeting the rational and irrational demands on them in the world away from home. Most important, parents and children acknowledge their own mistakes. They know how to forgive.

Strong family members adhere to family traditions and routines. They share power and decision making within the family. They communicate their feelings, concerns, and interests and listen and respond to what others have to say. Their styles of communication are clear, and individuals are encouraged to take responsibility for their feelings, thoughts, and actions. They spend time together but value individual privacy and pursue independent interests.

Strong families also are involved in the world in which they live. They have supportive attitudes toward each other and toward others outside of their families. A strong family contributes to the development of its members and to the well-being of its community and of society as well. Members of a strong family cultivate their relationships throughout life.

At the core of strong families is the legitimate use of parental authority.

PARENTAL AUTHORITY

American culture has moved away from the powerful father image that permeated the old-world order of family, church, and state. The image of the American Revolution throwing off the authority of a British king is reflected in the present-day extreme sensitivity to the abuse of power, to the extent that even legitimate parental authority has been undermined in American families.

As a result of this antiauthority ethos, many parents are not aware that freedom only has meaning in the context of legitimate restraint so that one individual's freedom does not restrict the freedom of others. We cannot avoid facing the effects of our freedom on other people. For this reason, legitimate authority is an ingredient of all successfully functioning groups. That authority flows from knowledge, wisdom, and experience that is respected by group members. In families those qualities generally reside in parents.

Two basic principles underlie the exercise of legitimate parental authority. The first is to recognize that from the time they are born, children are *individuals with valid needs and feelings*. The second is to *model effective living* for children, who are influenced more by what parents actually do than by what they say. When parents model controlling their impulses, their children learn how to behave civilly and tolerate the inevitable frustrations of life. When parents model delaying gratification, children learn how to schedule pleasant and unpleasant activities. In this context they learn the ingredients of effective living.

The attachment bonds that form between parents and children are the foundations for loving relationships with other people in later life. The limits parents set on their children's behavior help them develop respect for other persons. Those limits help children learn how to postpone gratification and to tolerate frustration of their impulses and desires. Through parents' beliefs in hopeful visions for the future, children learn how to surmount obstacles in their daily lives. They also gain inspiration for making the world a better place in which to live. All of this is nurtured by an atmosphere of respected parental authority.

Parental authority is exercised through the creative use of power, the practice of morality, the setting of family priorities, the affirmation of children, and a family's participation in its community and society.

The Creative Use of Power

The word *power* comes from the Latin *poder,* meaning "to be able." Everyone needs to be able, to be capable, to have a sense of personal power. At the heart of personal power is the sense that we are in charge of our lives. By accepting responsibility for our own selves and for our own behavior, we gain personal power.

The two sides of love in childrearing are showing affection and caring enough to help a child learn self-discipline. Although the negativistic behavior of young children is frustrating for all those involved in their care, it is a sign of their growing independence. At the same time, they need reasonable limit setting of their behavior. They also need parental models of self-discipline so that they can learn how to tolerate frustration and to delay gratification of their impulses themselves.

Parental authority is most appropriately exercised when parents gradually relinquish power to their children. The focus is on creatively sharing power among family members, not controlling them. In contrast with authoritarian parents, authoritative parents share power by helping their children find their talents and decide what they want to do with their lives. The legitimate exercise of power is the opposite of mutual victimization that occurs when parents and children struggle to control each other.

Throughout childhood, there are times when a parent leads a child and times when a child leads a parent. For example, during infancy a child actually wields great power and leads a parent by setting the feeding-sleep cycle. The challenge for parents is learning how to appropriately shift back and forth between leader and follower roles with their children. In order to do this, a parent needs to respect and trust a child, and more fundamentally, to respect and trust himself or herself.

Later on parental power is introduced around limit setting. Many parents do not realize how important it is to set limits for toddlers. It is easy to give in to their demands. The more difficult but rewarding course is to help them learn the limits of their power. During this stage prior to the appearance of the capacity for reasoning, nonverbal communication in the form of physical redirecting is necessary in order to establish a child's respect for the parent's appropriate use of the word *no*.

Most toddlers naturally test limits and push for all they can get. They are quick to assert themselves over siblings and peers. They want what they want when they want it. This means that parents are well advised to set clear limits and to help toddlers realize that the parents mean what they say. Physical redirection and restraint are necessary in order to demonstrate that a parent's words are to be taken seriously. Verbal commands across a room can be easily ignored, so that a toddler can conclude that what a parent says need not be heeded. Using one's feet and hands instead of one's voice is the most effective way of conveying a message to toddlers.

In contrast, when the easy way of appeasing a whining or tantruming child is taken, the message is that those behaviors can be used to manipulate adults. A whining or out-of-control toddler should be given a "time-out" and placed in a setting that will permit the child to regain self-control without unduly disrupting family life. Letting the child rejoin the parent when ready to do so conveys the message that regaining self-control is the purpose of the time-out, not punishment.

Family Priorities

Parental authority involves setting family priorities for mothering, fathering, homemaking, careers, managing stress, and family routines.

Because parenthood involves costs that are not borne by adults without children, parents must plan for financial consequences that increase as their children grow up. An appropriate balance needs to be found between childrearing, financial, and career objectives. Seldom can they all be met completely at one time in life.

The prudent management of family income and time based on the values and goals of a family is an increasingly urgent issue. It involves at least:

- family financial planning
- careful purchasing to ensure value received
- ongoing maintenance of a residence and personal needs
- planned use of time for personal, family, and community opportunities and obligations
- adequate nutrition and health care

Most important, financial goals need to be guided by setting a lower priority on material things than on family time. In later years, many parents wish they had spent more time with their children and less time making money.

Stress in families can be minimized by programming family time for relaxation, recreation, and play. This includes scheduling time away from children for parents. Otherwise, busy schedules, television, and computers leave few informal moments for parents and children to enjoy each other.

Family administration includes planning activities that can be programmed, such as traditions, celebrations, and routines. Traditions are celebrations of the past, such as Thanksgiving and Christmas. Celebrations are special events that accentuate the present, such as anniversaries and birthdays. Routines are regular daily and weekly activities.

A useful principle for guiding housekeeping routines is that all members of the family are responsible for contributing to the common good of the family as much as they are able to do.

THE PRACTICE OF MORALITY

Whether we like it or not, "good" and "bad" are real polarities in life. That polarity has been the foundation of philosophy throughout the centuries. For young children, "good" and "bad" are the only value judgments that have meaning.

The word *bad* is not appropriate when children do not comply with parental desires or expectations and are exercising their independence through noncompliance. *Bad* should be reserved for mean, unjust behavior toward others. "Bad" and "good" can be dealt with most usefully by facing issues of "right" and "wrong" in the family.

"Right" and "wrong" obviously depend on the perspective of the one making the judgment. The ancient Greeks pondered this question, as illustrated by Plato's observation that killing lambs was right for human beings but wrong for wolves.

Children have the inherent capacities to distinguish right from wrong and to be generous, compassionate, and altruistic. Early in life they have predispositions to attend to and respond to others' emotional states.[3] These predispositions are reinforced by parental attachment bonds and modeling. They wither away in the absence of attachment bonds to others. Children also acquire prosocial or antisocial values, fashions, and interests from their peers, teachers, religion, movies, literature, and television.

"Good" (right) and "bad" (wrong) can be broken down into manageable pieces. Good revolves around the truth (reality-trust) and love (giving to others). The core issues for the good are emotional honesty (accepting responsibility for one's feelings and actions) and the creative use of power (influencing others constructively). Bad essentially is deception (altering reality–mistrust) and hurting others (blaming-hating).

The irrational aspects of family life provide ample opportunities for children and parents to learn how to express and deal with "good" and "bad." Most family conflicts involve parents and children deceiving or hurting each other and, therefore, are opportunities for learning how to accept responsibility for one's feelings and actions and for learning how to constructively manage impulses to deceive and hurt others.

Distinguishing "right" from "wrong" in family life in terms of justice places interactions between parents and children on moral grounds rather than on arbitrary definitions based on the convenience or desires of parents. It introduces justice into the rearing of children rather than the simple exercise of parental power. For example, children can be expected to be courteous to others because respecting other people's rights is a moral good rather than because failing to do so annoys the parents.

A strong family is one in which there is mutual respect and in which no individual's personal needs or desires dominate. But families cannot always be "just" communities. Guidelines about telling the truth or about not interrupting when others are speaking tend to be unequally enforced for parents and children. Parents expect a degree of privacy that they do not accord their children. Often one family member is expected to do most of the compromising, or another tends to be unjustly accused of starting squabbles among siblings. The best efforts to establish justice in a family cannot succeed completely, because a family is a flawed institution composed of imperfect creatures. Consequently, as is all of life, family life is a struggle between right and wrong in the quest for justice. Being questioned and challenged by children compels parents to clarify their own moral values and become stronger persons themselves.

The family is the ideal proving ground for coping with human frailties by trying to be slow to lose patience and quick to be gracious; trying to be understanding when provoked; trying not to impress others with one's own importance; trying to think the best, not the worst, of others; and trying not to gloat over the faults and failures of others. Most mistakes in family life are harmless omissions and errors in judgment resulting from selfishness, jealousy, and irrationality rather than "bad" actions or omissions.

Still, because family emotional bonds are so intense, family members' faults can be the most difficult to forgive. At the same time, because it is impossible to hide human imperfections in a family, it is the place in which forgiveness is the most needed and appreciated.

MUTUAL AFFIRMATION

Internalized mental images of our parents and other influential persons are central components of our personalities.

Each of us grows up carrying an assortment of "good" and "bad" internalized images that carry previous family interactions with our parents and siblings into our present lives. These images constitute the "internal family" that stays with each one of us throughout our lives. These internal images "look over our shoulders" in present interactions and influence them. They can cause us to react inappropriately when unresolved conflicts from our own childhoods are activated. In turn, as parents, we become images in our children's internalized families.

For these reasons, children need to develop "good internal images" that flow from having their maturity affirmed by parents who expect and respect the highest level of maturity of which their children are capable. From the beginning, children need affirmation of their individuality and of their competence. Parents, in turn, are affirmed when their children become competent and responsible persons in later life.

Learning to Communicate Ideas and Emotions Verbally

Affirmation in family relationships relies upon open communication, so that parents and children understand each other's ideas, emotions, and needs. That communication depends upon listening, expressing ideas and feelings, and reaching mutual understanding.

Children especially need to learn from their parents how to find words to communicate their feelings to others. They are inclined to act out their feelings rather than use words to express them. Parents can model communication by verbally expressing their feelings instead of simply acting upon them. For example, an explanation that a parent has a headache helps a child understand a parent's irritable mood more than do angry actions.

When helped to learn to use words instead of actions to communicate their feelings effectively, children gain confidence in themselves. When they do not learn to use words, they ineffectively relieve their tensions in emotional outbursts. Misunderstandings because of faulty verbal communication lie behind most family conflicts.

How we handle our emotional reactions to other people is our personal responsibility. We can counterattack emotionally, or we can use words to express our feelings. The most useful response when others hurt our feelings is to honestly say that our feelings are hurt. We are better served by verbally communicating our feelings to others instead of blindly acting upon them.

The ways parents handle their own arguments provide models for their children. Still, arguments between siblings tax the ingenuity of parents. Separating them until they "cool off" usually is more effective than taking sides. In spite of the emphasis placed on sibling rivalry, most sibling relationships are congenial over the years.[4] Siblings usually are not as close to each other as friends during adolescence or as spouses and children in later life, but they do feel loyal to each other and see themselves as good rather than as best friends.

When parents and children are able to verbally communicate their feelings and needs to each other, blind emotional outbursts are minimized. They are able to put themselves in the position of the other person. This promotes children's capacities for empathy.

Building Self-Esteem by Affirming Individuality

Affirmation of each child's individuality facilitates developing that child's self-esteem. In turn the evidence of self-esteem in a child enhances a parent's self-esteem.

Affirmation differs from approval because seeking approval can lead children to conform to expectations and to squelch their own individuality, whereas affirmation of children enhances their individuality. The aim of parental affirmation is to build a child's self-esteem. On this foundation of affirmation, there is an additional need for approval and disapproval, so that children can learn to recognize and regulate the impact of their behavior on others.

Affirmation of a child begins with mirroring a child's innate sense of vigor during infancy through eye contact and mimicking sounds. This reinforcement of an infant's spontaneous expressions fosters development of the child's true self in contrast with an imitative self. When a parent does not respond to an infant's gestures, but instead substitutes his or her own, imitation is encouraged rather than individuality. In the same vein, parents later affirm when they touch, kiss, hold, wrestle, and play with their children. Younger children who are not touched in these ways may regard themselves as unattractive and ultimately unlovable.

Building Self-Esteem by Affirming Personal Competence

In addition to affirming a child's individuality, affirmation of a child's personal competence also builds that child's self-esteem.

Happiness is not a series of isolated pleasures. It is not "fun" from pleasurable or exciting activities. It is a feeling that one's self and the world are in harmony. It is a subjective sense of well-being and satisfaction, the intensity of which varies from one individual to another.[5] It is reflected in self-esteem that derives from early childhood experiences of being able to master one's body and of being effective in the world. Its prototype is a baby's smile on taking the first steps of walking. The feeling of self-esteem is an inner measurement of personal competence.

Self-esteem is enhanced by using language to guide our actions. As a medium of thought and communication, language enhances problem solving, learning from the consequences of one's actions, forming rewarding relationships with others, and engaging in long-range planning.[6] When thought accompanies actions, there need be no conflict between our basic drives and our self-esteem. The self-esteem that flows from personal competence is not so much the result of suppressing our innate drives as of integrating them into the thoughtful pursuit of our legitimate interests.

In order to foster self-esteem, parents need to insure that their children know that their love for them is not contingent on their behavior. Therefore, it is better to see children as doing "bad" or "good" things rather than as being "bad" or "good"; to help children avoid making the same mistake again rather than criticizing them when they make a mistake; to accept children as they are rather than to compare them with other children; to avoid talking in front of children as if they were not there; and to be aware of children's sensitivity about their physical appearance and avoid pet names.

Children need firm limits, but how limits are handled determines what they will learn. For example, when children's behavior is unacceptable, they first can be asked if they understand why their behavior was not acceptable. Then they can be asked what would help them avoid that behavior in the future. This places the responsibility for self-control with the child. When a parent expresses confidence in a child's ability to do better, that child's self-esteem is enhanced.

A sense of competence is fostered when parents encourage their children to take risks by giving them responsibilities instead of overprotecting them. They then affirm their children for trying new things even when they fail. This encourages children to master risks rather than to avoid them. There is a point of convergence where fear is met, confronted, and used as a source of both caution and energy. Daring our children to accept responsibility for the consequences of their actions has far more to teach about risk taking than any Outward Bound wilderness trip.

Learning to cope with failure is the essence of learning to take risks. For teenagers, schoolwork and after-school risk-taking activities, like sports, may be better self-esteem builders than paid work in itself. Earning money for its own sake can build a sense of responsibility for adolescents, but it also can foster self-centered materialism when the money is used simply to purchase luxury items.

For both parents and children, the most important aim is achieving self-confidence. In order to value themselves as competent persons, children need to develop a realistic sense of their own assets and liabilities. They need to learn how to tolerate frustration and to postpone gratification. They need to experience the satisfaction of pleasing others. Then they will be valued by others and value themselves.

If we value ourselves, we do not need to put others down in order to build ourselves up. Awareness of our own imperfections enables us to accept the imperfections of others. In this way seeking power over others through wealth, physical strength, weapons, and criticism can be replaced by affirming each other.

FAMILY PARTICIPATION IN COMMUNITY AND SOCIETY

Families are strengthened by involvement in their communities and in social and environmental issues. In fact, families are the foundation of their communities and of society. They are fundamental parts of the ecosystem in which we all live. Involvement in social and environmental causes encourages the idealism of children and adolescents and tempers it with reality.

The responsibility of human beings to care for the human family and for the Earth can be a central theme in family life. Family discussions and activities can be focused on participating in community, national, and global issues related to peace and the conservation of the Earth. In this way, the family can be a source of support for creative, reconciling community life. These kinds of active participation in their communities help young people relieve their anxieties about the future.

Families also can play key roles in advocating and modeling alternatives to violence as a way of solving problems. In so doing they can become involved in movements that oppose injustice and that foster peace. Children can be helped to see that poverty and oppression make people feel helpless and desperate and thereby breed violence. They can be helped to relate the violence they encounter in their own lives to the violence in the world. They can be inspired to be peacemakers in their own realms and thereby develop a peacemaking stance in the broader world.

CONCLUSION

The vital issues in family life revolve around intimacy, identification, influence, irrationality, and industry. In symbolic terms, the expression of these qualities of individual persons' "I's" makes it possible to fulfill the "we" of family life.

Intimacy in the family develops emotional bonds that integrate ambivalent love-hate emotions and that balance personal needs for interaction and privacy.

Identification is the process in which parents, children, and siblings reciprocally absorb each other's qualities and vicariously share experiences.

The *influence* that family members have on each other is expressed in the power structure of the family and in the behavior of individuals in the family.

Irrationality is an essential part of family life so that irrational fantasies, emotions, and behavior can be expressed and channeled into realistic outlets.

Industry in families is developing the coping abilities of family members through planning, resolving conflicts, allocating responsibilities in the family, acquiring tangible and intangible resources, and adapting to change.

Children become mature persons in their families by learning how to be responsible for themselves and for their actions, by learning how to tolerate frustration, by learning how to postpone gratification, by learning how to control their impulses, by learning how to solve problems, and by learning how to work. Children develop self-esteem by identifying with competent parents and by being affirmed as competent, unique individuals in an atmosphere of mutual trust and respect.

NOTES

1. Long, J. V. E., & Vaillant, G. E. (1989) Escape from the underclass. In T. E. Dugan & R. Coles (eds.), *The children in our times: Studies in the development of resilience.* New York: Brunner/Mazel; Quinton, D., & Rutter, M. (1988) *Parenting breakdown: The making and breaking of iintergenerational links.* Aldershot, U.K.: Avebury; and Werner, E. E., & Smith, R. S. (1992) *Overcoming the odds: High risk children from birth to adulthood.* Ithaca, N.Y.: Cornell University Press.

2. McCubbin, H. I., & Figley, C. R. (eds.) (l983) *Stress and the family.* Larchmont, N.Y.: Brunner/Mazel.

3. Zahn-Waxler, C., Cummings, E. M., & Iannotti, R. (eds.) (1986) *Altruism and aggression.* New York: Cambridge University Press.

4. Faber, A., & Mazlish, E. (l987) *Siblings without rivalry.* New York: Norton.

5. Lykken, D. (1999) *Happiness: What studies of twins show us about nature, nurture, and the happiness set point.* New York: Golden Books.

6. Shure, M. B., & Spivack, G. (l987) Competence-building as an approach to prevention of dysfunction: The ICPS model. In J. A. Steinberg & M. M. Silverman (eds.), *Preventing mental disorders.* Rockville, Md.: National Institute of Mental Health.

7

Combining Love and Limits in Authoritative Parenting

ROBERT E. LARZELERE

Childrearing advice to American parents has always been diverse, swinging between an emphasis on love or limits from one generation to the next. In the 1920s, John Watson, the founder of behaviorism, advocated strictness to the extent of warning mothers against the dangers of expressing love toward their children.[1] Benjamin Spock introduced a better balance between love and discipline, while affirming the common sense that most parents have.[2]

Thomas Gordon's book *Parent Effectiveness Training* emphasizes communication. Not only does he advocate good communication, he is against forceful disciplinary tactics. He said that "each and every time parents force a child to do something by using their power or authority, they deny that child a chance to learn self-discipline."[3]

At the other extreme is James Dobson's book *Dare to Discipline*. The first of his five key elements in childrearing is "Developing respect for parents is the critical factor in child management." Elsewhere he said, "When a youngster tries . . . stiff-necked rebellion, you had better take it out of him, and pain is a marvelous purifier."[4]

Fitzhugh Dodson presents a balance between the extremes of Gordon and Dobson, emphasizing both nurturance and control in his book *How to Discipline with Love*. He says: "I believe it is far better to solve a conflict by negotiation and agreement rather than through power. However, in extreme cases . . . I believe we have to fall back on sheer power."[5]

The same polarization between love and limits exists in scientific studies. The fields of cognitive developmental psychology and clinical behavioral psychology have produced the most empirical studies on parental discipline. They complement each other in many important ways. However, they often hold contradictory views about optimal disciplinary responses.

Cognitive developmentalists often recommend reasoning as a disciplinary response.[6] In contrast, clinical behaviorists favor the consistent use of nonphysical punishment, especially in managing disruptive children.[7] They generally regard reasoning as ineffective, except when describing the contingencies of punishment and reinforcement.[8]

A few experts have bridged this conceptual gap, most notably the child psychologist Diana Baumrind in her work on parenting styles.[9] She contrasts three major parenting styles: authoritarian, authoritative, and permissive. Authoritarian parents emphasize firm control; permissive parents emphasize nurturance; authoritative parents emphasize both. In addition, authoritative parents emphasize communication with their children and encourage age-appropriate skills and autonomy. In Baumrind's studies, the children of authoritative parents generally showed more individual initiative and social responsibility compared to children of the other two types of parents.

The contradictory recommendations of cognitive developmental and clinical behavioral research concerning reasoning versus punishment pose an important puzzle that needs to be solved in order to build a solid scientific foundation for advising parents. Something is wrong when reasoning, the most recommended disciplinary tactic in developmental psychology, is ignored in clinical behavioral work with parents and when the punishment supported by clinical research is denigrated in the developmental literature.

This strange situation is reflected in research questions and methods, which often assume the correctness of a researcher's implicit beliefs. For example, few studies investigate differences between effective and counterproductive use of a particular disciplinary tactic, whether reasoning or punishment. Instead, the implicitly preferred disciplinary tactic is assumed to be invariably effective and the other one invariably ineffective, regardless how either one is used. In contrast, our research program compares the effectiveness of reasoning and punishment against each other and in combination with each other.

COMBINING REASONING WITH PUNISHMENT

Our most important studies focused on maternal disciplinary responses to misbehavior of two- and three-year-olds. Mothers were asked to record all occurrences of disobedience or fighting over a four-week period. Using the Discipline Record,[10] they recorded the time of each incident and the discipline tactics they used to respond to it. The most important outcome was the delay until the next recurrence of the same kind of misbehavior. Presumably, the more effective the disciplinary response, the longer that delay.

Reasoning and Punishment More Effective

We found that the combined use of reasoning and punishment was more effective in delaying fighting and disobedience recurrences than was either one alone. For example, fighting recurred an average of twenty hours after mothers used both reasoning and punishment, but an average of less than ten hours later following either reasoning or punishment alone.[11]

The superior effectiveness of a reasoning-punishment combination over either reasoning or punishment has been shown by others in terms of immediate compliance[12] and a decrease in subsequent misbehavior, a potential precursor of moral internalization.[13]

Punishment Enhances Reasoning

A reasoning and punishment combination enhances the subsequent effectiveness of later reasoning when used by itself. Three different analyses of our data showed that disciplinary reasoning with two- and three-year-olds was ineffective unless it was backed up with punishment periodically. The children whose behavior improved the most over the next twenty months were those whose mothers frequently used reasoning without punishment, but also backed up the reasoning with punishment when necessary.[14] In contrast, the children whose behavior deteriorated the most had mothers who frequently used reasoning alone, but rarely backed it up with punishment.

THE CONDITIONAL SEQUENCE MODEL

A related backup sequence is used in behavioral parent training, which has been shown to be particularly effective in managing disruptive children.[15] It includes five major components: (1) positive reinforcement of appropriate behavior, (2) clear instructions, (3) a single warning of impending time-out, (4) time-out, and (5) a backup for time-out noncompliance, usually a two-swat spank for two- to six-year-olds. With particularly noncompliant children, a time-out is often ineffective without a backup procedure to enforce compliance. The spank backup is effective in enforcing compliance with the time-out, thus making the time-out effective and minimizing the subsequent need for the spank backup.

Roberts and Powers investigated three alternative backup procedures, but a brief room isolation was the only one that proved to be as effective as the original spank backup.[16] Consistent with my research, contingent use of a more severe backup procedure enhanced the subsequent effectiveness of a less severe disciplinary tactic, in this case a time-out.

The Conditional Sequence Model combines these two backup sequences. It begins with reasoning first. If that does not achieve the disciplinary goal, then it is backed up with a time-out. If the child does not comply with the time-out, it is backed up with a consequence, such as a two-swat spank or a brief room isolation.

This Conditional Sequence Model has several important features:

- First, it is consistent with authoritative parenting, as opposed to either authoritarian or permissive parenting. Authoritative parents use both reasoning and firm control. Authoritarian parents tend to skip the reasoning and go immediately to punishment. Permissive parents are less likely to try to change children's behavior with either reasoning or punishment.
- Second, this model tries gentler love-motivated disciplinary responses first, followed by firm punishment only when necessary.
- Third, this model is consistent with empirical research that shows that the effectiveness of milder disciplinary tactics depends upon their being backed up by more severe disciplinary tactics when necessary.[17]
- Fourth, this model has the potential of reconciling the contradictory recommendations of cognitive developmentalists and behavioral clinicians. It implies that particularly disruptive children need contingent punishment more often. Successful use of this model will result in parents using reasoning effectively and rarely needing to resort to punishment.

Predictions of the Model

The Conditional Sequence Model makes a variety of predictions that are consistent with the research evidence.

First, it predicts that the superiority of reasoning over punishment will be more evident among easily managed children than among difficult children. This is consistent with an overview of cognitive developmental studies.[18] Disciplinary reasoning was associated with better child outcomes than was punishment in studies of middle-class mothers. Studies of fathers, working-class families, preschoolers, boys, and temperamentally difficult children have generally failed to find such associations.

A second prediction is that the superiority of punishment over reasoning will be most evident among particularly difficult children. The psychologist Gerald Patterson initially tried to help parents manage their disruptive children by emphasizing the reinforcement of appropriate behaviors. Later he concluded, "If I were allowed to select only one concept to use in training parents of antisocial children, I would teach them how to punish more effectively," referring to time-out as the punishment of choice.[19]

Third, the Conditional Sequence Model predicts that children's aggression will be decreased more by conditional recommendations against spanking than by unconditional recommendations against spanking. Unconditional antispanking advice may make gentler disciplinary tactics less effective unless an equally effective backup replaces spanking. Some evidence from Sweden is consistent with that prediction. The frequency of child abuse and assaults by minors against minors increased dramatically after Sweden banned spanking in 1979.[20] A possible reason is that Swedish parents are less likely to use alternative disciplinary tactics such as reasoning and time-out and are more likely to use ineffective yelling and restraining.[21]

The conditional use of spanking is consistent with behavioral parent training, which discourages spanking except to enforce time-out compliance. Outcome studies support the effectiveness of this treatment for reducing disruptive behavior.[22] In addition, four studies found that behavioral parent training actually reduced parental spanking. Two of them used the spanking backup for noncompliance with time-outs,[23] and two of them used alternative backups for time-outs.[24] How spanking is used is more critical than whether or not it is used.

A fourth prediction of the Conditional Sequence Model is that programs that discourage the use of parental punishment will be more effective for general populations than for populations at risk of child abuse. Social work professor Neil Guterman reviewed the eighteen most rigorous evaluations of early parenting programs to prevent child abuse.[25] He found that eight of the ten programs targeted to general populations were effective in reducing subsequent child abuse, but only one of the eight programs showed similar effectiveness for at-risk populations.

Expanding the Model

To this point, I have focused on a simple three-step Conditional Sequence Model. Although it suggests a way to reconcile contradictory recommendations and successfully makes several innovative predictions, actual parental practices are more varied. There is empirical evidence to suggest helpful ways to expand the simple model.

First, there is some evidence that a single warning can dramatically reduce the need to move to the next level of consequences without compromising the effectiveness of the overall disciplinary strategy. Psychologist Mark Roberts found that a single time-out warning reduced the need to use a time-out by 74 percent without diminishing the effectiveness of the overall parental disciplinary sequence.[26] Multiple warnings reduce the effectiveness of the overall discipline.[27]

Psychologist Carolyn Zahn-Waxler and her colleagues explored the emotional intensity of maternal explanations to fifteen- to twenty-nine-month-old preschoolers in some detail.[28] They found that verbal explanations were used in 40 percent of disciplinary incidents. In most of these cases, the mothers communicated intensely with moralizing and judgmental remarks. Emotionally and morally charged explanations were positively associated with child reparations and altruism. Neutrally communicated explanations were the only form of explanations that failed to correlate positively with child reparations. Similarly, one of our earlier studies found that, when reasoning alone resulted in no child distress, it was a less effective disciplinary response than when it resulted in some child distress for about a minute or two.[29]

The emotional intensity is an aspect of verbal tactics that makes them effective either by themselves or when combined with an action component. Further research is needed to clarify when such emotional intensity becomes counterproductive.

Consistent with previous punishment research, we found that the more the punishment distressed the child, the more effective it was.[30] However, when reasoning was used, whether by itself or in combination with punishment, an intermediate level of child distress was associated with optimal effectiveness. This is consistent with previous research that found that, when reasoning was added to punishment, its effectiveness no longer depended on either the severity or the timing of the punishment.[31]

CONCLUSION

In contrast to the common practice of pitting love and limits against each other, this chapter has outlined a Conditional Sequence Model of optimal disciplinary responses that begins with less severe tactics, such as reasoning, but proceeds to firmer disciplinary tactics when the initial tactic achieves neither compliance nor an acceptable compromise. The firmer tactics can be nonphysical punishment initially, with nonabusive physical punishment or a brief room isolation reserved as a backup for it.

The Conditional Sequence Model is supported by many studies showing that a combination of reasoning and punishment is more effective than either one alone and by new evidence that this sequence enhances the subsequent effectiveness of milder disciplinary tactics with preschoolers. This model is consistent with Diane Baumrind's classic work on authoritative parenting.

The disciplinary process must be considered within the overall parenting context. Nurturance, age-appropriate autonomy, skill development, family routines, and family rituals are characteristics of optimal parent-child relationships. These characteristics are important in their own right and also are important in setting the stage for optimal disciplinary responses. Those responses should reflect a balance of love and firmness. Hopefully, the Conditional Sequence Model will help parents and parent educators clarify that balance.

NOTES

1. Watson, J. B. (1928) *Psychological care of infant and child.* New York: Norton.
2. Spock, B. (1968) *Baby and child care* (rev. ed.). New York: Pocket Books.
3. Gordon, T. (1975) *Parent effectiveness training: The tested new way to raise responsible children.* New York: Guilford Press, p. 158.
4. Dobson, J. (1970) *Dare to discipline.* Wheaton, Ill.: Tyndale, pp. 14, 16.
5. Dodson, F. (1977) *How to discipline with love.* New York: Rawson Associates, p. 121.
6. Grusec, J., & Kuczysnki, L. (eds.) (1997) *Parenting and children's internalization of values.* New York: Wiley; Grusec, J. E., & Goodnow, J. J. (1994) Impact of parental discipline methods on the child's internalization of values: A reconceptualization of current points of view. *Developmental Psychology* 30: 4–19; Hoffman, M. L. (1977) Moral internalization: Current theory and research. In L. Berkowitz (ed.), *Advances in experimental social psychology* (vol. 10, pp. 85–133). New York: Academic Press; and Weiss, B., Dodge, K. A., & Bates, J. E. (1992) Some consequences of early harsh discipline: Child aggression and a maladaptive social information processing style. *Child Development* 63: 1321–1335.
7. Barkley, R. A. (1987) *Defiant children: A clinician's manual for parent training.* New York: Guilford; Eyberg, S. M., & Boggs, S. R. (1989) Parent training for oppositional-defiant preschoolers. In C. E. Schaefer & J. M. Briesmeister (eds.), *Handbook of parent training: Parents as co-therapists for children's behavior problems* (pp. 105–132). New York: Wiley; Forehand, R. L., & McMahon, R. J. (1981) *Helping the noncompliant child.* New York: Guilford; and Patterson, G. R. (1982) *Coercive family process.* Eugene, Ore.: Castalia Press, p. 111.
8. Blum, N.J., Williams, G. E., Friman, P. C., & Christopherson, E. R. (1995) Disciplining young children: The role of verbal instructions and reasoning. *Pediatrics* 96: 336–341.
9. Baumrind, D. (1967) Child care practices anteceding three patterns of preschool behavior. *Genetic Psychology Monographs* 75: 43–88; Baumrind, D. (1973) The development of instrumental competence through socialization. In A. D. Pick (ed.), *Minnesota Symposia on Child Psychology* (vol. 7, pp. 3–46). Minneapolis: University of Minnesota Press; and Baumrind, D. (1991) The influ-

ence of parenting style on adolescent competence and substance use. *Journal of Early Adolescence* 11: 56–95.

10. Larzelere, R. E., & Merenda, J. A. (1994) The effectiveness of parental discipline for toddler misbehavior at different levels of child distress. *Family Relations* 43: 480–488.

11. Larzelere, R. E., Schneider, W. N., Larson, D. B., & Pike, P. L. (1996) The effects of discipline responses in delaying toddler misbehavior recurrences. *Child & Family Behavior Therapy* 18: 35–57.

12. Chapman, M., & Zahn-Waxler, C. (1982) Young children's compliance and noncompliance to parental discipline in a natural setting. *International Journal of Behavioural Development* 5: 81–94; Crockenberg, S., & Litman, C. (1990) Autonomy as competence in two-year-olds: Maternal correlates of child defiance, compliance, and self-assertion. *Developmental Psychology* 26: 961–971; Davies, G. R., McMahon, R. J., Flessati, E. W., & Tiedemann, G. L. (1984) Verbal rationales and modeling as adjuncts to a parenting technique for child compliance. *Child Development* 55: 1290–1298; Goodenough, F. L. (1931) *Anger in young children.* Minneapolis: University of Minnesota Press; and Lytton, H., & Zwirner, W. (1975) Compliance and its controlling stimuli observed in a natural setting. *Developmental Psychology* 11: 769–779.

13. Cheyne, J. A., & Walters, R. H. (1969) Intensity of punishment, timing of punishment, and cognitive structure as determinants of response inhibition. *Journal of Experimental Child Psychology* 10: 352–364; Dix, T., & Grusec, J. E. (1983) Parental influence techniques: An attributional analysis. *Child Development* 54: 645–652; Hoffman, M. L. (1977) Moral internalization: Current theory and research. In L. Berkowitz (ed.), *Advances in experimental social psychology* (vol. 10, pp. 85–133). New York: Academic Press; LaVoie, J. C. (1974) Aversive, cognitive, and parental determinants of punishment generalization in adolescent males. *Journal of Genetic Psychology* 124: 29–39; and Parke, R. D. (1969) Effectiveness of punishment as an interaction of intensity, timing, agent nurturance, and cognitive structuring. *Child Development* 40: 213–235.

14. Larzelere, R. E., Sather, P. R., Schneider, W. N., Larson, D. B., & Pike, P. L. (1998) Punishment enhances reasoning's effectiveness as a disciplinary response to toddlers. *Journal of Marriage and the Family* 60: 388–403.

15. Kazdin, A. E. (1987) Treatment of antisocial behavior in children: Current status and future directions. *Psychological Bulletin* 102: 187–203.

16. Roberts, M. W., & Powers, S. W. (1990) Adjusting chair timeout enforcement procedures for oppositional children. *Behavior Therapy* 21: 257–271.

17. Larzelere, R. E., Sather, P. R., Schneider, W. N., Larson, D. B., & Pike, P. L. (1998) Punishment enhances reasoning's effectiveness as a disciplinary response to toddlers. *Journal of Marriage and the Family* 60: 388–403; and Roberts, M. W., & Powers, S. W. (1990) Adjusting chair timeout enforcement procedures for oppositional children. *Behavior Therapy* 21: 257–271.

18. Grusec, J. E., & Goodnow, J. J. (1994) Impact of parental discipline methods on the child's internalization of values: A reconceptualization of current points of view. *Developmental Psychology* 30: 4–19.

19. Patterson, G. R. (1982) *Coercive family process.* Eugene, Ore.: Castalia Press, p. 111.

20. Wittrock, U. (1992) Barnmisshandel i kriminalstatistiken, 1981–1991. *KR Info* 1992:7 (Kriminalstatistik vid SCB, Stockholm); and Wittrock, U. (1995) Barnmisshandel, 1984–1994. *KR Info* 1995:5 (Kriminalstatistik vid SCB, Stockholm).

21. Palmerus, K., & Scarr, S. (1995, April) How parents discipline young children: Cultural comparisons and individual differences. Paper presented at the Society for Research in Child Development, Indianapolis.

22. Kazdin, A. E. (1995) *Conduct disorders in childhood and adolescence* (2e). Thousand Oaks, Calif.: Sage.

23. Eyberg, S. (1993) The spank back-up in time-out with preschool children. Unpublished paper, University of Florida; and Roberts, M. W. (1984) An attempt to reduce timeout resistance in young children. *Behavior Therapy* 15: 210–216.

24. McNeil, C. B., Clemens-Mowrer, L., Gurwitch, R. H., & Funderburk, B. W. (1994) Assessment of a new procedure to prevent timeout escape in preschoolers. *Child & Family Behavior Therapy* 16(3): 27–35; and Webster-Stratton, C. (1990) Enhancing the effectiveness of self-administered videotape parent training for families with conduct-problem children. *Journal of Abnormal Child Psychology* 18: 479–492.

25. Guterman, N. B. (1997) Early prevention of physical child abuse and neglect: Existing evidence and future directions. *Child Maltreatment* 2: 12–34.

26. Roberts, M. W. (1982) The effects of warned versus unwarned time-out procedures on child noncompliance. *Child & Family Behavior Therapy* 4: 37–53.

27. Sherrill, J. T., O'Leary, S. G., & Kendziora, K. T. (1992, November) The effects of warnings and response cost on classroom behavior. Paper presented at the Association for Advancement of Behavior Therapy, Boston.

28. Zahn-Waxler, C., Radke-Yarrow, M., & King, R. (1979) Child rearing and children's prosocial initiations toward victims of distress. *Child Development* 50: 319–330.

29. Larzelere, R. E., & Merenda, J. A. (1994) The effectiveness of parental discipline for toddler misbehavior at different levels of child distress. *Family Relations* 43: 480–488.

30. Ibid.

31. Cheyne, J. A., & Walters, R. H. (1969) Intensity of punishment, timing of punishment, and cognitive structure as determinants of response inhibition. *Journal of Experimental Child Psychology* 10: 352–364; and Parke, R. D. (1969) Effectiveness of punishment as an interaction of intensity, timing, agent nurturance, and cognitive structuring. *Child Development* 40: 213–235.

8

Modeling Values for Children in Families

DAVID POPENOE

A *Wall Street Journal* poll revealed that "moral decline" was the biggest problem that America will face in the next twenty years. When asked what the biggest change in American character has been since the 1950s, the leading answer was "less stable marriages and families."[1]

I agree with these popular assessments. The available empirical evidence indicates that deterioration of stable marriages and families has been a principal generator of moral decline. This is because children learn moral values mainly within their families, and mainly by relying on their parents as role models. When families are unstable, when parents are absent, emotionally distant, or preoccupied, or when parents themselves are immoral, the learning of moral values by children is greatly hindered.

In this chapter, I will discuss why parents have been failing at modeling moral values for children, focusing on parenting time and other family conditions for childrearing.

MODELING

When something appears to be "not right" or out of order, as when a common pattern of behavior is suddenly not followed, my twenty-two-month-old granddaughter points and says, "oh, oh." For example, when she was in the backseat of our car strapped in her car seat, and I started to drive off without first securing my seat belt, she pointed at me and said, "oh, oh."

The *New York Times* recently ran an article with the headline "If Drivers Buckle Up, Children Do, Study Finds."[2] The study, conducted by the Air Bag Safety Campaign, reported that "the evidence is clear: to get children buckled up, we must get drivers buckled up." Seat-belt use studies from more than ten states showed that "more than 80 percent of children were buckled in when their adults used their seat belts. But when parents were not buckled up, restraint use for younger children ranged from 11 to 56 percent." To make sure no one misunderstood the true nature of this phenomenon, the *Times* turned to Transportation Secretary Rodney Slater, who said, "Parents must buckle up because children follow their example." I can only add that, when children are as well socialized as my granddaughter, the process can work in reverse.

In the world of the social sciences, this phenomenon is known as modeling. And it is one of the most fundamental dimensions of raising a moral, prosocial child. Children pay more attention to what an adult does than to what an adult says. As psychologist Nancy Eisenberg reports, "socializers who preach . . . but do not model . . . may have little positive effect on children's prosocial development."[3]

This, of course, is a common and simple insight, yet it opens up a profound perspective on modern society and its effects on children. For in order to determine what values children are learning as they grow up, we must look first at what adults are doing, not what they are saying, and at the way things appear to children, not the way things appear to us. Most important of all, for children to learn values from their parents through modeling, the parents must have a regular, active, and continuing presence in the lives of their children. Unfortunately, parents in modern times are increasingly absent from their children's lives during the growing-up years.

Everything we know about human behavior suggests that the family is the institution in which most children learn about character and morality. The schools, the churches, and the law can all help in the process of character development, but they have much less independent force of their own. Their main function is to reinforce what has already been taught in the home. If morality and character are not taught in the home, other institutions cannot be relied on to undo the damage. That is why the quality of family life is so important, and why the family is society's most fundamental institution.

Childhood in the Past

The changes in Western childhood over the past few centuries have been remarkable. In the preindustrial era in Europe, an era of high infant and child mortality when life for many was "nasty, brutish and short," childhood does not seem to have been regarded as a sphere of life entirely separate from adulthood. Children were considered "little adults" and, as soon they were able, were expected to perform adult duties. With the struggle for existence dominating all of life, there was little time for childhood or childrearing as we think of them today.

With the rise several centuries ago of the industrial revolution and the modern nuclear family—the family of husband and wife living apart from other relatives—childhood became a very different phenomenon. The new economic conditions enabled many mothers to devote themselves full-time to childrearing, the home became a mostly private sphere, and the view of children and childhood significantly changed. Children came to be regarded as very different from adults, and childhood became a time of play, diminished work responsibilities, and formal learning. The quality of early childhood experiences began to be conceived of as having a major influence on adult outcomes. Each child was considered to have a unique personality to be developed, rather than to have been born with vices that needed to be expunged. The new family put child development at its highest level of priority. To help families, the commercial toy industry came into being, along with the children's book industry and a great variety of facilities and services designed especially for children.

While these changes may not have generated a "golden age" for children, they certainly represented a monumental improvement over the way children had been raised in the past. Moreover, a strong case can be made that the family form that pioneered this new notion of childhood was instrumental in generating many of the social achievements of modern times, especially achievement-oriented individualism and liberal democracy. The character of the family shapes the character of the society as much as vice versa, and these were the values that were taught in the new bourgeois home.[4]

Today, much of modern society is beginning to revert to the earlier preindustrial pattern. While life is far more secure economically and medically for more children than ever before, and childrearing methods have grown increasingly less punitive and authoritarian, many aspects of the domestic scene have grown worse for children. With the incursions of advertising and the organized entertainment industry, and the often sex- and violence-saturated popular culture they are driving, childhood is no longer the relatively protected period that it has been in recent centuries. Children are thrust into an adult culture at an early age, just as they were in the older era.

The environment of childrearing has deteriorated in other respects as well. Many communities have become less safe and more anonymous, making childrearing families feel even more isolated. Reports of child abuse and neglect have quintupled over the past two decades since detailed records have been kept. Perhaps worst of all because it is so widespread and so consequential, the crucial amount of time that parents spend raising their children has diminished, largely due to absent fathers and to mothers in the workplace.

This new set of childrearing conditions has had unfortunate and predictable consequences for the well-being of children. Juvenile delinquency has increased nearly 600 percent in the past three decades, and teen suicide has tripled. Juvenile violence has become much more lethal. Marked increases among teenagers have been seen in substance abuse, in eating disorders, and in rates of depression. In other words, while societies have advanced economically, the moral and emotional condition of children and youth has deteriorated. The tragic irony is that economic advance was supposed to improve the lives of the young, and thereby the quality of future generations.

WHAT DO CHILDREN SEE?

As they look around today, what do children see? In particular, what do they see that appears to be "not right," things that would cause my all-knowing granddaughter to say, "oh, oh," things whose values one would not wish children to try to copy? First, they see their parents breaking up. More than 50 percent of children today will spend some time living with just one parent by the time they reach age eighteen. Second, many will lose contact with their fathers. Some 40 percent of children today are living apart from their natural fathers, and most of these children see their fathers seldom, if at all. With nearly a third of children now born out of wedlock, many will grow up without ever knowing their fathers.[5]

Third, children see both parents rushing off to work, leaving them in the care of someone else, a "childcare provider." Fifty-two percent of children under five have mothers who are employed full- or part-time.[6] According to sociologist Arlie Hochschild, a growing number of parents face a time bind: the more time they spend at work, the more hectic home becomes, and the more they want to escape back to work. Eventually, work becomes their home, and home becomes work.[7]

Fourth, as children venture outside the home they encounter a local residential environment that is often crime-ridden and unsafe. Moreover, it has almost entirely been given over to the automobile rather than the pedestrian, especially the child-pedestrian. Many children can barely leave home except in an adult-driven car, and many new communities do not have sidewalks. With the automobiling of America, children have become largely disenfranchised from access to many community facilities and services and totally dependent on their parents for transportation. Unfortunately, the parents necessary to provide that transportation are often not around.

Fifth, children see a popular culture as produced by the organized entertainment industry and transmitted by the media that is overloaded with adult sexuality and violence and dominated by materialistic values. This is what their absent parents are supposed to protect them from.

In all of these ways, society today is turning away from the needs of children. Incredible though it may seem, because societal development has always implied a better future for our children, modern society is becoming ever more adult-centered. Adults have more freedom than ever, especially freedom for their own self-development and self-fulfillment, while children grow up in an ever more toxic environment.

The new toxic environment, of course, is different from the toxic environments of times past. Once children were beaten, now they are neglected; once they went hungry, now they are materially spoiled; once they lived in overcrowded conditions, now they sometimes live in virtual isolation. The most consequential change, particularly in recent decades, is a deterioration in the bond between parents and children. No longer can children count on what they need most: loving parents devoted to their well-being who act as good role models and protect them from harm.

The absence, emotional distance, or preoccupation of parents strikes at the very heart of those values which we hope children are learning: trustworthiness, respect for others, responsibility, fairness, caring, and citizenship. Each of these is learned primarily through interactions between parents and children, interactions in which it is mandatory for parents to be closely involved in the lives of their children.

HOW CHILDREN LEARN MORALITY

Within the family, there are three key processes by which children learn morality: forming emotional attachments, being taught prosocial behavior, and learning respect for authority and compliance with rules. All teaching of right and wrong begins with attachment, the warm, emotional tie that children have with their parents. Children learn from and are influenced most by those persons who are most meaningful to them. The most meaningful adults are those to whom the child is emotionally attached. If a child does not have a strong emotional attachment to a parent, the effectiveness of the parent as a teacher and moral guide is greatly diminished. As social psychologist Willard W. Hartup has concluded, "a child's effectiveness in dealing with the social world emerges largely from experience in close relationships."[8]

While many of the failures of moral development in children stem from poor attachment to parents, attachment alone is not enough. Prosocial behavior and moral values must be purposely taught, modeled, and reinforced by parents and other caregivers. A good example must continually be set. Indeed, strongly attached children will follow the example of parents' behavior even when it is undesirable.

One of the main approaches to teaching prosocial behavior is to build on a child's instinctive feelings of empathy, for example, through the regular use of reasoning in behavior management. This involves pointing out the consequences of the child's behavior on other people ("Look at the way you hurt her; now she feels bad"). Such an approach is far preferable to "power-assertive" forms of discipline that involve physical punishment or the deprivation of privileges. The latter can lead more often to the trait of self-protection than to the development of prosocial behavior.

Finally, it is important to instill in children a respect for authority and a sense of obligation to comply with social rules. Social psychologist William Damon puts the issue forcefully: "The child's respect for this authority is the single most important moral legacy that comes out of the child's relationship with the parent."[9] Character traits based on respect for authority and social rules, such as honesty, cooperation, responsibility, and self-reliance, are learned first within the family sphere. If learned well, these traits are then transferred beyond the family to dealings with society at large.

These processes by which character and morality are taught to children—attachment, prosocial behavior, and respect for authority and rules—all have one thing in common. They each require an immense amount of contact time between parents and their children. The parents must be physically present and emotionally, intellectually, spiritually, and morally engaged.

FAMILY STRUCTURE AND TIME

What kind of family is likely to be most successful at instilling character and moral values in its children? Here are its key characteristics: an enduring, two-biological-parent family that engages regularly in activities together; has many of its own routines, traditions, and stories; and provides a great deal of contact between adults and children. The children have frequent interaction with relatives, with neighbors in a supportive neighborhood, and with their parents' world of work, coupled without pervasive worry that their parents will break up. The family develops a vibrant family subculture that provides a rich legacy of meaning for children throughout their lives.

Time spent with children—quantity time—is arguably the central ingredient of the good family. There surely is a strong correlation between the amount of time parents spend with their children and the adult character of those children. The idea of "quality time" is largely a myth, the convenient rationalization of preoccupied parents. In good childrearing, time shortcuts are few and far between.

One should add that, in today's family-averse popular culture, strong, self-contained families are more important than ever. Childrearing families must do everything they can to insulate their children from many aspects of the outside world. The more time children can spend in family activities, and the less time spent with peers and the media, the better. Family subcultures need to incorporate something of an us-against-them philosophy, an issue around which it is no doubt useful for families to band together.

Most of the family characteristics noted above are self-evident. The issue of biological parenting is controversial and requires some clarification. All organisms have evolved through natural selection primarily to survive, reproduce, and parent so as to successfully pass on their genes into the next generation. Human beings have a set of cognitive, emotional, and behavioral predispositions that are encoded in their genes. It is almost certainly the case, therefore, that family behaviors—including courtship, mating, parenting, and relations with kin—are more than just arbitrary social constructs. Each of our relatives shares some of our genes, and it therefore makes evolutionary sense to nurture those genetic kin. This is why we tend to favor our relatives, and why parents tend to put so much effort into raising their biological offspring. Indeed, the parental relationship is unique in human affairs because the reciprocity of social benefits is not a major consideration.

This is not to say that stepparents are inherently unloving; many, of course, are intensely loving, as are adoptive families. But it is to say that parental feelings and parental love are inherently more difficult to develop among persons unrelated to a given child. The stepfamily is one of the fastest-growing family forms in America. An estimated one third of all children today may be expected to become stepchildren before they reach age eighteen. I do not mean to cast aspersions on all stepfamilies; many stepfamilies are necessary and inevitable. But the child outcomes of stepfamilies have been found to be markedly worse than the child outcomes of biological families, and the rapid growth of stepfamilies should certainly not be viewed as favorable from children's or from society's perspectives.

WHAT CAN WE DO TO STRENGTHEN FAMILIES?

What can we do to turn around the deterioration of childrearing conditions? Fundamentally, as parents, we must find ways to spend more time with our children. This may require working fewer hours and "voluntary simplicity" for those who can afford it; turning off the TV set; finding employment in firms that have family-friendly policies, such as flexible work hours; holding off having children until one can afford them; and living in areas where the cost of living is lower. Life is long and the child-rearing years are short. It is unconscionable that in this age of affluence so many of our children are left hanging out to dry.

For society as a whole, two fundamental changes are necessary.

- *Revitalize marriage.* Marriage is what holds men to the mother-child bond. As marriage weakens, fathers become disengaged from their children. To reengage men in childrearing, we must revitalize marriage, which means finding ways to build stronger marriages and to limit divorce and out-of-wedlock childbearing.
- *Reorganize work.* People are retiring from work at ever-earlier ages, when they are still healthy and fully functioning. At the same time, childrearing couples are under enormous pressure to work ever-longer hours. We have to find a way to reorganize our work lives so that we can take time off when our children are young and make up for the time when we are older and our children are grown.

CONCLUSION

Families today are under siege, and children are being hurt. More and more children are growing up with weak attachments, little empathy, and a weakened respect for law and order and civility. More than from anyone else children learn values from their parents, and they learn best by copying their parents' actions. Successful childrearing requires the active and continuing physical, emotional, intellectual, and spiritual presence of parents in the lives of their children. Those parents who spend the most time in childrearing, other things equal, will have the best child outcomes.

Children are our future. In the *Wall Street Journal* poll previously cited, when asked, "What ways do you think the American character is going to change in the twenty-first century?" only 20 percent of young adults answered, "More importance placed on marriage and children."[10] If the other 80 percent are right, if more importance is not placed on marriage and children, I suggest that this nation's future is in considerable peril.

NOTES

1. *Wall Street Journal* (1998) March 5, p. A14.
2. *New York Times* (1998) February 11, p. A15.

3. Eisenberg, N. (1992) *The caring child*. Cambridge: Harvard University Press.

4. See Berger, B. (1998) The social roots of prosperity and liberty. *Society* 35(3): 44–53.

5. See Popenoe, D. (1999) *Life without father: Compelling new evidence that fatherhood and marriage are indispensable for the good of children and society.* Cambridge: Harvard University Press.

6. U.S. Bureau of the Census. (1994 data) Who's minding our preschoolers? Washington, D.C.: USGPO.

7. Hochschild, A. R. (1997) *The time bind: When work becomes home and home becomes work*. New York: Metropolitan Books.

8. Hartup, W. W. (1989) Social relationships and their developmental significance. *American Psychologist* 44(2): 120–126.

9. Damon, W. (1988) *The moral child: Nurturing children's natural moral growth*. New York: Free Press, p. 52.

10. *Wall Street Journal* (1998) March 5, p. A-14.

9

Parenting Adolescents and Adolescents as Parents

A Developmental Contextual Perspective

RICHARD M. LERNER
E. REE NOH
and CLANCIE MAVELLO WILSON

Adolescence can be a confusing time for the young people experiencing this phase of life; for parents of adolescents; for other adults charged with enhancing the development of adolescents; and—with disturbing, historically unprecedented frequency—for adolescents who find themselves in the role of parents.

This chapter focuses on the parents of adolescents and on adolescents as parents in the context of their families, neighborhoods, communities, and society.

DEVELOPMENTAL CONTEXTUALISM

Developmental contextualism is a useful perspective for understanding the contemporary challenges involved in studying adolescents and parenting and for designing programs to promote the positive development of youth—both in relation to enhancing parenting adolescents and to addressing the challenges faced by adolescent parents.

As a theory of human development, developmental contextualism focuses on the changing relations (or, better, coactions)[1] between the developing individual and his or her human and physical environment.[2] It combines life course and human ecological theories and extends the analysis of the developmental process beyond the individual.

Through the diverse interactions a child has with his or her parents, the child influences the parents, who are in turn influencing him or her. In this sense, children are producers of their own development,[3] and the presence of a child constitutes the basis of bidirectional relations between parents and children. Of course, this bidirectional relation continues when the child is an adolescent and an adult. And corresponding relations exist between the person and siblings, friends, teachers, and indeed all other significant people in his or her life.

Moreover, the child-parent relationship is embedded in social networks, which, in turn, are embedded in still larger community, societal, cultural, and historical levels of organization. Time—history—cuts through all the systems. Diversity within time is created as change across time (across history) introduces variation into all the levels of organization involved in the system in figure 1, which depicts the developmental contextual view of human development: Parent-child relations and interpersonal and institutional networks are embedded in and influenced by particular community, societal, cultural, and designed and natural environments, all changing across time.

PARENT-ADOLESCENT RELATIONSHIPS AND CHILDREARING STYLES

Adolescents live in a variety of situations, such as two-parent and single parent biological, adoptive, and homosexual families; two-parent blended families; two- and single- parent grandparent and other relative-headed families; *in loco parentis* foster care, group, detention, and residential treatment facilities; and as homeless and runaway youth.

This wide variation in living circumstances influences both the way parents interact with youth and, in turn, the behavior of adolescents. For instance, in a study of urban, African American adolescents living in either (1) single-mother, (2) stepparent, (3) dual-parent, (4) mother-with-extended-family (e.g., grandparent, aunt, or uncle), or (5) extended-family-only settings (e.g., only an aunt is present), the social support (e.g., emotional encouragement, behavioral assistance) provided to youth was generally the same across family types, with one exception: youth living in single-mother families were given more support than the youth in the other four family types.[4]

Childrearing Styles in Adolescence

The classic research of Diana Baumrind identified three types of childrearing styles: authoritative, authoritarian, and permissive.[5] The first style of rearing is marked by parental warmth, the use of rules and reasoning to promote obedience and keep discipline, nonpunitive punishment (e.g.,

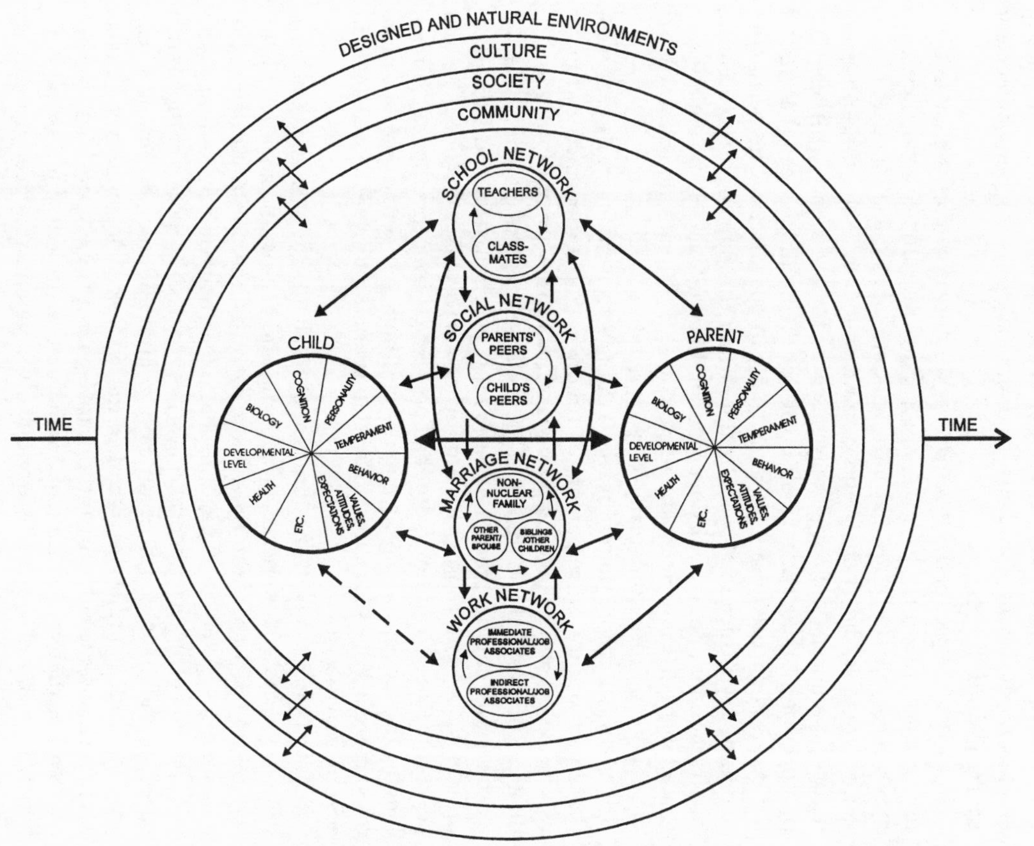
DESIGNED AND NATURAL ENVIRONMENTS
CULTURE
SOCIETY
COMMUNITY
TIME
TIME
SCHOOL NETWORK
TEACHERS
CLASS-
MATES
SOCIAL NETWORK
PARENTS'
PEERS
CHILD'S
PEERS
MARRIAGE NETWORK
NON-
NUCLEAR
FAMILY
OTHER
PARENT/
SPOUSE
SIBLINGS
/OTHER
CHILDREN
WORK NETWORK
IMMEDIATE
PROFESSIONAL/JOB
ASSOCIATES
INDIRECT
PROFESSIONAL/JOB
ASSOCIATES
CHILD
BIOLOGY
COGNITION
PERSONALITY
TEMPERAMENT
BEHAVIOR
VALUES,
ATTITUDES,
EXPECTATIONS
ETC.
HEALTH
DEVELOPMENTAL
LEVEL
PARENT
BIOLOGY
COGNITION
PERSONALITY
TEMPERAMENT
BEHAVIOR
VALUES,
ATTITUDES,
EXPECTATIONS
ETC.
HEALTH
DEVELOPMENTAL
LEVEL

using "time-out" or "grounding" instead of physical punishment), and consistency between statements and actions and across time.[6]

In the second style, authoritarian parents are not warm, stress rigid adherence to the rules they set ("Obey because we are setting the rules"), emphasize the power of their role, and use physical punishment for transgressions.[7]

In the third style, permissive parents do not show consistency in their use of rules, they may have a "laissez-faire" attitude toward their children's behaviors (i.e., they may either not attend to the child or let him or her do whatever he or she wants), and they may give the child anything he or she requests; their style may be characterized as being either more of a peer or an independent "observer" of their child. Indeed, because of the diversity of behavioral patterns that can characterize the permissive parenting style, Eleanor Maccoby noted that this approach to parenting can be thought of as two distinct types: indulgent (e.g., "If my child wants something, I give it to her") and neglectful (e.g., "I really don't know what my child is up to. I don't really keep close tabs on her").[8]

In a study of more than four thousand fourteen- to eighteen-year-olds, those with authoritative parents had more social competence and fewer psychological and behavioral problems than those with authoritarian, indulgent, or neglectful parents.[9] Those with neglectful parents were the least socially competent and had the most psychological and behavioral problems. In turn, those with authoritarian parents were obedient and conformed well to authority but had poorer self-concepts than the others. Finally, those with indulgent parents had high self-confidence but more often abused substances, misbehaved in school, and were less engaged in school activities.

Similarly, in a study of about ten thousand high school students, adolescents whose parents were accepting, firm, and democratic achieved higher school grades, were more self-reliant, were less anxious and depressed, and were less likely to engage in delinquent behavior than were youth with parents using the other rearing styles;[10] this influence of authoritative parenting held for youth of different ethnic and socioeconomic backgrounds and regardless of whether the adolescent's family was intact. Moreover, adolescents with authoritative parents were more likely to have peer groups that valued academic achievement, athletics, and social popularity.[11] In contrast, youth with uninvolved parents had peer groups that did not support adult norms or values, and boys with indulgent parents were in peer groups that stressed fun and partying.

Considerable additional research confirms the generally positive influence on adolescent development of authoritative parenting and, conversely, demonstrates the developmental problems that emerge in youth when parents are authoritarian, permissive, indulgent, or uninvolved.[12] Moreover, this research shows that the positive influences of authoritative parenting extend to the adolescent's involvement with peers.[13]

How successful are parents' attempts at socialization? During adolescence very few families—estimates are between 5 and 10 percent—experience a major deterioration in the parent-child relationship.[14] Moreover, not only do parents expect to see change in their sons' and daughters' behaviors as they socialize them during adolescence,[15] but through their interactions on a day-to-day basis parents can model and influence the cognitive, emotional, and behavioral attributes they desire to see in their offspring.[16]

Supportive Parent-Adolescent Relationships

Among American youth, warm parental interactions are associated with effective problem-solving ability in both the adolescent and the family as a whole; however, hostile interactions are associated with destructive adolescent problem behaviors.[17] Similarly, among German adolescents, parental behaviors marked by approval and attention to positive behavior are associated with an adolescent who feels he or she is capable of controlling events that can affect him or her;[18] however, when parental behaviors disparage the child and fail to attend to his or her specific behavior, the adolescent feels that chance determines what happens to him or her in life. Feelings of closeness between parents and adolescents are related to parents' satisfaction in their parenting and to the youths' self-esteem and participation in family activities.[19]

Parental support also has been associated with adolescents' better school grades and scholastic self-concept;[20] with adolescents' perceiving that social relationships can be more beneficial than risky to one's development;[21] with adolescents' satisfaction with life;[22] and with a decreased involvement of adolescents in drinking, delinquency, and other problem behaviors.[23]

Close parent-child relationships are linked to feeling cohesive with one's family and are associated with high self-perceived competence, especially across the transition to junior high school, low levels of problematic behavior, and low levels of depression or anxiety.[24]

Stressful Parent-Adolescent Relations

At the same time, conflicts are ubiquitous in families.[25] Many adolescents report that conflicts often arise because they feel that their parents are not providing the emotional support they want, because either youth or parents believe that the other is not meeting their expectations, or because of a lack of consensus about family or societal values.

In a study of more than eighteen hundred Latino, African American, and European American parents of adolescents, conflicts occurred in the main over everyday matters, such as chores and style of dress, rather than in regard to substantive issues such as sex and drugs.[26] Parents from all racial/ethnic groups reported arguing about the same issues; however, European American parents reported more conflict than parents from the other two groups.

Although adolescents and their parents are in conflict about a common set of issues—chores, appearance, and politeness—these arguments decrease as adolescents mature.[27] However, conflict over finances tends to increase at older age levels. As youth develop they are less likely to concede an argument to parents; as a result, conflicts may be left unresolved, especially with boys.[28]

Family conflicts may lead an adolescent to think negatively about himself or herself and can even lead to suicidal thoughts.[29] In addition, conflict is associated with "externalizing" problems (such as hostility) among youth.[30] For adolescent girls, the experience of menarche is associated with increased conflict, especially in the mother-daughter relationship, causing fewer positive emotions and more negative exchanges.[31] A vicious cycle may be created when adolescent problems increase parent-adolescent conflicts.[32]

The negative emotions of parents can result in problems for adolescents. For example, fathers' feelings of stress are associated with adolescents' emotional and behavioral problems. Maternal stress is associated with "internalizing" problems (e.g., anxiety, depression) for adolescent boys and with poor school grades for adolescent girls.[33] The link between parental stress and adolescent problems seems to involve depression in parents, which disrupts effective parental discipline and leads to adolescent depression and problem behaviors.[34] Ineffective parenting behaviors (e.g., low self-restraint among fathers) are associated with problem behaviors of offspring.[35]

Parents of tenth graders with conduct problems have been found to be more hostile than parents of tenth graders with depression.[36] In addition, parents of tenth graders who were both depressed and showing problem behaviors had high levels of hostility and low levels of warmth when their children were in the seventh, eighth, and ninth grades. Similarly, depression among both European American and Asian American adolescents is associated with family relations marked by low warmth and acceptance and high levels of conflict with their mothers and fathers.[37] In addition, anger, hostility, coercion, and conflict shown by both parents and siblings have a detrimental effect on adolescent adjustment.[38]

Psychiatric disorders of parents are related to the occurrence of antisocial and hostile behaviors among adolescents.[39] In addition, the problem drinking or alcoholism of parents is associated with alcohol use and abuse among adolescent offspring in European American, African American, and Latino families.[40]

Similarly, parental drug use results in a host of behavioral, cognitive, and self-esteem problems in their offspring.[41] Maternal smoking is associated with smoking in adolescent children,[42] and parental substance use in general is linked to numerous problems of adolescent personal and social behavior, including experience with the same substances (drugs, alcohol, cigarettes, etc.) used by parents.[43]

Moreover, when fathers have an emotionally distant relationship with their wives and turn to their adolescent daughters for intimacy and affection, the daughters show depression, anxiety, and low self-esteem.[44] In turn, IQ scores for youth are lower in larger families, in families where the mother's educational attainment and the family's social support are low, and in families of poor, minority background.[45]

A considerable body of research indicates that divorce is associated with social, academic, and personal adjustment problems in affected adolescents, including problems associated with early initiation of sexual behavior.[46] In addition, parent-child relations are less hierarchical and children are pushed to grow up faster in divorced families.[47] The period following separation and divorce is quite stressful for youth,[48] especially if the adolescent is caught between divorced parents engaged in continuing, conflictual, and hostile interactions.[49]

In some cases there are gender differences in the reaction of adolescents to divorce. Although girls tend to react more negatively than boys prior to the parents' separation, they also tend to adapt better than boys after the divorce.[50] In the case of remarriage, there is evidence that although both male and female adolescents may have difficulty interacting with stepfathers, girls may have more specific problems.[51] Moreover, even two years or more after the remarriage both male and female adolescents show no improvement in relationships with their stepfathers or in behavior problems (e.g., school grades) associated with the divorce.[52]

In contrast, living under the custody of one's birth father is linked to problems for both male and female adolescents.[53] For instance, adolescents living with their fathers adjust more poorly than youth living in other arrangements (e.g., with their mothers). This seems to be due to the closeness they have with, and the monitoring provided by, the parent with whom they are living.[54] In the same vein, living with a stepfather and mother, as compared to living with a father and stepmother, is associated with more positive self-esteem among both male and female adolescents.[55]

ADOLESCENTS AS PARENTS

According to the data presented in the *1993 Kids Count Data Book,* 45 percent of the 1.7 million new American families started in 1990 by the birth of a baby were at major risk of experiencing problems, such as having inadequate family resources or witnessing negative developments for the child (e.g., poor school performance), because of the presence of at least one of three factors: (1) the mother had fewer than twelve years of schooling; (2) the mother was not married to the child's father; or (3) the mother was a teenager at the time of the birth of her first baby.[56]

Families headed by adolescents have an elevated probability of experiencing financial and developmental risks. Illustrations of the magnitude of these risks include the following:

- Each year, one million adolescents become pregnant;[57] about half give birth, so that about every minute, an American adolescent has a baby.[58]
- Of adolescents who give birth, 46 percent go on welfare within four years; of unmarried adolescents who give birth, 73 percent go on welfare within four years.[59]
- By age eighteen, 25 percent of American females have been pregnant at least once.[60]
- Youth between fifteen and nineteen years of age account for 25 percent of all cases of sexually transmitted disease each year. Moreover, 6.4 percent of adolescent runaways, of which there are between 750,000 and 1,000,000 each year in America, have positive tests for the AIDS virus.[61] These runaway youth often engage in unsafe sex, prostitution, and intravenous drug use. Thus, each year in America up to sixty-four thousand "time bombs" are going out onto the streets of our towns and cities and spreading a disease that will kill them and the other people with whom they engage in behaviors related to drug use and unsafe sex.
- About $25 billion in federal funds is spent annually to provide social, health, and welfare services to families begun by teenagers.[62]
- About 20 percent of adolescent girls in grades eight through eleven are subjected to sexual harassment, and 75 percent of girls under the age of fourteen who have had sexual relations are victims of rape.[63] Thus, sex among young adolescent girls is usually forced sex.[64]
- Over the last three decades, the age of first intercourse has declined. Higher proportions of adolescent girls and boys reported being sexually experienced at each age between fifteen and twenty in 1988

than in the early 1970s. In 1988, 27 percent of girls and 33 percent of boys had intercourse by their fifteenth birthday.[65]

- Pregnancy rates for girls younger than fifteen rose 4.1 percent between 1980 and 1988, a rate higher than for any other teenage age group.[66]
- In 1993, 71.8 percent of all births to teenagers were to unmarried teenagers. This rate represents an increase of 399 percent since 1963.[67]
- Women who become mothers as teenagers are more likely to find themselves living in poverty later in their lives than women who delay childbearing. In their twenties and thirties, 28 percent of women who gave birth as teenagers were poor, while only 7 percent of women who gave birth after adolescence were living in poverty.[68]
- In 1992, the federal government spent nearly $34 billion on Aid to Families with Dependent Children, Medicaid, and food stamps for families begun by adolescents.[69]
- In 1997, 49 percent of high school males and 48 percent of females reported having become sexually active.[70]
- In 1997, in a survey of sexually active female adolescents, 49 percent reported not using a condom during their most recent sexual intercourse. The corresponding rate for males was 37 percent.[71]
- By age twenty, 74 percent of males, and 57 percent of females, who became sexually active at age fourteen or younger have had six or more sexual partners.[72]
- In 1991, 38 percent of pregnancies among fifteen- to nineteen-year-olds ended in abortion.[73]
- By age nineteen, 15 percent of African American males have fathered a child; the corresponding rates for Latinos and European Americans are 11 percent and 7 percent respectively.[74]
- 39 percent of the fathers of children born to fifteen-year-olds and 47 percent of the fathers of children born to sixteen-year-olds are over age twenty.[75]

The magnitude and diversity of these problems is challenging the educational, health care, and social service systems of America. The complexity of resolving issues raised by these behaviors is due at least in part to the connection of unsafe sexual practices to the other risk behaviors of adolescence and to numerous individual and contextual influences on adolescents.[76]

The peers of adolescents influence their sexual behavior. For example, peer rejection in the sixth grade is positively associated with the number of sexual partners females will have over the next four years.[77] In turn, however, peer acceptance, when it is associated with both intense dating and use of alcohol with classmates, is positively associated as well with the number of sexual partners adolescents have by tenth grade. The number of sexually active girlfriends, as well as the number of her sexually active sisters and whether she has an adolescent childbearing sister, is linked to an adolescent girl's permissive sexual attitudes, having intentions for future sex, and being a nonvirgin.[78]

About 20 percent of girls report that they have been involved in unwanted sexual experiences within the past year.[79] Approximately one third of these encounters involved forced sexual intercourse; the other two thirds involved unwanted touching. A girl's history of sexual abuse, a tendency to conform to peers, and having parents whose rearing style was either authoritarian or reflective of low monitoring were predictive of being a target of an unwanted sexual advance. Similarly, in divorced families, a mother's dating behavior and whether she has sexually permissive attitudes influences both her daughters' and sons' sexual activity.[80]

The community context also influences adolescent sexuality. In poor communities, youth have higher rates of abortion and lower rates of marriage.[81] In turn, among both African American and European American female adolescents, living in a socially disorganized, low-income community where family planning services are not readily available increases the likelihood of initiating sexual intercourse at an early age.

CONCLUSION

Parents are charged with an awesome responsibility by society. Society expects parents to create healthy and productive citizens—to develop the human resources of the future. Most parents fulfill these expectations. However, there are failures.

The existing diversity in parenting styles and in family structures has pervasive implications for adolescent development, which all too often are problematic. Although family influences are not the only source of problems in adolescence, they covary with other sources in affecting the incidence of problem behavior. In many cases problematic outcomes are associated with the adolescent himself or herself being a parent. At the same time, the family of origin can protect youth from the occurrence of problem behaviors.

Most adolescents have the personal, emotional, and social context resources necessary to successfully meet the biological, psychological, and social challenges of adolescence—either by themselves or as a consequence of intervention programs that capitalize on their "plasticity," that is, on their potential for developmental change. But a critical number do not have these resources.

The challenges we must address to produce positive outcomes on a more regular and sustained basis are more daunting when an adolescent is a parent. A key task for future research is to identify the bases of successful development under such circumstances and then to translate such successes into appropriate, sustained programs and policies.

NOTES

1. Gottlieb, G. (1997) *Synthesizing nature-nurture: Prenatal roots of instinctive behavior.* Mahwah, N.J.: Erlbaum.

2. Lerner, R. M. (1986) *Concepts and theories of human development* (2e). New York: Random House; Lerner, R. M. (1991) Changing organism-context relations as the basic process of development: A developmental contextual perspective. *Developmental Psychology* 27: 27–32; Lerner, R. M. (1992) *Final solutions: Biology, prejudice, and genocide.* University Park: Pennsylvania State University Press; and Lerner, R. M. (1995) *America's youth in crisis: Challenges and options for programs and policies.* Thousand Oaks, Calif.: Sage.

3. Lerner, R. M. (1982) Children and adolescents as producers of their own development. *Developmental Review* 2: 342–370.

4. Zimmerman, M., Salem, D., & Maton, K. (1995) Family structure and psychosocial correlates among urban African-American adolescent males. *Child Development* 66: 1598–1613.

5. Baumrind, D. (1967) Child care practices anteceding three patterns of preschool behavior. *Genetic Psychology Monographs* 75: 43–88; and Baumrind, D. (1971) Current patterns of parental authority. *Developmental Psychology Monographs* 4 (no. 1, pt. 2).

6. Baumrind, D. (1971) Current patterns of parental authority. *Developmental Psychology Monographs* 4 (no. 1, pt. 2); and Lamborn, S. D., Mounts, N. S., Steinberg, L., & Dornbusch, S. M. (1991) Patterns of competence and adjustment among adolescents from authoritative, authoritarian, indulgent, and neglectful families. *Child Development* 62: 1049–1065.

7. Baumrind, D. (1971) Current patterns of parental authority. *Developmental Psychology Monographs* 4 (no. 1, pt. 2); and Belsky, J., Lerner, R. M., & Spanier, G. B. (1984) *The child in the family.* Reading, Mass.: Addison-Wesley.

8. Maccoby, E., & Martin, J. (1983) Socialization in the context of the family: Parent-child interaction. In E. M. Hetherington (ed.), *Handbook of child psychology: Socialization, personality, and social development* (vol. 4, pp. 1–101). New York: Wiley.

9. Baumrind, D. (1971) Current patterns of parental authority. *Developmental Psychology Monographs* 4 (no. 1, pt. 2).

10. Steinberg, L., Mounts, N. S., Lamborn, S. D., & Dornbusch, S. M. (1991) Authoritative parenting and adolescent adjustment across varied ecological niches. *Journal of Research on Adolescence* 1(1): 19–36.

11. Durbin, D. L., Darling, N., Steinberg, L., & Brown, B. B. (1993) Parenting style and peer group membership among European-American adolescents. *Journal of Research on Adolescence* 3(1): 87–100.

12. Almeida, D. M., & Galambos, N. L. (1991) Examining father involvement and the quality of father-adolescent relations. *Journal of Research on Adolescence* 1(2): 155–172; Baumrind, D. (1991) The influence of parenting style on adolescent competence and substance use. *Journal of Early Adolescence* 11(1): 56–95; Brown, B. B., Mounts, N., Lamborn, S. D., & Steinberg, L. (1993) Parenting practices and peer group affiliation in adolescence. *Child Development* 64(2): 467–482; Feldman, S. S., & Wood, D. N. (1994) Parents' expectations for preadolescent sons' behavioral autonomy: A longitudinal study of correlates and outcomes. *Journal of Research on Adolescence* 4(1): 45–70; Melby, J. N., & Conger, R. D. (1996) Parental behaviors and adolescent academic performance: A longitudinal analysis. *Journal of Research on Adolescence* 6(1): 113–137; Paulson, S. E. (1994) Relations of parenting style and parental involvement with ninth-grade students' achievement. *Journal of Early Adolescence* 14: 250–267; Simons, R. L., Johnson, C., & Conger, R. D. (1994) Harsh corporal punishment versus quality of parental involvement as an explanation of adolescent maladjustment. *Journal of Marriage and the Family* 56: 591–607; and Wentzel, K. R., Feldman, S. S., & Weinberger, D. A. (1991) Parental child rearing and academic achievement in boys: The mediational role of social-emotional adjustment. *Journal of Early Adolescence* 11(3): 321–339.

13. Brown, B. B., Mounts, N., Lamborn, S. D., & Steinberg, L. (1993) Parenting practices and peer group affiliation in adolescence. *Child Development* 64(2): 467–482; and Lerner, R. M., & Galambos, N. (1998) Adolescent development: Challenges and opportunities for research, programs, and policies. In J. T. Spence (ed.), *Annual Review of Psychology* (vol. 49, pp. 413–446). Palo Alto, Calif.: Annual Reviews.

14. Steinberg, L. (1990) Autonomy, conflict, and harmony in the family relationship. In S. S. Feldman & G. R. Elliott (eds.), *At the threshold: The developing adolescent.* Cambridge: Harvard University Press, pp. 255–276.

15. Freedman-Doan, C. R., Arbreton, A. J., Harold, R. D., & Eccles, J. S. (1993) Looking forward to adolescence: Mothers' and fathers' expectations for affective and behavioral change. *Journal of Early Adolescence* 13(4): 472–502.

16. Eisenberg, N., & McNally, S. (1993) Socialization and mothers' and adolescents' empathy-related characteristics. *Journal of Research on Adolescence* 3(2): 171–191; Larson, R. W., & Richards, M. H. (1994) Family emotions: Do young adolescents and their parents experience the same states? *Journal of Research on Adolescence* 4(4): 567–583; Simons, R. L., Whitbeck, L. B., Conger, R. D., & Conger, K. J. (1991) Parenting factors, social skills, and value commitments as precursors to school failure, involvement with deviant peers, and delinquent behavior. *Journal of Youth and Adolescence* 20(6): 645–664; and Whitbeck, L. B. (1987) Modeling efficacy: The effect of perceived parental efficacy on the self-efficacy of early adolescents. *Journal of Early Adolescence* 7(2): 165–177.

17. Ge, X., Best, K. M., Conger, R. D., & Simons, R. L. (1996) Parenting behaviors and the occurrence and co-occurrence of adolescent depressive symptoms and conduct problems. *Developmental Psychology* 32(4): 717–731; and Rueter, M. A., & Conger, R. D. (1995) Interaction style, problem-solving behavior, and family problem-solving effectiveness. *Child Development* 66: 98–115.

18. Krampen, G. (1989) Perceived childrearing practices and the development of locus of control in early adolescence. *International Journal of Behavioral Development* 12(2): 177–193.

19. Paulson, S. E., Hill, J. P., & Holmbeck, G. N. (1991) Distinguishing between perceived closeness and parental warmth in families with seventh-grade boys and girls. *Journal of Early Adolescence* 11(2): 276–293.

20. Dubois, D. L., Eitel, S. K., & Felner, R. D. (1994) Effects of family environment and parent-child relationships on school adjustment during the transition to early adolescence. *Journal of Marriage and the Family* 56: 405–414.

21. East, P. L. (1989) Early adolescents' perceived interpersonal risks and benefits: Relations to social support and psychological functioning. *Journal of Early Adolescence* 9(4): 374–395.

22. Young, M. H., Miller, B. C., Norton, M. C., & Hill, E. J. (1995) The effect of parental supportive behaviors on life satisfaction of adolescent offspring. *Journal of Marriage and the Family* 57: 813–822.

23. Barnes, G. M., & Farrell, M. P. (1992) Parental support and control as predictors of adolescent drinking, delinquency, and related problem behaviors. *Journal of Marriage and the Family* 54: 763–776.

24. Papini, D. R., Roggman, L. A., & Anderson, J. (1991) Early-adolescent perceptions of attachment to mother and father: A test of the emotional-distancing and buffering hypotheses. *Journal of Early Adolescence* 11(2): 258–275; and Kenny, M. E. (1993). Contributions of parental attachments to view of self and depressive symptoms among early adolescents. *Journal of Early Adolescence* 13(4): 408–430.

25. Fisher, C. B., & Johnson, B. L. (1990) Getting mad at mom and dad: Children's changing views of family conflict. *International Journal of Behavioral Development* 13(1): 31–48.

26. Barber, B. K. (1994) Cultural, family, and person contexts of parent-adolescent conflict. *Journal of Marriage and the Family* 56: 375–386.

27. Galambos, N. L., Sears, H. A., Almeida, D. M., & Kolaric, G. C. (1995) Parents' work overload and problem behavior in young adolescents. *Journal of Research on Adolescence* 5 (2): 201–223.

28. Smetana, J. G., Yau, J., & Hanson, S. (1991) Conflict resolution in families with adolescents. *Journal of Research on Adolescence* 1(2): 189–206.

29. Shagle, S. C., & Barber, B. K. (1993) Effects of family, marital, and parent-child conflict on adolescent self-derogation and suicidal ideation. *Journal of Marriage and the Family* 55: 964–974.

30. Mason, C. A., Cauce, A. M., Gonzales, N., Hiraga, Y., & Grove, K. (1994) An ecological model of externalizing behaviors in African-American adolescents: No family is an island. *Journal of Research on Adolescence* 4(4): 639–655.

31. Holmbeck, G. N., & Hill, J. P. (1991) Conflictive engagement, positive affect, and menarche in families with seventh-grade girls. *Child Development* 62: 1030–1048; and Steinberg, L. (1987) Impact of puberty on family relations: Effects of pubertal status and pubertal timing. *Developmental Psychology* 23: 451–460.

32. Maggs, J. L., & Galambos, N. L. (1993) Alternative structural models for understanding adolescent problem behavior in two-earner families. *Journal of Early Adolescence* 13(1): 79–101.

33. Compas, B. E., Howell, D.C., Phares, V., & Williams, R. A. (1989) Risk factors for emotional/behavioral problems in young adolescents: A prospective analysis of adolescent and parental stress and symptoms. *Journal of Consulting and Clinical Psychology* 57(6): 732–740.

34. Conger, R. D., Patterson, G. R., & Ge, X. (1995) It takes two to replicate: A mediational model for the impact of parents' stress on adolescent adjustment. *Child Development* 66: 80–97; and Gallimore, M., & Kurdek, L. A. (1992) Parent depression and parent authoritative discipline as correlates of young adolescents' depression. *Journal of Early Adolescence* 12(2): 187– 196.

35. Baumrind, D. (1991) The influence of parenting style on adolescent competence and substance use. *Journal of Early Adolescence* 11(1): 56–95; D'Angelo, L. L., Weinberger, D. A., & Feldman, S. S. (1995) Like father, like son? Predicting male adolescents' adjustment from parents' distress and self-restraint. *Developmental Psychology* 31(6): 883–896; Feldman, S. S., & Weinberger, D. A. (1994) Self-restraint as a mediator of family influences on boys' delinquent behavior: A longitudinal study. *Child Development* 65: 195–211; and Simons, R. L., Whitbeck, L. B., Conger, R. D., & Conger, K. J. (1991) Parenting factors, social skills, and value commitments as precursors to school failure, involvement with deviant peers, and delinquent behavior. *Journal of Youth and Adolescence* 20(6): 645–664.

36. Ge, X., Best, K. M., Conger, R. D., & Simons, R. L. (1996) Parenting behaviors and the occurrence and co-occurrence of adolescent depressive symptoms and conduct problems. *Developmental Psychology* 32(4): 717–731.

37. Greenberger, E., & Chen, C. (1996) Perceived family relationships and depressed mood in early and late adolescence: A comparison of European and Asian Americans. *Developmental Psychology* 32(4): 707–716.

38. Pike, A., McGuire, S., Hetherington, E. M., Reiss, D., & Plomin, R. (1996) Family environment and adolescent depressive symptoms and antisocial behavior: A multivariate genetic analysis. *Developmental Psychology* 132(4): 574–589.

39. Ge, X., Conger, R. D., Cadoret, R. J., & Neiderhiser, J. M. (1996) The developmental interface between nature and nurture: A mutual influence model of child antisocial behavior and parent behaviors. *Developmental Psychology* 32(4): 574–589.

40. Barrera, M., Li, S. A., & Chassin, L. (1995) Effects of parental alcoholism and life stress on Hispanic and non-Hispanic Caucasian adolescents: A prospective study. *American Journal of Psychology* 23(4): 479–507; Hunt, E., Streissguth, A. P., Kerr, B., & Olson, H. C. (1995) Mothers' alcohol consumption during

pregnancy: Effects on spatial-visual reasoning in 14-year-old children. *American Psychological Society* 6(6): 339–342; and Peterson, P. L., Hawkins, J. D., Abbott, R. D., & Catalano, R. F. (1994) Disentangling the effects of parental drinking, family management, and parental alcohol norms on current drinking by black and white adolescents. *Journal of Research on Adolescence* 4(2): 203–227.

41. Kandel, D. B., Rosenbaum, E., & Chen, K. (1994) Impact of maternal drug use and life experiences on preadolescent children born to teenage mothers. *Journal of Marriage and the Family* 56: 325–340.

42. Kandel, D. B., & Wu, P. (1995) The contributions of mothers and fathers to the intergenerational transmission of cigarette smoking in adolescence. *Journal of Research on Adolescence* 5(2): 225–252.

43. Andrews, J. A., Hops, H., Ary, D. V., & Tildesley, E. (1993) Parental influence on early adolescent substance use: Specific and nonspecific effects. *Journal of Early Adolescence* 13(3): 285–310; and Stice, E., & Barrera, J. (1995) A longitudinal examination of the reciprocal relations between perceived parenting and adolescents' substance use and externalizing behaviors. *Developmental Psychology* 31(2): 322–334.

44. Jacobvitz, D. B., & Bush, N. F. (1996) Reconstructions of family relationships: Parent-child alliances, personal distress, and self-esteem. *Developmental Psychology* 32(4): 732–743.

45. Sameroff, A. J., Seifer, R., Baldwin, A., & Baldwin, C. (1993) Stability of intelligence from preschool to adolescence: The influence of social and family risk factors. *Child Development* 64: 80–97; and Taylor, R. D. (1996) Adolescents' perceptions of kinship support and family management practices: Association with adolescent adjustment in African American families. *Developmental Psychology* 32(4): 687–695.

46. Brody, F., & Forehand, R. (1990) Interparental conflict, relationship with the noncustodial father, and adolescent post-divorce adjustment. *Journal of Applied Developmental Psychology* 11: 139–147; Carson, A., Madison, T., & Santrock, J. (1987) Relationships between possible selves and self-reported problems of divorced and intact family adolescents. *Journal of Early Adolescence* 7(20): 191–204; Demo, D. H., & Acock, A. C. (1988) The impact of divorce on children. *Journal of Marriage and the Family* 50(3): 619–648; Doherty, W. J., & Needle, R. H. (1991) Psychological adjustment and substance use among adolescents before and after a parental divorce. *Child Development* 62: 328–337; Hetherington, M. E. (1991) Presidential address: Families, lies, and videotapes. *Journal of Research on Adolescence* 1(4): 323–348; Hetherington, M. E., Cox, M., & Cox, R. (1985) Long-term effects of divorce and remarriage on the adjustment of children. *Journal of the American Academy of Child Psychiatry* 24: 815–830; Simons, R. L., Johnson, C., & Conger, R. D. (1994) Harsh corporal punishment versus quality of parental involvement as an explanation of adolescent maladjustment. *Journal of Marriage and the Family* 56: 591–607; Wallerstein, J. S. (1987) Children of divorce: Report of a ten-year follow-up of early latency-age children. *American Journal of Orthopsychiatry* 57(2): 199–211; and Whitbeck, L. B., Simons, R. L., & Kao, M. (1994) The effects of divorced mothers' dating behaviors

and sexual attitudes on the sexual attitudes and behaviors of their adolescent children. *Journal of Marriage and the Family* 56: 615–621.

47. Smetana, J. G. (1993) Conceptions of parental authority in divorced and married mothers and their adolescents. *Journal of Research on Adolescence* 3(1): 19–39.

48. Doherty, W. J., & Needle, R. H. (1991) Psychological adjustment and substance use among adolescents before and after a parental divorce. *Child Development* 62: 328–337.

49. Buchanan, C. M., Maccoby, E., & Dornbusch, S. M. (1991) Caught between parents: Adolescents' experience in divorced homes. *Child Development* 62: 1008–1029.

50. Doherty, W. J., & Needle, R. H. (1991) Psychological adjustment and substance use among adolescents before and after a parental divorce. *Child Development* 62: 328–337; and Hetherington, M. E., Cox, M., & Cox, R. (1985) Long-term effects of divorce and remarriage on the adjustment of children. *Journal of the American Academy of Child Psychiatry* 24: 815–830.

51. Lee, V. E., Burkam, D. T., Zimiles, H. & Ladewski, B. (1994) Family structure and its effect on behavioral and emotional problems in young adolescents. *Journal of Research of Adolescence* 4(3): 405–437.

52. Hetherington, M. E. (1991) Presidential address: Families, lies, and videotapes. *Journal of Research on Adolescence* 1(4): 323–348; and Lee, V. E., Burkam, D. T., Zimiles, H., & Ladewski, B. (1994) Family structure and its effect on behavioral and emotional problems in young adolescents. *Journal of Research of Adolescence* 4(3): 405–437.

53. Lee, V. E., Burkam, D. T., Zimiles, H., & Ladewski, B. (1994) Family structure and its effect on behavioral and emotional problems in young adolescents. *Journal of Research of Adolescence* 4(3): 405–437.

54. Buchanan, C. M., Maccoby, E. E., & Dornbusch, S. M. (1992) Adolescents and their families after divorce: Three residential arrangements. *Journal of Research on Adolescence* 2: 261–291.

55. Fine, M. A., & Kurdek, L. A. (1992) The adjustment of adolescents in stepfather and stepmother families. *Journal of Marriage and the Family* 54: 725–736.

56. *Michigan Kids Count 1992 data book: County profiles of child and family well-being.* Available from the Michigan League for Human Services, 300 N. Washington Avenue, Suite 401, Lansing, MI 48933.

57. di Mauro, D. (1995) *Sexuality research in the United States: An assessment of social and behavioral sciences.* New York: Social Science Research Council.

58. Children's Defense Fund (1995) *The state of America's children yearbook.* Washington, D.C.: Children's Defense Fund.

59. Lerner, R. M. (1995) *America's youth in crisis: Challenges and options for programs and policies.* Thousand Oaks, Calif.: Sage.

60. Ibid.

61. Ibid.

62. di Mauro, D. (1995) *Sexuality research in the United States: An assessment of social and behavioral sciences.* New York: Social Science Research Council.

63. Ibid.

64. Carnegie Corporation of New York (1995) *Great transitions: Preparing adolescents for a new century.* New York: Carnegie Corporation of New York; and *Kids Count Special Report* (1998) When teens have sex: issues and trends. Baltimore, Md.: Annie E. Casey Foundation.

65. Ibid.

66. Ibid.

67. Ibid.

68. Ibid.

69. Ibid.

70. Ibid.; and Alan Guttmacher Institute. (1994) *Sex and America's teenagers.* New York: Alan Guttmacher Institute.

71. Carnegie Corporation of New York (1995) *Great transitions: Preparing adolescents for a new century.* New York: Carnegie Corporation of New York; *Kids Count Special Report* (1998) When teens have sex: Issues and trends. Baltimore, Md.: Annie E. Casey Foundation; and U.S. Department of Health and Human Services. (1996) *Trends in the well-being of America's children and youth: 1996.* Washington, D.C.: U.S. Department of Health and Human Services, Office of the Secretary for Planning and Evaluation.

72. U.S. Department of Health and Human Services. (1996) *Trends in the well-being of America's children and youth: 1996.* Washington, D.C.: U.S. Department of Health and Human Services, Office of the Secretary for Planning and Evaluation.

73. Ibid.

74. Lerner, R. M. (1995) *America's youth in crisis: Challenges and options for programs and policies.* Thousand Oaks, Calif.: Sage.

75. U.S. Department of Health and Human Services. (1996) *Trends in the well-being of America's children and youth: 1996.* Washington, D.C.: U.S. Department of Health and Human Services, Office of the Secretary for Planning and Evaluation.

76. Luster, T., & Small, S. A. (1994) Factors associated with sexual risk-taking behaviors among adolescents. *Journal of Marriage and the Family* 56(3): 622–632.

77. Feldman, S. S., Rosenthal, D. R., Brown, N. L., & Canning, R. D. (1995) Predicting sexual experience in adolescent boys from peer rejection and acceptance during childhood. *Journal of Research on Adolescence* 5(4): 387–412.

78. East, P. L., Felice, M. E., & Morgan, M. C. (1993) Sisters' and girlfriends' sexual and childbearing behavior: Effects on early adolescent girls' sexual outcomes. *Journal of Marriage and the Family* 55: 953–963.

79. Small, S. A., & Kerns, D. (1993) Unwanted sexual activity among peers during early and middle adolescence: Incidence and risk factors. *Journal of Marriage and the Family* 55: 941–952.

80. Whitbeck, L. B., Simons, R. L., & Kao, M. (1994)The effects of divorced

mothers' dating behaviors and sexual attitudes on the sexual attitudes and behaviors of their adolescent children. *Journal of Marriage and the Family* 56: 615–621.

81. Sullivan, M. L. (1993) Culture and class as determinants of out-of-wedlock childbearing and poverty during late adolescence. *Journal of Research on Adolescence* 3(3): 295–316.

PART II

Parenthood in the Community

Some parenting functions can be delegated to childcare workers, teachers, coaches, and mentors, but certain responsibilities clearly lie with parents. They are (1) reliable availability throughout childhood and adolescence; (2) an unconditional relationship that fosters a child's moral and emotional development; (3) arranging for a child's education and health care; and (4) acting with a child's interests in mind.

Parenthood blends into grandparenthood with the arrival of grandchildren. In most instances, grandparents offer ties for grandchildren away from their homes. Grandparents can offer approval, loving delight in their grandchildren, and reliable support for their own offspring. As senior citizens, grandparents are gaining increasing power in the political arena and in the moral leadership of our society. As a grandparent himself, Jack Westman concludes that grandparents are the link between the past and the present—and most significantly between the present and the future. Humanity flows in the endless stream of life through parents, children, and grandchildren.

Divorce directly involves communities in family life through the intervention of courts in establishing custodial, visitation, and financial arrangements. Divorce alters the living arrangements of parents and children and often adds stepfamily relationships. Although mothers and fathers remain the mothers and fathers of their sons and daughters, children often feel personally that the part of them identified with the noncustodial parent has been divorced as well. For all of these reasons, the divorce lifestyle is stressful for both parents and children. Judith Wallerstein's twenty-five-year follow-up of children of divorce shows conclusively that children continue to experience the effects of divorce during adult life with residues of sadness, anger, and anxiety about the potential unreliability of relationships. She outlines the tasks confronting children and their parents before, during, and after divorce. She also offers pointers for parents in beginning and continuing a dialog with their children about divorce.

Lois Hoffman reviews the literature and describes her study of the effects of mothers' employment on the socially competent behavior of their children. Her general finding is reassuring for the 70 percent of all mothers who are employed either part- or full-time: maternal employment is not a serious social problem. On the negative side, the more time a child spends in childcare and the less stable that care, the more likely are later problems in child behavior. Hoffman's findings should not be construed to mean that nothing needs to be done to improve the relationship between the workplace and family life. Forty-four percent of the mothers of children under the age of six are in the workforce full-time, and 20 percent part-time. Our evolving society has yet to accommodate parenthood well. More adjustments are needed: affordable, high-quality childcare; after-school programs; and appropriate family leave policies.

Diane Adams describes the issues involved in seeking childcare of good quality. After outlining the history of childcare in the United States, she describes the three mazes confronting parents—cost, regulations, and quality—and offers pointers for parents in their search for good childcare. She envisions a time in which the complexities of childcare will be unraveled so that parents will not have to "go it alone" in their quest for childcare for their children.

Research shows that well-to-do children with college-educated parents tend to do well no matter what school they attend. However, across social classes the critical factor in student achievement is the involvement of parents in the education of their children. M. Elizabeth Graue describes a useful model for thinking of parent-child-school relationships in terms of who is responsible for what aspects of education. She concludes that responsibility lies with students, schools, parents, communities, and society. Ben Benson, a classroom teacher, outlines ways in which parents can support their children's education through encouraging their children; teaching them how to accept responsibility, organize and set goals, and cope with adversity; being positive role models; and demonstrating that learning is a lifelong process.

Beverley Johnson addresses how to connect families with the health care of their members. She outlines the principles of family-centered care as they apply to parents, parent educators, and family support organizations; she illustrates how these concepts can help make health care facilities and providers more supportive of families. She points to changes that institutions, providers, and families can make in order to move toward a family-centered approach to care. She then suggests strategies that community organizations can use to collaborate with health care leaders, clinicians, medical educators, and policy makers to improve health care. Implementing family-centered approaches to health care takes time. It requires that institutions, their staffs, and patients and families take a new look at traditional approaches to health care and create new ways of working together.

10

Grandparenthood

JACK C. WESTMAN

Too many folks spend their lives aging rather than maturing.
President Jimmy Carter, *The Virtues of Aging*

A seven-year-old girl described her grandmother: "She may be old on the outside, but she acts like she's young on the inside." Grandparents like to hear this said about them!

Most grandparents remain active today with some still working into their seventies and eighties. Some who retire during their sixties may spend as much as one third of their lives in retirement. A few families span five generations.

By the middle of the next century as the "baby boomers" become the elderly, the entire United States will resemble present-day Florida in the proportion of the population composed of older adults. In 1790 less than 2 percent of the population was over 65. In 1990 that figure was 12 percent; by 2030 it will be over 20 percent.[1]

OUR THIRD LIFE

Living longer means that more of us now lead three lives: first as children, second as adults with careers and most likely as parents, and third as retirees from employed careers and for the vast majority as grandparents. The 1990 census revealed that 94 percent of adults over fifty-five are grandparents and that 90 percent of all adults over twenty-five are or have been parents.[2]

During each of these three lives we continually discover and learn new things. We often find sides of ourselves that we did not know existed. Our third life is a time for discovering new talents and creative possibilities. It is a time for reflection and for applying the wisdom of the ages to ourselves. It is a time for discovering the full meaning of life and for preparing for the future, whatever that may be. It is a time for sharing our thoughts and discoveries with others.

One's third life as a grandparent varies in significance. Although grandparenthood is not the dominant aspect of most grandparents' lives, it is more important than most initially realize. For some who are actively raising their grandchildren, it is the most important part of their lives. Others are estranged from their children and from their grandchildren because of strife in their families. However, most live at some distance from their grandchildren and manage to maintain an active role in their lives though the mail, telephone, Internet, and visits.

Grandparents have important symbolic and practical functions in cultures. They are important simply because they are the oldest living representatives of their families. They can be matriarchs or patriarchs for their families. They can be family historians, mentors, and role models.

Without grandparents, there is no tangible family line. Children who have had no contact with grandparents miss knowledge of their ancestry. They may not have a confident sense of the future that comes from interacting with older people who have seen their futures become the present and the past.

Grandparents are links to the past in their families. They are conveyers of traditions in their families and in their cultures. They can recall when the parents of their grandchildren were young—not always to the liking of those parents! They are the repositories of information about their genealogies (they are well advised to record as much as they can). That information often becomes useful material for themes that their grandchildren write in school, and sometimes it flowers into full-fledged interest in building family trees.

Grandparents can provide advice to their children and grandchildren. However, that is best done tactfully and when asked for! They can bring their families together and foster and maintain communication between them. They can play healing roles in assuaging the challenges, hurts, and disappointments in their families. In doing so, they need to carefully avoid stirring up difficulties, the potential for which especially lies beneath the surface in in-law relationships.

Grandparents have much to offer their families and their communities. They are the people who "have been there, done that." Whatever wisdom is should reside in them. They can see through the posturings of our everyday world. They can identify with the life stream and the cycles of human existence. They know what really is important and what is not. They know that disappointments, heartaches, and pain are natural parts of life.

Grandparents know that life goes on without them. They have been a part of history and often have an interest in learning more about the past. They have seen enough to know that everything is not sensible and rational. They have had enough dreams and life experiences to know that the mystical may be more real than the rational. They have learned that whatever it is—good or bad—"it will pass."

OUR AGELESS INNER "I"

Charles Horton Cooley, one of the founders of the field of sociology, called attention to how a healthy mind needs change and renewal throughout life:

> There is no health in mind except as it keeps expanding, taking in fresh life, feeling love and enthusiasm. . . . But if love closes, the self contracts and hardens: the mind, having nothing else to occupy its attention and give it that change and renewal it requires, busies itself more and more with self-feeling, which takes on narrow and disgusting forms, like avarice, arrogance, and fatuity.[3]

Grandparenthood offers many opportunities for change and renewal. In order to maintain vitality in their lives, grandparents are well advised to manage their diets and to engage in regular physical exercise so that their bodies can serve them as well as possible.

If grandparents have been reasonably wise in the conduct of their own lives, they have attended to their physical health and to their spiritual and emotional needs. They know that their bodies age, that their minds fail, but that their seemingly ageless inner "I" remains the same throughout their lives.[4] If they think about it, they can recognize that the present moment is in the "eternal now." This means that the flow of time is unchanging now as it was in the past and will be in the future. It is as if our "I" is in a boat floating down a stream. We can see the changing landscape around us, but our "I" is not changing.

There is something reassuring about the fact that the material world continuously changes, but the passage of time does not change our "I's." This is why we feel old in our bodies and minds but not in our spirits (our "I's"). This is why we do not feel that the image in the mirror accurately reflects who we are. We truly know that we can be old on the outside but young on the inside.

Grandparents also have the luxury of living their lives more or less as they wish. They have more control over their schedules by relinquishing the responsibilities of the workplace. They have time to reflect and to enjoy the simple things in life. They can take time to appreciate the pleasures of being alive. They can enjoy the clouds, the trees, the flowers, and the smell of the air. They also can devote their time and energies to helping those who are less fortunate.

Most important, grandparents can relive and resolve the past in their memories and reveries. The past is part of their lives today—they know what it feels like to lapse into the past as if it is the present. Their storehouse of memories leads most of them to relinquish the wish to live their lives over again.

GRANDCHILDREN

Grandchildren can give grandparents a new lease on life. All of us gain profound meaning in life from the love and respect of our juniors. The attachment between grandparent and grandchild is second in emotional power only to the bond between parent and child. The arrival of a grandchild usually triggers a dormant instinct to nurture. This is accompanied by joy in the birth or adoption of a grandchild; by recalling one's own experiences as a parent and as a grandchild; and by thoughts of continuing one's own life in the next generation.

Grandchildren have as much to offer grandparents as grandparents have to offer them. Grandparents can enjoy pleasures with grandchildren without the responsibilities of rearing them. The love and attention of the older build the younger's self-esteem. Grandchildren's interest in the company and stories of their grandparents reminds grandparents of how important they are to their families. Grandparents and grandchildren offer each other the sense of belonging not only to their own families but to the human family. Grandparents also can relive memories of their own parenting years.

PARENTING GRANDCHILDREN

Grandparents have always stepped in when needed to help raise their grandchildren and the children of others. In the United States, the number actually raising their grandchildren has increased by more than 50 percent over the last ten years. Almost four million are doing so today.[5] This figure represents only those grandparents who are raising their grandchildren through legal measures, such as judicially ordered custody or guardianship. There are many more who care for their grandchildren informally.

Grandparents are motivated by love and duty and at times by the desire to keep their grandchildren out of foster care. Drug and alcohol abuse by the children's parents accounts for about 80 percent of the reasons grandparents rear their grandchildren.[6]

Those who parent their grandchildren can feel like they are riding an emotional roller coaster with feelings of anger, sadness, and guilt. They often express less satisfaction with life when compared with nonparenting grandparents.[7] They have to make lifestyle changes that entail financial, housing, medical, and educational challenges. They may have to postpone retirement. They may have to learn over again how to give children the love and limits they need, although their own past childrearing experience is invaluable.

Even though the responsibilities of raising grandchildren are exhausting, expensive, and emotionally draining, many grandparents derive satisfaction from feeling needed and useful and having opportunities to make a difference in the lives of their grandchildren. Some even report feeling more energetic than before. Receiving the love of their grandchildren is their greatest reward.

Resources and support groups for childrearing grandparents are provided by a number of national, state, and local organizations.[8]

GRANDPARENT POWER

As senior citizens, grandparents are gaining an increasing amount of power in our society not only in the political arena but in moral leadership. They really do have much to offer even though some younger folks tend to disparage the elderly. In fact, many in their seventies and eighties remain active in the power structures of our society.

Grandparents can advocate the interests of the elderly, not only for themselves but for those who are subjected to elder ageism and abuse. Most important, grandparents are aware of the interests and needs of future generations. They are in a position to be powerful advocates for children and parents. Because they are not likely to be motivated by advocacy for children that really is advocacy for adult interests, they can truly advocate the interests of children.

CONCLUSION

Grandparents are crucial resources for their families. But the art of grandparenting requires commitment, understanding, practice, and perseverance.

Grandparents can offer approval, loving delight in their grandchildren, and reliable support for their own offspring. They are the link between the past and the present and even the future! It is through grandchildren that humanity flows in the endless stream of life.

Achieving maturity for grandparents means accepting unfulfilled hopes, illness, disability, and death as natural parts of life. The philosopher Robert Nozick said it well:

We all might seriously weigh spending our penultimate years in endeavors to benefit others, in adventures to advance the cause of truth, goodness, beauty, or holiness not going gentle into that good night or raging against the dying of the light but, near the end, shining our light most brightly.[9]

NOTES

1. Bureau of the Census (1989) *Projections of the population of the United States, by age, sex, and race.* Washington, D.C.: U.S. Department of Commerce.
2. Bureau of the Census (1998) *Current population reports: August 1998.* Washington, D.C.: U.S. Department of Commerce.
3. Cooley, C. H. (1998) *On self and social organization.* Chicago: University of Chicago Press, p. 167.
4. Westman, J. C. (1997) *Born to belong: Becoming who I am.* Lima, Ohio: CSS Publishers, pp. 99–113.
5. Bureau of the Census (1998) *Household and family characteristics: March 1997.* Washington, D.C.: U.S. Department of Commerce.
6. deToledo, S., & Brown, D. (1995) *Grandparents as parents: A survival guide for raising grandchildren.* New York: Guilford Press.
7. Dannison, L., & Nieuwenhuis, A. (1996) *Second time around: Grandparents raising grandchildren.* Kalamazoo, Mich.: Strong Families/Safe Families.
8. Senior Help Line, (800) 252–8966; AARP Grandparent Information Center, (202) 434–2296; Grandparents United for Children's Rights, 137 Larkin Street, Madison, WI 53705–5115, (608) 238–8751.
9. Nozick, Robert (1989) *The examined life: Philosophical meditations.* New York: Simon & Schuster.

11

The Challenges of Divorce for Parents and Children

JUDITH S. WALLERSTEIN

The theme of this chapter is the impact of divorce on parenthood and children. In order to focus the discussion, I will describe six tasks for parents following divorce and six tasks for children of divorce.

My colleagues and I followed the course of a significant sample of divorcing families for twenty-five years after the time of the decisive marital separation and the initial filing for divorce.[1] Because of the time period covered by this study, the vast majority of parents with legal custody were the mothers. Most children by far, throughout the country, still remain in the physical custody of the mother, although legal custody had shifted in the direction of joint legal custody in many states.

PARENTHOOD AFTER DIVORCE

Divorce shifts the husband-wife relationship to an ex-husband and ex-wife status, but mother-child and father-child relationships continue throughout life. In this context, I have identified six tasks for parents after divorce.[2]

Task I: Ending the Marriage

The first task of divorce is to bring the marriage to an end in as civilized a manner as possible, without one partner giving away his or her rights, taking flight just to get it over with, playing saint or sinner, or being controlled by the wish to inflict pain or get revenge. Although it is extremely difficult, parents should negotiate and conclude financial and child custody arrangements with as much reality, morality, emotional stability, and enlightened self-interest as they can muster.

When well done, this task has the potential to ease future years for adults and children. Done poorly, it can set the stage for years of continued anger, deprivation, and suffering for everyone involved.

Task II: Mourning the Loss

Each ex-spouse should acknowledge the loss and mourn the dreams and hopes that were never fully realized. Crying reduces anger to human size. Through mourning, a person can regain or maintain perspective on what was lost. Even the most miserable marriage embodied some expectation of a better life, and, although no tears may be shed for the lost partner, the symbolic meaning of the marriage should be gently put to rest.

An unmourned marriage continues psychologically and keeps the feelings associated with the separation alive at their most hurtful levels.

Task III: Reclaiming Oneself

Reclaiming or establishing a new sense of identity signifies detachment from the marriage. There are many ways to do this. One is for each partner to reach back into his or her early experience and find other images and roots for independence, for being able to live alone, and for undertaking the second chances provided by divorce.

Most of all, the voice of the ex-partner—carping or demeaning, petulant or demanding—needs to be exorcised from within, so that the person does not carry the old marital failure into new relationships and ventures.

Task IV: Resolving or Containing Passions

The experience of divorce engenders feelings that can engulf people for years, coming as unbidden flashbacks and bitter memories of exploitation and betrayal. These feelings are often refueled by subsequent events: the remarriage of the ex-partner, the failure of one's own remarriage, financial inequity, the stresses of single parenting, and the inevitably different courses each person follows after divorce. The reason to try to resolve them is not to "turn the other cheek" but to save oneself from being dominated by the trauma of divorce.

Task V: Venturing Forth Again

To restore a sense of competence and self-esteem, a divorced parent has to find the courage to try new relationships, new roles, and new solutions to old problems in both the workplace and the sexual arena. In trying to move out of the lingering shadow of divorce, people encounter the inescapable fact that failure is always possible, that danger is the flip side of opportunity. Confidence is not achieved in one large step but in many small steps along the way, and hardly ever in a straight line. This task is especially difficult for older people who have spent most of their adult life in the marriage.

Task VI: Rebuilding

The goal is to create a new adult relationship that will be better than the one left behind and will include the children or to establish a gratifying life without marriage that includes but does not overburden the children. In finding postdivorce stability, a person should allow obligations, memories, and lessons of the past to coexist peacefully with experiences in the present.

CHILDREN'S EXPERIENCE OF LOSS

Divorce is not an event that stands alone in the experience of children and their parents. It is one event in a way of life that begins in an unhappy marriage and extends through separation, divorce, subsequent cohabitation, remarriages and second or third divorces, and the remainder of the lives of those involved.

Many divorcing families make their way through the acute phase of the divorce experience and after several years of disequilibrium reach stability and closure in the postdivorce or remarried family.

Chronically litigating couples remain in conflict-fixated behavior, but others who never enter the court arena may also remain fixated at the acute, conflict-ridden phase. Children in these families are especially hindered in their efforts to reach closure. While they may sometimes succeed in addressing the tasks imposed by divorce, they are more likely to falter or to fail along the way.[3] Conversely, if the parents resolve their conflicts and overcome their hurt following the divorce and successfully use the second chance provided by the divorce to improve the quality of life for themselves and their children, the children are more likely to emerge happy and well.

Indeed, it is clear that years after the marital rupture the divorce remains for many children and adolescents the central event of their childhood and casts a long shadow over these years for both boys and girls.[4] These effects are incorporated within the character, attitudes, relationships, self-concept, expectations, and worldview of the child. Over the course of time they are modified by the unfolding developmental stages and by subsequent life experiences and life decisions related and unrelated to events within the family.

For the children in our study, the postdivorce years brought the following:[5]

- Half saw their mother or father get a second divorce in the ten-year period after the first divorce.
- Half grew up in families where parents stayed angry at each other.
- One in four experienced a severe and enduring drop in their standard of living and went on to observe a major, lasting discrepancy between economic conditions in their mothers' and fathers' homes.
- Three in five felt rejected by at least one parent.
- Very few were helped financially with college, even though they continued to visit their fathers regularly. Because their fathers were relatively well off, they were ineligible for scholarships.

PSYCHOLOGICAL TASKS FOR CHILDREN OF DIVORCE

Six tasks fall into an unfolding sequence with varying time spans attached for accomplishing each. The tasks for the children are related to factors within the family following divorce and to the children's mastery of specific threats to development. These tasks add substantially to the usual challenges of growing up.

Task I: Acknowledging the Reality of the Marital Rupture

The first task for a child is to acknowledge the reality of the marital rupture and to understand the family and household changes that ensue separate from the frightening fantasies evoked in the child's mind.

Younger children are especially disadvantaged in grasping the meaning of divorce. Their limited grasp of time, the calendar, space, distance, marriage, separation, and divorce burdens their struggle to understand the course of events in the family.

The lacunae in young children's understanding foster greater dependence on fantasy and further block understanding. Their age-appropriate difficulty in separating reality and fantasy render them especially vulnerable to intense, frightening fantasies and to developmental regressions, such as losing toilet usage.

Yet older youngsters are not spared. Many preadolescents and young adolescents respond to their parents' announcement of their decision to divorce as if it is a cataclysm. Overcome by the fantasy of being in grave danger, several youngsters in our study ran shrieking through the house or to a neighbor to ask for help. Others developed acute vomiting and other symptoms verging on panic that further reduced their capacity to discern and understand the reality.

Task II: Disengaging from Parental Conflict and Distress and Resuming Customary Pursuits

The second task for a child is to return to customary activities and relationships at school with the capacity for learning and at play with appropriate interests and pleasure unimpaired by the family crisis.

This task poses a dual challenge. At a time of family disequilibrium, when one or both parents may be troubled, depressed, or angry, when the household is likely to be in disarray, the child seeks to find and maintain some measure of psychological distance and separation from the adults. In order to achieve this distance, the child needs to actively and painfully disengage from the parental distress or conflict despite what may be profound worry over a parent and despite what may be the intense need of one or both parents for nurturance and support from the child. Often with little or no expectation of parental help, the child needs to take appropriate steps to safeguard his or her individual identity and separate life course.

The second part of this task requires the child to remove the family crisis from its commanding position in his or her inner world. The achievement of this task rests in turn on the mastery, or at least the diminution, of anxiety, depression, and the many conflicting feelings that attend the marital rupture in order to gain or regain the perspective and composure sufficient to enable the child's return to usual activities.

Following the marital rupture, many youngsters at every age feel too wretched, worried, or dispirited to find interests anywhere. A significant subgroup in our study stayed at home or close to home. It was not uncommon for many children following the marital rupture to respond to a request for their three greatest wishes with "I have no wish except to get my family back together again." The pervasive sense of desolation we observed in a significant number of the children was such that it was difficult to evoke even a brief pleasurable response: Arthur, a nine-year-old, told us soberly, "I'm at a dead end in the middle of nowhere." Roberta, age seven, volunteered sadly, "No one likes me because I don't have a house."

Teachers described children at this time as unable to concentrate, daydreaming, preoccupied, bored, restless, inattentive in the classroom, irritable, manipulative, aggressive, or withdrawn. A full half of the fifty-seven children in our sample between the ages of seven and eleven suffered a significant decline in school grades during the year following the marital rupture.[6]

Unlike the first task, the mastery of this task of disengagement was not easier for the older children. It may have been rendered more difficult by the fine shading between an all too realistic worry and phobic anxiety. Many youngsters paced the floor nervously when the parent was late in returning home. Some children begged the custodial parent to quit smoking, asking, "What will happen to me if you get cancer?" A few children had a parent confide suicidal preoccupation and realized full well that their presence was needed by the parent in order to stave off a suicide attempt.

Adolescent commitments to school and their usual extracurricular activities seem particularly vulnerable to disruption at this time. Some adolescents in our study became newly involved at this time in sexual activity or delinquency, most notably stealing. Several became acutely depressed: one fourteen-year-old, who had distinguished herself at school and competitive sports, was truant for the remainder of the school year following her parents' separation and was found to be riding local buses six hours daily, preoccupied with suicidal thoughts.

Task III: Resolution of Loss

Divorce brings multiple losses in its wake, of which the most central is the partial or total loss of one parent from the family. But the losses of divorce may include, as well, the loss of the familiar daily routines; the loss of the symbols, traditions, and continuity of the intact family; and the loss of the protective, physical presence of two parents who can spell and buffer each other as needed. Often, as well, the losses of divorce include the loss of the family home, school, and neighborhood, and sometimes the loss of a more privileged way of life, including private school and a wide range of pleasurable, exciting activities.

The departure of a parent who has been physically or psychologically brutal or demeaning to the child or other parent provides relief. But by and large children who have not been frightened on their own behalf or on behalf of a parent are likely to mourn the loss of one parent's departure even in the absence of a close relationship during the marriage.

The task of absorbing loss is perhaps the single most difficult task imposed by divorce. The child is required to mourn multiple losses in order to come to terms with the constraints, limitations, and potentialities of the postdivorce or remarried family. At its core, one parent's departure often demands that the child overcome his or her sense of rejection, humiliation, unlovability, or powerlessness. Children at all ages are likely to feel rejected. "He left me," they say, and are likely secretly to conclude, "He left because I was not lovable enough." Children in the custody of their father because their mother has relinquished or abandoned them have even stronger feelings of unlovability, unworthiness, and rejection.

This task is greatly facilitated by the establishment of a reliable visiting pattern that can enable parent (usually the father) and child to restore a sense of psychic wholeness in their respective new roles of part-time parent and part-time child. At times a visitation parent and a child spend more time together than they did prior to the divorce. However, only if the loss of the full-time presence of the departed parent is accepted by both parent and child does the potential of the visiting relationship become fully realizable.[7] The quality of a child's relationship to a stepparent is important in this mourning process.

The resolution of this task often lasts many years. The voluntary nature of both the divorce and the parent's departure burdens the child's coping efforts and increases the child's suffering, making this loss more difficult to assimilate than the involuntary loss associated with bereavement. This task is most easily accomplished when the loss of the relationship with the father (or the mother) is partial and the outside parent and child are able to establish and maintain a loving relationship within an ongoing, reliable visiting pattern. Even under ideal conditions this is no small achievement.

Task IV: Resolving Anger and Self-Blame

In order to understand this task it is important to understand the social context of marital dissolution. Unlike bereavement or a disaster, divorce is a voluntary decision for at least one of the marital partners.

The children are aware that divorce is not inevitable, that its immediate cause is the decision of one or both parents to separate, and that its true cause is an unwillingness or failure to maintain the marriage. Moreover, the children, like the community, have different responses when the divorce is sought to remedy a brutal or an unhappy marriage, to pursue a postponed career, or because of one adult's impulsive decision to join a lover.

Our work indicates clearly that children and adolescents do not believe in no-fault divorce. They may blame one or both parents, or they may blame themselves. Divorce characteristically gives rise to anger at the parent who sought the divorce or both parents for their perceived self-centeredness or unresponsiveness to the wishes of the child to maintain an intact family. The anger that these children experience sometimes is likely to be intense and long-lasting, especially among older children and adolescents who disapprove of the conduct of one or both parents. In a school composition written five years after the marital rupture, a fourteen-year-old boy in our study wrote: "My father picked up his suitcase one day and walked out because, as he said, he wanted his freedom. We thought we were a close-knit family, and it was an unexpected shock. It was the death of our family."

Among the distinguishing attributes of some of the parent-child relationships at the ten-year mark is a growing closeness between youngster and parent which seems to have the hallmarks of a significant, long delayed reconciliation. Barbara reported at the age of seventeen, ten years after the marital rupture: "My mom and I are real close now. I stopped being angry at her when I was fifteen when I suddenly realized that all of the kids who lived in intact houses with picket fences were not any happier than I was. It took me a long, long time to stop blaming her for not being in one of those houses."

Task V: Accepting the Permanence of Divorce

Closely related to all of the foregoing tasks, and particularly to the task of successfully mastering the distress evoked by a father's departure, is the child's gradual acceptance that the divorce is permanent. We have observed children, adolescents, and adults decades after the divorce persisting in the expectation that the family will be restored, weeping for the father they hardly knew, and finding omens of reconciliation in a handshake or a friendly nod. Even the remarriage of both parents sometimes does little to diminish the intensity of this persistent fantasy, wish, hope, or expectation. Our clinical experience includes a middle-aged woman patient who sought help from a male and a female therapist simultaneously. She finally confessed to each her central wish to bring both therapists together, so that they could hold hands and restore the family that she had lost as a preschool child.

Task VI: Achieving Realistic Hope Regarding Relationships

Finally, we come to the task that may be the most important both for the child and for society. It is resolving relationship issues in such a way that the adolescent or young adult is able to reach and sustain a realistic vision regarding his or her capacity to love and to be loved. This task brings together and integrates the coping efforts of earlier years and provides in this way an opportunity for reworking the impact of the divorce experience.

As the adolescents in our study examined their parents and themselves and considered their future, many were frightened at the possible repetition of marital or sexual failure in their own lives. Pamela, at the age of twenty-four, told us at the ten-year follow-up, "I'm afraid to use the word *love*. You can hope for it but you can't expect it." A significant number of young people during late adolescence turned away in anger from a parent's behavior, having measured it and found it wanting, as expressed at the ten-year follow-up by one twenty-six-year-old young man who had elected to follow a lifestyle entirely different from his father's: "Someday

I will say to my dad, 'Are you proud of what you have done with your life?'" But, he said bitterly, "What can he answer me?"

The following pointed and poignant comments of adolescents illustrate their efforts to evolve strategies that might safeguard them from failure and help consolidate a separateness from their parents' experiences: "My parents cheated and lied, but I decided never to do that." "I will live with a guy for a long time. I won't rush into marriage." "They should both have been more considerate. My mother is selfish, and my father should never have married." "The trouble with my parents is that they each gave too little and asked too much."

Nevertheless it seems evident that youngsters whose adjustment was otherwise adequate foundered on this last task. Sometimes the cynicism expressed was startling: Jay, at the age of fourteen, told us, "Dad left because Mom bored him. I bored him all the time."

Other adolescents insisted that they would never marry because they were convinced that their marriages would fail. Still others were caught in a web of promiscuity and low self-esteem and spoke cynically and hopelessly of ever achieving a loving relationship or other goals. We have noted the emergence of what appears to be a delayed depression among adolescent girls many years following the marital rupture.[8]

THE PARENT-CHILD DIALOG ABOUT DIVORCE

Parent's support is critical in preparing children for the divorce, the turmoil surrounding it, and the lifestyle of divorce. The following points represent a useful model for creating an open dialog between parents and children about divorce.[9]

The first step is at the time of the impending separation before one parent leaves. Parents should take very seriously what they say and how they say it, for what they say or fail to say will long be remembered. If possible, parents should tell the children together. It is better to tell all the children at once rather than each separately. The children can help each other.

Children should be told about the divorce when it has become a firm decision. Parents should offer a clear explanation of what is going on in the family consistent with what a child knows or has observed. The explanation varies with the age of the child. For young children it should be something like this: "When Mommy and Daddy married, we loved each other and hoped that we would live together for the rest of our lives. We were very happy when you were born. But now we find that we are making each other unhappy, and we have decided it is better that we do not stay together." Detailed descriptions of the legal process are appropriate for adolescents. The ideal aim is for the parents to admit they made a serious mistake, tried to rectify the mistake, and now are embarking on a socially acceptable remedy.

Parents' expression of sadness about the divorce is important because it gives children permission to cry and mourn without having to hide their feelings of loss from the adults or from themselves. Clarity is important so that children will not be encouraged to undertake efforts at reconciliation and will not have a realistic basis for blaming themselves for the divorce. Parents should tell their children they are sorry for all the hurt they are causing their children.

Parents need to prepare their children for the changes that lie ahead in as much detail as possible. Everyone will need to be brave. Children should be informed of major developments and invited to ask questions, which initially often relate to details, such as what will happen to their possessions. They should also be invited to make suggestions that will be seriously considered so that they can feel they have a voice in what is happening to them without being made to feel responsible for major decisions.

Children should be told that the parents are divorcing each other, not their children, but they realize that the divorce profoundly affects the children. Parents need to give children permission to love and respect both parents. This may be a difficult task, but children need to feel that their individual integrity is respected, that they have a right to have and to express their own feelings, and that they are not being asked to ally with one parent against the other.

These points usually need to be revisited with children as they reach later developmental stages.

IMPLICATIONS FOR PUBLIC POLICY

Although policy makers, legislators, and judges have increasingly sought support from the behavioral sciences and guidance from the mental health professions, the accumulation of psychological knowledge has not kept up with the rapid evolution of family law.[10]

Knowledge about children and parent-child relationships in the post-divorce family is still fragmentary and insufficient to support many of the legislative changes in family policy that have powerful adherents. The subtleties of psychological thinking and shadings of individual differences that are so critical to behavioral scientists translate poorly into the arenas of the courts and legislatures.

In fairness to the children involved, child support following divorce should include automatic cost-of-living increases, and effective methods of ensuring prompt payment should be included. In order to protect long-married homemakers who have had little or no job experience, judges should redistribute a husband's postdivorce income so that the wife can be supported in circumstances that are fair and appropriate to her former lifestyle, including health insurance. Selling of the family home should be delayed as long as possible in order to minimize disruption of the children's lives. Child support should continue into the college years, if the parent can afford it and the values of the family are such that the child would have been supported in college had the couple remained together.

Our studies show no difference in psychological outcome between children in voluntary joint physical custody and those in voluntary sole physical custody. Time spent with a parent also is not a factor. What matters is the parent-child relationship, the psychological health of the mother, the degree of cooperation and civility between the two parents, and the psychological health of the child. Children in high-conflict families, who have been court-ordered into joint physical custody over the objections of one or sometimes both of the parents, deteriorate markedly in their school performance and their psychological adjustment. Courts also should take into account the ages of children and their developmental stages in writing custody and visitation orders.

From the point of view of expert testimony in family litigation, the several years of follow-up required to assess the impact of changed circumstances on altered family structures are ill suited to the pressured agenda of the judicial process. And, despite the widespread acknowledgment given to the interface between family law and mental health, the major task of building cooperation and mutual understanding on the firm basis of empirical knowledge and shared values in these fields still lies ahead. Because of the complexity and pitfalls of legal and legislative approaches to family breakdown, a combination of educational efforts devoted to preparation for marriage and parenthood with workplace policies that strengthen families and prevent family instability would be much more effective.

CONCLUSION

A child's long-range adjustment following marital disruption is related to many factors within the family that reflect the quality of family life following divorce as compared with that within the failing marriage. Nevertheless, the child's own capacity and efforts at mastery are significant in the final outcome.

Efforts at mastery and readjustment that are required of a child in order to maintain psychic integrity and development have been conceptualized and presented as a series of six coping tasks, which are closely related, hierarchical, and in a temporal sequence that begins at the time of the marital rupture and culminates with the close of adolescence. These tasks represent substantive additions to the usual tasks of growing up. Successful resolution would enable the child to achieve closure to the divorce experience, a well-earned sense of independence and pride, and an intact capacity to trust and to love. My twenty-five-year findings show conclusively that children of divorce continue to suffer during adult life with residues of sadness, anger, and anxiety about the potential unreliability of relationships.[11]

One important goal in formulating the tasks a child of divorce confronts during his or her developmental years is to construct the conceptual building blocks that are needed for formulating preventive interventions designed specifically for this population.

NOTES

1. Kelly, J., & Wallerstein, J. (1976) The effects of parental divorce: Experiences of the child in early latency. *American Journal of Orthopsychiatry* 46: 20–32; Kelly, J., & Wallerstein, J. (1977) Part-time parent, part-time child: Visiting after divorce. *Journal of Clinical Psychology* 6: 51–54; and Wallerstein, J. (1983) Children of divorce: The psychological tasks of the child. *American Journal of Orthopsychiatry* 53: 230–243.

2. Cherlin, A. J., Chase-Lansdale, P. L., and McRae, C. (1998) Effects of parental divorce on mental health throughout the life course. *American Sociological Review* 63: 239–249; and Japel, C., Tremblay, R. E., Vitaro, F., & Boulerice, B. (1999) Early parental separation and the psychosocial development of daughters 6–9 years old. *American Journal of Orthopsychiatry* 69(2): 49–60.

3. Wallerstein, J. S., & Blakeslee, S. (1989) *Second chances: Men, women, and children a decade after divorce*. New York: Ticknor & Fields, pp. 277–294.

4. Cherlin, A. J., Chase-Lansdale, P. L., & McRae, C. (1998) Effects of parental divorce on mental health throughout the life course. *American Sociological Review* 63: 239–249; and Japel, C., Tremblay, R. E., Vitaro, F., & Boulerice, B. (1999) Early parental separation and the psychosocial development of daughters 6–9 years old. *American Journal of Orthopsychiatry* 69(2): 49–60.

5. Hunter, J., & Schuman, M. (1976) Chronic reconstitution of a family style. *Social Work* 24: 446–451.

6. Wallerstein, J., & Kelly, J. (1980*) Surviving the breakup: How children and parents cope with divorce*. New York: Basic Books.

7. Wallerstein, J., & Kelly, J. (1980) Effects of divorce on the visiting father–child relationship. *American Journal of Psychiatry* 137: 1534–1539.

8. Wallerstein, J. (1984) Children of divorce: Stress and developmental tasks.

In N. Garmezy & M. Rutter (eds.), *Stress, coping, and development*. New York: McGraw-Hill.

9. Wallerstein, J. S., & Blakeslee, S. (1989) *Second chances: Men, women, and children a decade after divorce*. New York: Ticknor & Fields, pp. 285–288.

10. Wallerstein, J. S., & Corbin, S. B. (1996) The child and the vicissitudes of divorce. In M. Lewis (ed.), *Child and adolescent psychiatry* (2e). Baltimore: Williams & Wilkins.

11. Wallerstein, J. S., Lewis, J. A., & Blakeslee, S. (in press) *The legacy of divorce: A twenty-five-year landmark study*. New York: Hyperion.

12

The Effects of Maternal Employment on Families and Children

LOIS WLADIS HOFFMAN

Maternal employment has steadily risen in the United States. In 1940, 9 percent of mothers with children under the age of eighteen were employed away from home; by 1996, it was 70 percent. Employed married mothers of preschoolers tripled between 1960 and 1996 to 63 percent. Employed married mothers of infants doubled between 1975 and 1995 to 59 percent.[1]

The path linking a mother's employment status with outcomes for a child is a long one with many steps in between. This chapter will review research on the effects of maternal employment on children interwoven with the results of our University of Michigan study of school-age children in the mid-1990s.[2] In evaluating how maternal employment affects a child, the father's role, the mother's sense of well-being, and the parents' childrearing patterns will be taken into account.

EMPLOYED AND NONEMPLOYED MOTHERS

Earlier and current research does not reveal meaningful differences between children simply because their mothers are employed or not employed. Other factors, such as social class, the mother's marital status, whether the employment was full- or part-time, the parents' attitudes, and the child's gender, need to be considered. Differences found in research include the following:

- *Daughters of employed mothers* have higher academic achievement, greater career success, more nontraditional career choices, and greater occupational commitment. They also have been found to be more independent, particularly in interaction with their peers in a school setting, and to score higher on socioemotional adjustment measures. Our Michigan study also found that daughters with employed mothers, across different socioeconomic and marital groups, showed more positive assertiveness and less acting-out behavior, as rated by the teacher. When mothers are employed, girls view women as more competent. This view mediated the girls' own higher sense of efficacy and higher academic performance as rated by teachers as well as by the test scores.

- A few earlier studies found that *sons of employed mothers* in the middle class showed lower school performance and lower IQ scores during the grade school years than full-time homemakers. One finding from the 1970s was that lower-class sons of employed mothers did well academically, but there was a strain in the father-son relationship. In the 1980s two studies found no academic differences, but a third did.[3] In our Michigan study, controlling for the mothers' education, the children of employed mothers obtained higher scores on three achievement tests in language, reading, and math across gender, socioeconomic status, and marital status—middle-class boys included. Lower-class boys showed more positive social adjustment when their mothers were employed as well; this was true for both one-parent and two-parent families. For the middle-class boys, although their academic scores were higher, there was little evidence of social adjustment benefits from their mothers' employment. In fact, there was some evidence that those with employed mothers showed more acting-out behavior than the sons of full-time homemakers.
- Previous research found that *sons and daughters of employed mothers have less traditional gender-role attitudes.* Our Michigan study found that girls with employed mothers were more likely than girls whose mothers were full-time homemakers to indicate that women could be competent in the traditionally male domain. This result held for girls in two-parent homes and girls in one-parent homes. For boys, however, employment status was not related to their view of women's competence in traditional male activities. On the other hand, in two-parent families, both sons and daughters of employed mothers felt that men could do female activities, while children with full-time homemaker mothers did not. This effect was because fathers with employed wives were more active in traditionally female tasks and in childcare.
- Studies of *children in poverty* found higher cognitive scores for children in both two-parent and single-mother families as well as higher scores on socioemotional indices.

THE FATHER'S ROLE

Since the 1950s, fathers have been found to be more active in household tasks and childcare when mothers are employed. However, recent studies found that the greater involvement of fathers with children is confined to functional interactions, not leisure/play interactions.[4] There is an interesting gender effect: fathers in single-wage families interact more with sons than daughters, but fathers in dual-wage families interact with sons and daughters equally.

In the Michigan study, higher involvement of fathers in their daughters' lives was directly related to their daughters' better academic performance and greater sense of efficacy. In addition, although maternal employment was directly related to daughters' views that women are competent in activities generally seen as male activities, higher father involvement increased this effect. The view that women are competent was a major link to girls' greater sense of efficacy and higher test scores. The fathers' higher involvement in childcare also was related directly to both boys' and girls' higher test scores. The amount of time fathers spend with their children in leisure/fun activities, on the other hand, showed no relationship to test scores for either boys or girls.

Thus, there is a path from the mother's employment status to the father's role to the children's academic performance. In accommodating to the mother's employment, fathers take on a larger share of the household tasks and childcare. Their higher participation in childcare operates to increase the academic competence of both boys and girls, but particularly of girls.

THE MOTHER'S SENSE OF WELL-BEING

Numerous studies have compared employed mothers to full-time homemakers on indicators of mental health and life satisfaction. Most of this research has found a higher level of satisfaction and morale and lower scores on stress indicators and measures of depressive mood among the employed mothers. But some investigations conducted with middle-class women found no significant differences.

The mental health advantage of employment is more consistently found in lower-class and poverty samples. For these women, the satisfactions from employment are not from the job per se but from the increased social support and stimulation provided by coworkers, the marked advantages that their wages bring to their families, and the greater sense of control they feel over their lives. So a viable hypothesis is that the greater advantage of maternal employment for working-class children is because of its more positive effect on the mother's sense of well-being.

Furthermore, the possibility that a mother's well-being influences the relationship between maternal employment and child outcomes is bolstered by the fact that there is a large body of research demonstrating a positive relationship between maternal mental health and both more effective parenting and children's cognitive and emotional adjustment.

The role of maternal well-being was examined in our Michigan study. Employment did show a positive health advantage in the lower class for both single and married mothers. Employed mothers had lower scores on a measure of depressive mood and higher scores on a measure of positive morale.[5] However, no relationship between employment status and either measure was found in the middle class. Furthermore, the greater sense of well-being for the lower-class employed mothers was linked to their use of more positive parenting styles.

CHILDREARING PATTERNS

Differences in childrearing techniques associated with a mother's employment status affect outcomes for school-age children. Our Michigan study revealed that lower-class employed mothers were less likely than full-time homemakers to use either authoritarian or permissive parenting styles and more likely to use an authoritative style, a pattern in which parents exercise control but provide explanations rather than relying on power assertion and harsh discipline. In addition, lower-class employed mothers indicated a higher frequency of positive interactions with their children than did the full-time homemakers. The permissive parenting of married lower-class homemakers was associated with acting-out behavior in their sons, and authoritarian control was associated with acting-out behavior in daughters.

A number of researchers have suggested that childrearing that encourages independence, demands maturity, and grants autonomy is important. There is evidence that employed mothers encourage independence in their children more than nonemployed, perhaps because independence enables the family to function more effectively in the mother's absence. The developmental ecologists Urie Bronfenbrenner and Ann Crouter have suggested that encouraging independence and granting children autonomy may have a negative effect on boys because it increases the influence of the peer group, which is more likely to be counter to adult standards for boys.[6] The encouragement of independence and autonomy in girls, on the other hand, would be expected to have a positive effect since they are traditionally given too little encouragement for independence.

A number of studies have documented a general pattern of encouraging dependency in girls. For example, Beverly Fagot, a developmental psychologist, conducted a series of studies of toddlers and found that mothers of daughters reward dependency by responding too quickly to their bids for help, while mothers of boys are more likely to encourage them to work the problem out for themselves.[7] Such gender-based differences in childrearing are less prevalent in employed-mother families.

In our Michigan study, we found that, across social class, employed mothers, in contrast with full-time homemakers, showed less differentiation between sons and daughters in their discipline style and in their goals for their children. We also found that employed mothers, compared to full-time homemakers, were more likely to cite independence as a goal for their daughters and less likely to indicate that "obedience" or "to be feminine" was their goal. Mothers who had the goal of obedience or the goal "to be feminine" were more likely to have daughters who were shy and nonassertive in the classroom and had a lower sense of efficacy, while having the goal of independence showed the opposite effects.

Few studies have examined the relationship of the supervision and monitoring of children to maternal employment. For children from small communities and rural areas, Ann Crouter and her colleagues found no relationship between a mother's employment status and how well children were monitored.[8] However, they also found that when children were unmonitored, boys with employed mothers were the ones likely to show negative effects in conduct and school grades. In our Michigan urban sample, we found that dual-wage lower-class boys were more likely to be left unsupervised and unmonitored. Maternal employment was not related to supervision and monitoring in middle-class families, in single-mother families, or for lower-class girls. The negative effects of being unsupervised and unmonitored were found only for boys in poor lower-class families. Being left unsupervised but monitored by phone, however, showed no negative effects.

Our Michigan study was the first to consider a broad range of parenting attitudes and behaviors in the link between the mother's employment and child outcomes. As already noted, full-time lower-class homemakers used more authoritarian control, less authoritative control, and more permissiveness. In addition, across class and marital status, full-time homemakers used more authoritarian control and stressed obedience as a goal for their children. The higher use of authoritative controls by lower-class employed mothers was related to their children's higher academic performance. The more punitive style of the homemakers was related to conduct problems in school.

Middle-class full-time homemakers indicated more frequent positive and educational activities with their children than employed mothers; but in the lower class, more frequent positive and educational activities with daughters were reported by the employed mothers. There was no difference for sons. However, on a measure of how often mothers expressed overt affection toward their children, employed mothers were higher across class and marital status. In addition, employed married mothers held higher educational goals for their children, and this was reflected in the children's higher test scores.

It is important to point out, however, that although we took the most relevant variables into account, including the mother's education, it is still possible that self-selection factors are involved. For example, it could be that mothers who elect to stay home may be mothers who are particularly committed to obedience, and thus this difference may be not only an effect of employment status but also a cause. Similarly, higher educational goals for children could be a motivation for women to be employed. These possibilities were examined in the analyses, and the data still supported a direction of causality from the mothers' employment status to parenting styles to child outcomes. Nevertheless, it is almost impossible in a field study to entirely rule out self-selection factors.

MATERNAL EMPLOYMENT DURING THE EARLY YEARS

Research on infants and preschoolers has looked directly at parent-child interactions because valid outcome measures are difficult to obtain for infants and young children. These studies have evaluated the quantity and quality of the mother-child interaction, the home environment, and the parent-child attachment relationship.

In general, research indicates that full-time employed mothers spend less time with their infants and preschoolers than part-time and nonemployed mothers, but this effect diminishes with maternal education and with the age of the child. In addition, the effect also is less when the nature of the interaction is considered. The data indicate that employed mothers tend to compensate for their absence by spending more time with their children when they are at home. Several studies of mother-infant interaction showed that employed mothers were more highly interactive with their infants, particularly with respect to verbal stimulation. Some studies have examined the mothers' sensitivity in interactions with their infants and found no difference between employed and nonemployed mothers.[9]

Mother-infant attachment in dual-wage and single-wage families has been a particularly active area of maternal employment research since 1980. In most of these studies, no significant differences were found.

However, in a few studies the number of insecure attachments was higher when the mothers were employed full-time, although the majority of mother-infant attachments in the full-time employed-mother group was secure. Furthermore, in reviews that combined subjects across studies, full-time employed mothers were more likely than part-time employed and nonemployed mothers to have insecurely attached infants.[10]

The association between early maternal employment and mother-infant attachment has received a great deal of attention in the media. One problem with this research is that the measure of attachment used is a laboratory measure called the Strange Situation, which involves having the mother and toddler enter a room furnished with toys. A young woman comes in, and then the mother leaves. There are two maternal departures and reunions a few minutes later. This measure was set up as a "strange situation" to observe how the toddler acts toward the mother when anxious. Although this measure has proven useful in predicting subsequent childhood behavior, its validity had not been established for employed-mother families.

The problem is that the Strange Situation may not be anxiety-producing for a child who has experienced regular nonmaternal care; thus, the child's behavior may not be a valid basis for evaluating the attachment relationship. In studies that found more insecure attachment for children with full-time employed mothers, the type of insecure attachment was found to be the "avoidant" pattern. The avoidant infant is one who seems to be independent. This independence may be a defense against anxiety, but it may also be an appropriate behavior if the child is not anxious in the situation; thus, distinguishing between avoidant insecurity and lack of anxiety can be difficult.[11]

The most extensive investigation of nonmaternal care in early childhood is an ongoing, multisite study conducted by the National Institute of Child Health and Development (NICHD). Its data support the validity of the Strange Situation measure as used in this study. In this study, the amount of nonmaternal care (whether the infant received more than thirty hours a week or less than ten) was not related to the security of the attachment, nor was the child's age at onset of the mother's employment. The high quality of this investigation, and the fact that the consortium of investigators included researchers from both sides of this highly politicized issue, may have led to more precise coding operations, which eliminated the uncertainties sometimes involved in differentiating less anxiety from insecure-avoidant attachment. The results of this study indicate that the quality of the mother-child interaction, particularly her sensitivity to the child's needs, affects the security of the attachment, and the amount of nonmaternal care in itself does not. Neither does the mother's employment status nor the age of the child when the mother resumed work.[12]

The NICHD investigation has been following the children since infancy. Their latest reports are based on the data obtained when the children were three years old. Previous research on the effects of daycare suggested that although daycare experience was often associated with higher cognitive competence, it was also associated with less compliance and more assertiveness with peers, both positive and negative. The NICHD study found that on multiple measures of the child's negativity and behavior problems the major variables were again the mother's sensitivity and her psychological adjustment. Both higher quality of nonmaternal care and greater experience in groups with other children predicted socially competent behavior. However, more time in childcare and in less stable care predicted problematic and noncompliant behavior at twenty-four months. On the whole, the results of this investigation have indicated that the home environment is the major influence on child outcomes, but the quality and stability of the nonmaternal care do have an effect.[13]

CONCLUSION

The research results presented here are not consistent with the once prevalent view that maternal employment is a serious social problem. A mother's employment status does have effects on families and children, but few of these effects are negative. Indeed, most seem positive: higher academic outcomes for children; benefits in their behavioral conduct and social adjustment; and a higher sense of competence and effectiveness in daughters.

On the whole, these research results suggest that most families accommodate to the mother's employment and in doing so provide a family environment that works well. In two-parent families, the fathers take on a larger share of the household tasks and childcare, and this seems to have benefits for the children. Lower-class employed mothers indicate a higher level of well-being than full-time homemakers. This, in turn, affects their parenting in positive ways. Even in the middle class, where employed mothers did not show a higher level of well-being, neither did they show a lower one. While the quality and stability of nonmaternal care for infants and young children are important, the mother's employment itself does not seem to have serious negative effects.

Our findings should not be construed to mean that nothing needs to be done to improve the relationship between the workplace and family life. Our evolving society has yet to accommodate parenthood well. Necessary adjustments are needed: more affordable, quality childcare; after-school programs; and more liberal family leave policies.

NOTES

1. U.S. Bureau of the Census (1997) *Statistical abstract of the United States* (112e). Washington, D.C.: USGPO.

2. Hoffman, L. W., & Youngblade, L. M., with Coley, R. L., Fuligni, A. S., & Kovacs, D. D. (1999) *Mothers at work: Effects on children's well-being*. New York: Cambridge University Press. The Michigan study focused on socioeconomically heterogeneous third- and fourth-grade children living with four hundred mothers residing in a large industrial city in the Midwest. It included single-parent families as well as two-parent, and African American as well as European American families. The mother's employment had been stable for at least three years. The data collected were extensive, including questionnaires from mothers, fathers, and children; personal interviews with mothers and children; standard achievement test scores provided by the schools; teachers' ratings of the children's social and academic competence; and ratings by classroom peers of their behavior and how much they were liked.

3. Hoffman, L. W. (1989) Effects of maternal employment in the two-parent family: A review of the recent research. *American Psychologist* 44: 283–290.

4. Crouter, A. C., Perry-Jenkins, M., Huston, T. L., & McHale, S. M. (1987) Processes underlying father involvement in dual-earner and single-earner families. *Developmental Psychology* 23: 431–440; and Hoffman, L. W., & Youngblade, L. M., with Coley, R. L., Fuligni, A. S., & Kovacs, D. D. (1999) *Mothers at work: Effects on children's well-being*. New York: Cambridge University Press.

5. Radloff, L. (1977) The CES-D scale: A self-report depression scale for research in the general population. *Applied Psychological Measurement* 1: 385–401.

6. Bronfenbrenner, U., & Crouter, A. C. (1982) Work and family through time and space. In S. B. Kamerman & C. D. Hayes (eds.), *Families that work: Children in a changing world*. Washington, D.C.: National Academy Press, pp. 39–83.

7. Fagot, B. I. (1978) The influence of sex of child on parental reactions to toddler children. *Child Development* 49: 459–465.

8. Crouter, A. C., MacDermid, S. M., McHale, S. M., & Perry-Jenkins, M. (1990) Parental monitoring and perceptions of children's school performance and conduct in dual- and single-earner families. *Developmental Psychology* 26: 649–657.

9. Hoffman, L. W. (1989) Effects of maternal employment in the two-parent family: A review of the recent research. *American Psychologist* 44: 283–290.

10. Clarke-Stewart, K. A. (1989) Infant day-care: Maligned or malignant? *American Psychologist* 44: 266–273.

11. Ibid.; and Hoffman, L. W. (1989) Effects of maternal employment in the

two-parent family: A review of the recent research. *American Psychologist* 44: 283–290.

12. NICHD Early Child Care Research Network (1997) The effects of infant child care on mother-infant attachment security: Results of the NICHD Study of Early Child Care. *Child Development* 68: 860–879.

13. NICHD Early Child Care Research Network (1998) Early child care and self-control, compliance, and problem behavior at 24 and 36 months. *Child Development* 69: 1145–1170.

13

The Quest for Quality Childcare

DIANE B. ADAMS

My perspectives have been shaped by over thirty years in the childcare and early education fields. I have spent most of those years working on behalf of parents in their search for reliable and affordable childcare.

About thirteen million young children, many of whom are under two years of age, spend all or most of their days in childcare.[1] Many of the parents of these children devote considerable time to searching for appropriate, affordable, and reliable childcare. Those parents often confront a maze of childcare arrangements and may select less than desirable ones simply because of the dizzying array of choices—or sometimes no choices at all! This chapter addresses three of the most critical mazes parents must negotiate as they enter into childcare arrangements: cost, regulations, and quality.

Five assumptions guide my remarks. They are honed from years of experience with Head Start, childcare resource and referral, and early childhood international work. After listing them, I will outline the history of childcare, which will help explain the current childcare mazes for parents.

ASSUMPTIONS

First, most parents genuinely care about their children. Even incarcerated parents and those on death row are likely to truly want the best for their children. Of course, there are exceptions: parents who murder or abuse their children or who allow incest to occur in their families.

Second, all families experience stress in our society. Poor families have been the laboratories for almost all research on families, and the topics of family violence, Head Start success, school readiness, and family stress and coping were studied first in low-income families. But the stresses of parenthood are found in *all* social classes to some degree, even though more affluent parents have more resources. Drug abuse, alcoholism, violence, and teenage pregnancy know almost no social class boundaries, though poverty exacerbates many of these conditions.

Third, since about 1987 there has been a strident campaign to label childcare with the negative connotation of "institutional care" that is not as good as "parent care." In 1998, several congressional hearings included testimony that described childcare as "institutional care"—fraught with danger for children. These choreographed comments are part of a larger mixed message to society that children should be reared by "moms at home," except for low-income mothers who are required to be employed by welfare reform laws! By and large, these childcare critics are wrong. With the exception of a few childcare programs and providers who inadvertently harm children, almost all childcare programs follow a service motif. The caregivers are there to serve children and families and to support family life.

Fourth, both the families that use and the caregivers who offer childcare need all the support they can get. Most families need support in their two most prominent roles: raising their children and earning a livelihood.[2] Even the wealthiest families, who have the resources to purchase high-quality childcare, need support because they face a similar problem as other families: a lack of time with their children. And the caregivers—the family childcare providers, teachers, and directors in childcare center programs across the country—need support for doing what is a most difficult job. They need to be partners with families and share responsibility for the nurture and care of children, yet they have minimal resources to do so. In an example of professional concern and collaboration, the National Association of Child Care Resource and Referral Agencies recently worked with the Family Support of America to emphasize the need for support for both caregivers and parents.

Fifth, parental "guilt" for using childcare is exaggerated. Because childcare is a necessity of life for employed parents, and welfare reform initiatives require poor mothers to be employed, there is little room for "guilt." In fact, "guilt" should be felt by society for letting childcare develop without sufficient oversight and sound policy. Our neglectful society lets families wander, as if through a series of mazes, with no road map to guide them in finding good childcare. There are no stoplights to say: "Don't use this bad type of childcare." There is no highway patrol to say: "You can count on me to police the industry with regulations that make sense for families." Our society is guilty of relegating childcare decision making to an ill-informed public.

THE HISTORY OF CHILDCARE

The mazes that families must negotiate in their search for childcare are grounded in the three eras of childcare policy in the United States.

The Discovery of Child Development: 1920–1940

The federal Children's Bureau was established by government in the 1920s, and the focus of nine major federally funded research institutions was on child development. The balance beam, building blocks, discovery through play, and child growth measurements were demonstrations of our new "scientific" interest in children. Nursery schools and parent-teacher associations made their way onto the scene. Middle-class mothers, in particular, were seen as "good mothers" if they sent their children to nursery schools and learned child development theories.

Child Care for Emergencies: 1941–1989

Research continued through this next period as well. The fact that not all the children coming to public school were ready for school learning situations was documented. Projects studying low-income children from Appalachia, inner-city children, and Native American and immigrant populations led early childhood educators to project interventions that might be needed to make learning more successful for young children and families. This, in turn, helped prepare the early childhood field to respond to two large-scale emergencies.

The first was during World War II, when Congress passed the Lanham Act (1944), which mobilized the nation on behalf of the defense industries and enabled some communities to build excellent childcare facilities during wartime.

The second emergency came during the 1960s, when inner cities exploded with violence. Families out of the mainstream of success demanded access to more resources and better schools. Out of this chaos came the "War on Poverty" during the Johnson administration. Head Start, Community Action, and Legal Services were among the many programs designed to reflect researchers' new understanding of the devastating effects of poverty. Head Start became a major mobilization effort that showed we could respond to the needs of parents, if we wanted to.

Windows on Day Care (1972) condemned most childcare as inadequate in quality and quantity.[3] That influential book, based on interviews conducted by the National Council of Jewish Women, described childcare as needed primarily by parents in poverty. But throughout the 1970s and 1980s, childcare emerged as a multiclass and bipartisan concern to benefit the nation, business, and parents.

Childcare as Everyone's Issue: 1990–1998

Congress started the 1990s by passing and implementing the Child Care and Development Block Grant (CCDBG). Extra funding was provided for school-age care, childcare resource and referral (CCR&R), and the care of children at risk of neglect or abuse. The passage of CCDBG was possible partly because childcare had become a "public problem."[4] Midway through this decade welfare reform legislation placed responsibilities for welfare and childcare with the states and added more money to the childcare system. However, passing CCDBG did not significantly change national childcare policy.

The following current childcare topics illustrate how scattered childcare policy has become:

- the "mommy track" arguments for at-home mothers' equity with working women
- the "nannygate" incidents that scare parents about low-quality in-home childcare
- the debates on how much or how little regulation is needed
- the wars over "parent share" versus "government share" for subsidized childcare
- the debates about Head Start as a complement to regular childcare or as the building block for full-day care, especially for infants
- the recent "research" on the relative lack of parent influence as compared with peer influences on young children's development

In the context of heated debates, childcare and early childhood researchers, educators, and advocates have become experts on one or more of these themes. As a result, systemic problems are not being addressed. Few Congressional or state policy makers have a complete picture of how fragmented and vulnerable the entire childcare system has become. Some local agencies, including CCR&R agencies, can offer an overview of the entire childcare system in a community, but national childcare policy still remains fraught with inconsistency and lacks a clear commitment to quality.

THE MAZES

All of this leaves parents in a quandary, facing three mazes through which they must negotiate their way: cost, regulations and quality.

Cost

I had a heartening experience one morning. My husband and I were out for a restaurant breakfast, and just behind us sat four young businessmen dressed in suits and ties, with briefcases nearby. But the conversation was not about fourth-quarter profits or mergers. One man said: "Do you know they charge me even when my kid isn't there on Friday?" Another remarked: "I don't think they have a very good handle on the finances over at my child's center." And a third said: "It takes the two of us working just to pay for childcare." I knew we had "arrived"—for these working fathers were talking about childcare cost!

The amount parents "should" spend for childcare has been widely debated.[5] Across the country, under welfare "reform" low-income childcare subsidy recipients must contribute something for the cost of their childcare. In Oregon, unsubsidized families earning under twenty-five thousand dollars spend 25 percent of their income for childcare. In Wisconsin, families receiving subsidy may have to contribute up to 12 percent of their income for a childcare "copayment."[6] Unsubsidized families with incomes over fifty thousand dollars spend from 3 to 10 percent of their income for childcare expenses and 25 percent or more for housing.

Little is known about the economic supports needed for childcare. The first question many childcare are providers receive is "What do you charge?" Since most parents using childcare earn less than thirty-five thousand dollars a year, cost is not an inconsequential issue.

Understanding how the cost for childcare is computed is difficult for most parents to comprehend (for example, rates are based on *x* number of staff times *x* per hour of pay, plus facility rent, utilities, equipment, food, taxes, and other core budget items in childcare center programs). Parents are acquainted with their own family budgets, which usually are a fraction of a childcare center's budget. The maze of cost is clear only to those who understand childcare budgeting.

Regulations

Childcare regulations almost defy understanding. For example, in Wisconsin, to offer childcare to four or more children an individual must get a license and have forty hours of child development training. One could raise many questions about these regulations:

- Why four or more children? What about the first, second, and third child in care?
- Why forty hours of training? Why not eighty or a hundred and sixty hours, or the thousand hours required of licensed cosmetologists?

Wisconsin's childcare licensing law was written in 1949. Although revised many times, the law still is based on the premise that only when four children are in care is it a "serious" business. Since there are no national childcare regulations, each state must devise its own regulatory structure. The "hidden" regulations in childcare (such as the amount of food that must be served or the number of toys that must be present) should be more visible to the consumers. Though state agencies and CCR&R try to inform parents, only childcare providers and those who regulate them truly understand the meaning of the regulations. This is a disservice to parents, who need to understand more than anyone else and who face the maze of regulations almost as if blindfolded.

Quality

Finally, the quality maze is particularly complex. There are some quality factors that are easy to understand, such as small group sizes for young children, low children-to-staff ratios, and training that is focused on childcare and child development. These quality factors are based on child development research and are being more widely promoted since the advent of Child Care Aware, a national childcare marketing program begun by the Dayton Hudson Corporation and others in 1994. It uses marketing techniques to articulate quality questions and reminded parents to

- look
- ask
- count
- stay involved

However, because childcare is sought by so many families each year and the turnover among childcare providers is so high, the Child Care Aware message has not yet permeated society, even though it has been on Cheerios boxes of late.

When you send your children to college, you assume there will be professors who can teach them. Someone has accredited the college or university, and department committees have hired individuals with advanced degrees to teach. And, even though many college professors have not had teaching methods courses, we assume that these professors are adequate teachers.

But in individual childcare programs, there is little agreement about the level of quality needed for teaching young children. I have heard operators of childcare programs say: "I'm a licensed center. I offer quality childcare." They seem offended when they are reminded that the license is a permission to operate, not an indicator of quality. So the maze of quality continues to plague families, who pay (or are subsidized) for care whose regulations they seldom fully understand and whose quality may be questionable. Accreditation (meeting high quality standards) from the National Association for the Education of Young Children (NAEYC) has been achieved by less than 1 percent of Wisconsin childcare programs.

WHAT TO LOOK FOR IN CHILDCARE

The cost of childcare varies from one part of the country to the next. Full-day care in centers may range from $70 to $200 a week. Family childcare may cost $40 to $100 a week. Nannies may charge $300 to 500 a week and require room and board in addition. Despite cost as a major factor, families must look beyond the price of care. Some of the most important considerations for parents in seeking childcare are the following:

- What type of training and education do the caregivers have?
- How many staff members have left in the last three years? (High turnover is disruptive for children and may relate to low pay for teachers.)
- How many children does each adult care for? (There should be at least one adult for every three infants or toddlers.)
- How long has the caregiver or center been operating?
- Ask the provider to describe other children in the group. (If she uses negative or pejorative terms, she may be negative toward your child, too.)
- Spend some time observing the children and the caregivers. (When you visit, if most of the children run over to you, it may be a sign that they are bored; if they remain engaged in play, it's a good sign.)
- Assess the quality of the relationships between caregivers and children. (How they greet the child is a beginning step.)

CONCLUSION

There are many childcare experts: people who run parenting programs, family living agents, family resource center leadership, and child development specialists. The important thing for professionals in this field to recognize is that they only provide a "piece" of what parents need to become the consumers they want to be. There are no universal approaches for assisting parents in their workplaces and in childrearing.

Childcare is such an important experience for families that we ought to determine now that no parent should have to "go it alone." New books for parents in family-friendly language are being produced by CCR&Rs. Books are being written that do not "preach" about what parents ought to do but that help parents get a clearer picture of what childcare looks like. An example is *James Begins Child Care* (and its Spanish version), produced by the Child Care Group.[7] *The Good-Bye Window* by parent/author Harriett Brown helps parents understand what goes on in a childcare center.[8] These materials help parents learn more and perhaps choose more wisely.

Someone once said that God did not create the world in seven days. God really sat around for six days thinking, dreaming, and planning—and then pulled an all-nighter. We are facing an all-nighter for childcare, and the challenges are many. We need to be clearheaded thinkers. We need to stand for quality. We need to share the belief of many early childhood professionals that this system needs multipurpose legislation. Families should not continue to face the mazes described in this chapter or new ones. They should have sufficient support in their communities so that "parenthood in America" does not become the job you least want.

NOTES

1. Downs, S. W., Costin, L., & McFadden, Emily (1996) *Child welfare and family services: Policies and practice* (5e). London: Longman Group.
2. Adams, D., Foote, R., & Vinci, Y. (1996) *Making child care work*. Washington, D.C.: National Association of Child Care Resource and Referral Agencies.
3. National Council of Jewish Women (1972) *Windows on day care*. Revised (2000) as *Opening a new window on child care*. New York: NCJW.
4. Gormley, W. T. (1995) *Everybody's children: Child care as public problem*. Washington, D.C.: Brookings Institution.
5. Helburn, S., et al. (1996) *Cost, quality, and child care outcomes*. Denver: University of Denver Press; and Mitchell, A., & Stoney, L. (1997) *Financing child care in the United States: An illustrated catalog of current strategies*. Ewing Marion Kauffman Foundation and Pew Charitable Trusts.
6. Office of Child Care (1998). *W-2 child care subsidy* (internal document). Madison, Wisc.: Department of Workforce Development.
7. The Child Care Company (1997) 1212 Riverwalk Drive, Dallas, Tex.
8. Brown, Harriett (1998). *The good-bye window: A year in the life of a day-care center.* Madison: University of Wisconsin Press.

14

Children, Parents, and Schools

Part 1: A Theoretical View

M. ELIZABETH GRAUE

One way to think about home-school relations is in terms of responsibility—the ethical actions that set the stage for individuals to interact.

RESPONSIBILITY TO WHOM?

M. M. Bakhtin suggests that responsibility be conceived as *answerability:* you are answerable to others for what you do.[1] In addition, he speaks of *addressivity,* which calls attention to the fact that answerability includes specific other people to whom one is answerable. This dyad of answerability and addressivity is useful to depict responsibility as being "answerable to someone." In schools, parents, educators, community members, and students are all answerable to each other.

CONCEPTIONS OF RESPONSIBILITY

To illustrate how notions of responsibility have been conceived in the work of researchers, I will describe the work of three prominent scholars of home-school relations: Joyce Epstein, James Comer and colleagues, and Annette Lareau.

The Epstein Model

The foundation of Joyce Epstein's work is large-scale surveys that evaluate the success of activities that link homes and schools.[2] Her model describes what exists and reflects the status quo, rather than exploring what might or should be. She envisions schools, families, and communities as sharing responsibility through overlapping spheres of influence in children's education. She advocates a high degree of overlap of spheres of responsibility to leverage the most action.

Epstein uses economic terms to describe education. She suggests that families, communities, and governments should invest in schooling because of the economic payback that can come out of such investment. Capital is increased by creating effective partnerships, accounting for resources and investments, and looking for profits for all concerned. In Epstein's view, schools and parents do not produce successful students. Instead, she assumes that students can generate their own success when they have capital provided by relevant actors.

Epstein suggests multiple levels of responsibility for schools. First, we are all responsible for investing in children. Second, students are responsible for making the most of the investments made in them. Third, her model promotes including parents in the educational process through the efforts of school personnel, but she does not stress what parents can do to change the schools.

The Comer Model

James Comer and his colleagues developed a model that has been applied in many schools.[3] It conceptualizes education as a problem-solving system that puts the developmental needs of children at the center.

The Comer model is designed with specific attributes to leverage the most participation and power for all concerned. Three teams (a parent team, school planning and management team, and student and staff support team) work to develop a comprehensive school plan, formulate staff development, provide assessment and evaluation, negotiate collaboration, and promote a nonblaming ethos. The strength of the model is its focus on individuals working within systems with specific attention to balancing needs, voice, and power. Responsibility and relationships are at its core.

However, Comer's model lacks full attention to the social and political forces that shape the development of children. Relying on psychological models of development connects school activities to the needs of *some* children (traditionally white and middle-class) but may divert attention from more important issues in the homes and neighborhoods of other children.

The Lareau Model

Annette Lareau looks at the role social class plays in the ways schools and families relate to each other.[4] For example, lower-class parents usually do not assume that they can take a proactive role in their children's educational lives. Instead, they rely on teachers as professionals to do what is right for their children. They wait for guidance by school personnel, whom they regard as having expertise and responsibility for their children's education. In contrast, middle-class parents are more inclined to advocate actively for their children and to work *with* school personnel to get gain advantages for their children. They are more likely to know how institutions work and to use that knowledge to promote their children's school careers.

Lareau's model explores how interactions between individuals occur in the context of social and political forces in the broader society. She moves considerations of responsibility beyond individuals by recognizing that the opportunities for parents to interact with schools are not equal. She also helps us see that parent involvement can have unintended consequences. The influence of some middle-class parents may put undue pressure on their own children to achieve and at the same time may divert a teacher's attention from other children.

Lareau suggests that programs for parent involvement should help lower-class families develop the skills so deftly used by middle-class parents. While this could provide some advantages, it does not recognize the adaptive nature of some lower-class families' strategies. Reacting to longstanding inequities in schools, some lower-class parents may be inclined to resist a system that has not treated them fairly.

In addition, Lareau's model does not recognize the implications of "advantage." An advantage exists only if it is relatively uncommon. If everyone has something, having it is no longer an advantage. No one has considered what it means if everyone tries to get maximum resources for his or her children in schools with finite assets. We need to think this through more clearly as we try to increase connections between parents and schools.

CONCLUSION

The multiple levels of responsibility involved in relationships among schools, families, children, and social and political systems need to be taken into account in our efforts to make schools more responsive to the complex needs of children and the vital role parents can play in education. By asking who is answerable in schooling, we can better understand what needs to be done to improve the quality of education for our nation's children. We can see more clearly how issues of power shape home-school interactions and how we might change those dynamics to make them more equitable.

When we focus on responsibility in education we find that there are no simple answers to contemporary problems. We all share responsibility for children's education and for the relationships that would enhance the lives of all children, their families, and schools.

In part 2, Ben Benson offers the perspective of a classroom teacher on how parents can be answerable to their children and their schools. He suggests ways parents can enrich their interactions with schools and help their children to be more productive.

Part 2: A Teacher's View

BENJAMIN A. BENSON

Parents are the first and most significant teachers that children will ever have. For the first five to six years parents lay the foundation for the student-to-be. Even after beginning formal education, children usually spend only one third of each weekday in school. For the remaining two thirds, they are under more or less parental supervision away from the school environment. Although children learn academic skills and knowledge in schools, they learn the value of education and work in their homes.

SUGGESTIONS FOR PARENTS

As a classroom teacher, I have six suggestions for how parents can improve the performance of both students and teachers in school.

1. Provide physical and psychological support. A student who is not loved and respected by those who have given him or her life and is not encouraged to succeed in school is unlikely to be interested in the daily science lesson.

2. Encourage your child to take chances and make mistakes. It is easy to stay in the place that we know and have mastered. The unknown is a scary place, but we all can benefit from being encouraged by those we trust to enter uncharted areas and take chances and make mistakes so that we are open to learning something new. *Perfection is not the goal of education—improvement is.* While we are improving, we will make mistakes. Applaud effort, celebrate improvement, and encourage and support the next adventure in learning.

3. Teach your child to plan, organize, and set goals for success in learning. Setting goals and developing a plan to reach them provides the greatest opportunity for success and happiness in life. Children do not naturally know how to set goals; even when they do so, they are not fully aware of it. You can formalize the process and help your child develop the skill.

4. Be a positive role model. Value learning, school, effort, honesty, and other persons. "Do as I say, not as I do" is difficult, even impossible, for some children to comprehend. In their early years, children deal in the concrete, not the abstract. Children are literal in their interpretation of the world around them. Confusing messages lead to confusing conclusions and actions.

5. Teach your child to accept responsibility for what he or she does and does not do. This gives him or her the power to find solutions. When we blame other factors, we tend to wait for those factors to correct the problem. We are powerless; we mark time; we stagnate. By taking responsibility for our own actions and inactions, we gain control over our lives.

6. Explain that learning is a lifetime process and that knowledge can be found everywhere and in everything we do. We continue to learn until we draw our last breath. Embracing knowledge, whatever its source, is how we grow as individuals. Applying what we learn and incorporating it into our lives is how we mature.

CONCLUSION

The most important contribution parents can make to the education of their children is to teach them how to accept responsibility for their own actions and how to respect legitimate authority, which is essential for the exercise of their own rights in the context of the rights of others. When parents fulfill their responsibility to socialize and motivate their children, teachers are able to do their best job as educators.

NOTES

1. Bakhtin, M. M. (1990) Author and hero in aesthetic activity. In M. Holquist & V. Liapunov (eds.), *Art and answerability: Early philosophical essays by M. M. Bakhtin*. Austin: University of Texas Press.

2. Epstein, J. L. (1994) Theory to practice: School and family partnerships lead to school improvement and student success. In C. L. Fagnano & B. Z. Werber

(eds.), *School, family and community interaction: A view from the firing line.* Boulder, Colo.: Westview Press.

3. Comer, J. P., Haynes, N. M., Joyner, E. T., & Ben-Avie, M. (eds.) (1996) *Rallying the whole village: The Comer process for reforming education.* New York: Teachers College Press.

4. Lareau, A. (1989) *Home advantage.* London: Falmer Press.

15

Family-Centered Health Care

BEVERLEY H. JOHNSON

Over the last twenty years, parents and parent-led organizations have assumed key roles in creating change in the health care system. Despite this progress, a great deal of work remains to be done, but parent organizations are well positioned to spearhead further change.

The purposes of this chapter are to (1) introduce parents, parent educators, and family support organizations to the principles of family-centered care; (2) illustrate how these concepts can help make health care facilities and providers more supportive of families; (3) outline changes that institutions, providers, and families can make in order to move toward a family-centered approach to care; and (4) suggest strategies that community organizations can use to collaborate with health care leaders, clinicians, medical educators, and policy makers to improve health care.

CORE PRINCIPLES OF FAMILY-CENTERED HEALTH CARE

The following core principles of family-centered care evolve from the belief that the family has great influence over an individual's health and well-being:[1]

Family-centered health care treats people with dignity and respect.

Practitioners of family-centered care approach their patients and families as unique individuals with their own traditions, beliefs, and value systems. They acknowledge that the word *family* is variously defined, and they recognize the important influence of the larger community on the family. Family-centered practitioners respect patients' beliefs, experiences, and backgrounds and explicitly encourage their participation in health care decision making. This approach is reflected not only in staff attitudes and institutional policies but in the physical design, and even the signage, of a hospital or clinic.

In children's hospitals in St. Paul and Minneapolis, family members are recognized as the caregivers and decision makers for their children. Hospital signs welcome them. Members of the hospital staffs support and encourage family participation. When a five-year-old had surgery to repair an incision from previous cancer surgery, his mother, father, and new baby brother roomed in with him. This family's desire to stay together was a priority for the hospital staff. Because of the support they received while their son was hospitalized, the family could take their child home sooner, and they were more confident in caring for him at home.

In a hospital emergency department in Grand Rapids, Michigan, families decide whether or not they wish to remain present with a family member during medical procedures, including resuscitation. Some families choose to stay with their loved one; others decide to remain in the waiting room or chapel. The staff supports each family's choices.

In family-centered health care, health care providers communicate and share complete and unbiased information with patients and families in ways that are affirming and useful.

Information is essential to decision making. Practitioners of family-centered care provide patients and families with as much information as they want—in the ways they prefer to receive it. They use language that creates an emotional connection with the patient and family and does not focus only on the technical aspects of disease and treatment. They listen to and learn from patients. Together, families and providers develop a care plan, collaborate in its implementation, and revise it as necessary.

In a discussion with the mother of a child with significant speech and motor delays, a physical therapist asked about the mother's goals for her child and about her daily routine. In addition to offering practical suggestions based on the mother's response, the therapist worked with her to develop a care plan that was centered on the mother's customary parenting tasks and minimized additional demands on her time.

At Children's Hospital of Philadelphia, families participated in designing the Connelly Resource Center. This center offers a comfortable place for families to meet other families and to acquire information and support. Books, videos, and access to clinical and research information on the Internet and through CD-ROM searches are available. Classes are taught here, and there is an opportunity to practice new skills that may be required in caring for a child following hospitalization.

In family-centered health care, individuals and families build on their strengths by participating in experiences that enhance control and independence.

Family-centered practitioners invite families to build on their resources and strengths by participating in experiences that facilitate growth. Accumulating over time, these experiences enhance families' control, strengthen their decision-making abilities, and increase their capacity to make changes in their lives and the lives of others in their communities. This collaborative approach is also empowering for health professionals. No longer do they have to be the sole experts. If they do not have a ready answer, they can admit it and then together with the family seek answers to questions.

When women arrive at the Morris Heights Birthing Center in the Bronx, New York, each picks up her own chart, records her weight, and reads her chart, even the social work notes. Some of these women later become involved in peer support. They gain confidence and have an opportunity to give back to the system.

In the Maternal and Child Health HIV Program at Cook County Hospital in Chicago, a woman who is HIV positive coordinates a program to involve other women served by the program as advisers. She creates a variety of ways for women to become involved in providing peer support, participating in the development of educational materials, making presentations in the community, and providing training about counseling and testing to staff in community-based prenatal centers. Participating women discover new strengths within themselves and develop the capacity to take control of their lives.

In family-centered health care, collaboration among patients, families, and providers occurs in policy and program development and professional education, as well as in the delivery of care.

Families' perspectives can contribute to system-wide improvements and cost efficiencies in health care as well as to individual health care encounters. Opportunities for patient and family participation in the planning, implementation, and evaluation of health care policies, programs, facility design, and professional education are essential to family-centered care.

Under the leadership of the director for pediatric education in the Department of Pediatrics of the Uniformed Services University of Health Sciences, parents of children with special needs and disabilities identified physician competencies important to them. They suggested teaching strategies to foster the development of these competencies. Efforts are under way to integrate family-centered concepts and teaching strategies throughout the military health care system.

The Colorado Collective for Medical Decisions has brought families of children who have been hospitalized in newborn and pediatric intensive care units together with health care professionals and community members to develop guidelines for ethical decision making in health care.

Washington State's Department of Health and the Children's Hospital and Medical Center of Seattle are working together to bring about change in systems of care for children with special health needs. Families are part of this process. For example, first-year residents visit with a family at home to learn about how family members are incorporating and balancing the demands posed by a child with special needs with those of other family members. Families join health professionals as members of the Children with Special Health Care Needs Issue Investigation Group. Collaborative efforts with the state's Foster Parent Association provide foster parents with support they need to care for children with special health needs.

In Michigan, Children's Special Health Care Services, the Title V program serving children with special needs, has developed an approach to ensure that families' perspectives are incorporated into the policy discussions concerning Medicaid managed care contracts. A parent and a pediatrician co-chaired the committee that developed standards of care for managed care organizations. Families are part of the site-review teams that select contractors and monitor compliance. They also provide technical assistance and support to the managed care agencies.

In summary, family-centered care emphasizes collaboration rather than control; focuses on families' strengths rather than on their deficits; recognizes the family's expertise as well as that of professionals; fosters empowerment rather than dependence; promotes information sharing among patients, families, and providers rather than information "gatekeeping" by professionals; and emphasizes program flexibility rather than rigidity.

LAYING A FOUNDATION FOR FAMILY-CENTERED CARE

Family-centered care calls for fundamental changes in the ways in which patients, families, and health care providers in hospitals, clinics, and community agencies interact with one another. Hierarchical relationships yield to collaboration; paternalistic approaches yield to an environment in which each individual values the unique skills and experience of the other.

Individuals who have spearheaded the introduction of family-centered approaches in health care institutions concur that their efforts generally share key characteristics. Among the most important of these are the following:

Implementing family-centered approaches requires systemic as well as individual change.

It is truly gratifying when a single doctor, nurse, or social worker works respectfully and collaboratively with families. But that is not enough. If the clinic where that doctor or nurse works is open only during the week when children are in school or parents are working, the system is not very "family friendly." If there is no place in a clinic examination room or a patient's hospital room for family members, it is difficult for the family to be a partner in care. Health care administrators and clinicians make decisions about clinic hours, facility design, and space allocation. In family-centered health care institutions, decisions about such routine matters as hours of service are based on factors other than staff convenience.

Health care institutions that have been most successful in implementing family-centered care have senior leaders committed to this approach to care. As a result, they make decisions that are consistent with family-centered values, and they articulate these values to all stakeholders. These leaders also recognize that family-centered changes in policies, programs, and practices take time; effecting change is a long-term commitment.

Because the impact of family-centered care is so extensive, it is advisable that an institution's commitment to it be expressed in a mission and philosophy of care statement. Such documents help shape organizational priorities and the policies, programs, facility design, and interactions of its staff. For example, an institution that has stated in writing its belief that families bring unique and essential resources to their children's health care will have difficulty labeling families as "visitors" and limiting their access to their children during a hospital stay. When family-centered principles are explicitly articulated in an institution's mission and philosophy of care statements, visiting policies are replaced with guidelines that welcome and encourage family participation.

Family-centered care involves engaging families directly in all phases of organizational operations: program planning, implementation, and evaluation; hospital design; staffing decisions; and professional development and training.

Organizations committed to a family-centered approach to care create a variety of ways for families to participate in planning, implementing, and evaluating policies and programs. The most visible symbol of this commitment is often a family advisory workgroup or council. Other indications include appointing families as members of committees or task forces and creating family liaison staff positions.

Additional roles that parents can take include the following:

- serving as members of design planning teams and participating in site visits to other facilities to learn about family-centered hospital renovation or design
- participating in hospital- or clinic-based quality-improvement initiatives
- reviewing written materials that have been prepared for patient or family use
- testifying at local or state hearings on issues relating to health care
- organizing fund-raising projects

- leading parent-to-parent support groups
- participating in family faculty programs

Systems must be in place to ensure that families have access to information and support.

Information and support are key to helping parents promote the health and well-being of their children and their families. Family-centered health care programs ensure that staff members are available and able to provide information and support. Additional information is available in a variety of formats, languages, and reading levels; and there is easy access to a family resource center or medical library.

For many families, the opportunity to meet and learn from other families who have had similar experiences provides a unique and important kind of support that is different from and supplements the kind of support provided by professionals. Systems need to be in place to enable families to connect with other families.

Institutions must take specific measures to prepare families for new collaborative roles in policy and program development.

Health care providers and institutions must make a conscious effort to reach out to families and prepare them for their new advisory roles. Families who have been empowered by their collaborative experiences must reach out to other parents and draw them into the work. Publications such as *Essential Allies: Families as Advisors* and *Words of Advice* available from the Institute for Family-Centered Care provide practical guidance for family members and professionals.

Strategies for reaching out to families and involving them effectively in health care policy and program development include the following:

- Provide concrete examples of the impact that parents can have on policy and program issues when recruiting families. Let them know that their participation will make a difference.
- Make a special effort to include families with a wide variety of special interests, backgrounds, and needs.
- Provide training and support for families to develop skills for collaboration and being effective advisors.
- Offer mentors to help build collaborative skills over time.
- Consider the priorities and needs of families when setting meeting times and find ways to ensure that child care and transportation are available. Offer parents a modest compensation for their time.
- Create the setting, format, and tone that encourages family participation and permits them to participate in a nonthreatening way. In setting up committees, for example, it is best to have family

members outnumber professionals. Committee chair responsibilities should be held jointly by a parent and a professional.
- Conduct ongoing outreach to bring in new families to the process.

Staff need opportunities to learn from families and practice collaborative skills.

Collaborating with families in caregiving, not to mention program and policy development, is a new role for many health professionals and administrators. Like parents, staff members need preparation for these roles. Training sessions should be held to introduce staff to the concepts of collaboration. Such sessions should emphasize the benefits of partnerships not only for patients and families but for the staff. Ideally, such sessions should provide opportunities for staff to role play or practice collaborative skills and to discuss their concerns candidly.

As support for family-centered care grows, many hospitals find it particularly useful to involve parents directly in staff orientation and continuing education programs. Many hospitals and clinics have created family-faculty programs in which families share their stories and experiences with health care professionals and students who have an opportunity to ask questions and explore issues candidly with families outside of the clinical encounter.

PARENTS AND PARENTING GROUPS AS CATALYSTS FOR CHANGE

The goals of family-centered care are consonant with those of individual parents as well as those of parenting and family support organizations. A common focus is on communication, collaboration, and empowerment.

Parent leaders, parent educators, and family support organizations can be powerful catalysts for family-centered change. They can do so by capitalizing on the base of support they have already earned in the community and creating links between parents and the health care community. Before undertaking such activity, even the most well-established group needs to familiarize itself with the local health care environment and with the advantages that can be achieved through family/professional partnerships. This process involves the following steps.

Assess Families' Perceptions of Health Care

Begin by finding out more about how families in your organization or community feel about the quality of health care they receive. What is working for them and what is not?

Although some families may be vocal in expressing their preferences, others may be reticent. Some patients and families have been conditioned to be passive recipients of care. As a result, they may not even be aware of options. You may find it useful to use a checklist to help families assess the quality of care they receive. A tool such as the following might lead to productive discussions:

- Describe one positive experience you and your family had at the hospital, clinic, or managed care organization.
- Describe one negative experience you and your family had at the hospital, clinic, or managed care organization.
- Did staff ask about your views or observations about your child? Did they listen to your responses? Did staff respect the decisions and choices you made for your child and your family?
- Do you feel that you have trust in your care providers?
- Did you receive the information and support you wanted or needed to participate in or provide your child's care?
- Was the information you received useful and understandable?
- If you could make only two changes in the care you and your family received, what would these changes be?

Responses to these questions, coupled with a review of families' verbal comments, will give you a good understanding of how well your local health systems are responding to family needs.

Complete your assessment by creating a list that summarizes what families with whom you are associated feel is important in a health care experience. With the help of some of the family members, rank the issues on the list in order of priority. You may also want to categorize them in terms of type of care (e.g., inpatient care, outpatient care, care in the emergency department, or care for infants and young children or care for older children and teens).

Identify a Potential Partner

While your discussions with families may reveal several hospitals or clinics where you might work to further the implementation of family-centered care, it is better to focus your effort on a single place than to touch several places only superficially.

The families served by your organization will have suggestions concerning this choice. Ask them to suggest the names of physicians, nurses, or other providers who have been particularly supportive during a health care encounter. These individuals can help you gain entree to the health system.

Pediatrics and maternity care may be good places to begin; it is there where support for family-centered care is often strongest. Ensuring that women's health services, prenatal care programs, childbirth education programs, birthing centers, hospital-based maternity programs, and home visiting services are committed to family-centered approaches will better prepare parents for parenthood and partnership relationships with health care providers. These programs and services can reinforce the concept of informed consumerism and build the competence and confidence of parents to be advocates for their children and their families. You can call or write a letter to the administrator or the medical director for pediatric, maternity, or women's health services.

Another suggestion is to contact the hospital's or clinic's consumer/patient relations department. The Title V program (a state program serving mothers and children) in the public health department is another possibility. The Parent to Parent organization or the Parent Training and Information Center in your state may have efforts already under way to influence the quality of care in your local health agencies. You could join with their efforts.

When you contact the individual or organization you have selected, explain that you would like to offer your organization and its parent members as a resource in their efforts to make their services more responsive to family needs. Your objective should be to schedule a one- or two-hour meeting at which you will present ideas about how such collaboration might take place.

Before the meeting, find out as much as you can about the organization—its size, scope of services, and services, for starters. Become familiar with the current trends and health care issues facing health care administrators and providers today.[2]

Present Your Case

Decide on how you want to present your message—who will participate and what points they will make. Make sure that your presentation is not overly structured or hurried. You will want to provide ample opportunity for discussion and questions.

Create a feeling of partnership from the beginning. Be positive. It is useful to share information about things that are working well before moving on to areas for improvement. It is likely that there are some changes that families want that would benefit the health agency as well; the goals of providers and patients are usually quite similar. At the beginning it is best not to tackle the most complex problems. Your goal is to initiate a trusting, long-term relationship that will lead to substantive change.

Ask if consumers are currently involved as advisors for policies and programs. Then explore some ways that families can be involved in the hospital, clinic, or managed care organization. When appropriate, give examples from other hospitals and clinics.

You may wish to offer representatives of the hospital or health system with whom you are meeting a self-inventory or checklist that will enable them to assess whether their services are consistent with a family-centered approach. Such a checklist might ask, does our institution:[3]

- Offer services in a coordinated and flexible manner, in ways convenient for patients and families?
- Encourage and support physicians and other health care professionals in developing collaborative relationships with individual patients and their families?
- Work with patients and families in designing systems for information sharing and support in the hospital or in all types of health care organizations within the network?
- Systematically assess patients' and families' perceptions of care and create collaborative processes to respond to their needs and concerns?
- Offer those served by the institution or network the opportunity to participate in planning, implementing, and evaluating all quality initiatives?
- Create a variety of ways for patients and families served to be advisors for institution and network policies, programs, and practices?
- Create opportunities for patients and families to participate as faculty in developing and presenting orientation and continuing education for staff across all disciplines and levels?
- Apply core principles of family-centered care to systems of care for individuals of all ages, but especially for childbearing women, young children, children with special needs, and the elderly?

Identify Next Steps

As the meeting draws to a close, discuss what can be done to increase the momentum for family-centered care. You may note that many health care organizations have found it beneficial to establish a family advisory workgroup to begin the process of learning to work together and implementing a family-centered approach to health care. In time, this workgroup often leads to a more structured family advisory council. To begin this process, you might offer to facilitate such an effort with a key staff person from the health care agency.

Schedule a follow-up meeting in a month. This will give the leaders enough time to follow through on ideas suggested at your first session but will be sufficiently close to sustain the momentum and enthusiasm.

MANAGED CARE: A SPECIAL WORD

Because managed care organizations are having such a significant impact on the financing of health care, they influence the organization of care and how patients and families experience health care. If you become involved in discussions with managed care organizations, you might find the following strategies useful:

- Use the contracting process as leverage for making family-centered care an integral part of managed care.
- Work with managed care leaders to create staff development programs to enhance the communication and collaborative skills of all staff working with patients and families. Ensure that families are part of the faculty for these programs.
- Encourage the managed care organization to create family liaison positions staffed by members of families who use the system.
- Assist the managed care organization in providing information and education to families on how to access care.
- Work with managed care leadership to create demonstration projects for family-centered approaches that document patient and family satisfaction and other outcome measures.

CONCLUSION

The experience of health care providers, decision makers, families, and patients in hospitals and clinics of all types and sizes in this country has shown that family-centered partnerships can improve the quality and reduce the costs of health care. The examples provided in this article give insight into what family-centered care looks like in action; the strategies suggest how parent leaders, parent educators, and family support organizations can collaborate with others to introduce family-centered approaches in their communities.

One final word may be helpful: implementing family-centered approaches to health care takes time. It requires that institutions, their staff, and patients and families take a new look at traditional approaches to health care and create new ways of working together. It cannot happen overnight. But, with dedication and perseverance, it will happen. And it will truly make a difference.

NOTES

The author expresses her appreciation to Linda Harteker for her assistance in preparing this chapter, which was developed with support from the Nathan Cummings Foundation.

1. This section was adapted from a Briefing Paper prepared by the Institute for Family-Centered Care (IFCC), Bethesda, Maryland, in 1997. A longer version was published in the summer 1998 issue of the IFCC semiannual newsletter, *Advances in Family-Centered Care.*

2. Packard Foundation (1998) Children and managed health care. *Future of Children* 8(2). Palo Alto, Calif.: David and Lucile Packard Foundation; IFCC (1996) Family-centered care and managed care. *Advances in Family-Centered Care* 3(1); IFCC (1998) Family re-union 7 puts family-centered care in the spotlight. *Advances in Family-Centered Care* 4(1); Family Voices (a national grassroots network of families and friends speaking in behalf of children with special health care needs), P.O. Box 769, Algodones, NM 87001, (505) 867–2368, www.familyvoices.org; Hanson, J. L., Johnson, B. H., Jeppson, E. S., Thomas, M. J., & Hall, J. H. (1994) *Hospitals moving forward with family-centered care.* Bethesda, Md.: IFCC; Jeppson, E. S., & Thomas, J. (1995) *Essential allies: Families as advisors.* Bethesda, Md.: IFCC; Children Now (1998) *Right time right place: Managed care and early childhood development.* Available from Children Now, 1212 Broadway, 5th floor, Oakland, CA 94612, (510) 763–2444, www.childrennow.org; *The ABC's of managed care standards and criteria: A report from the Egg Harbor family summit,* March 1996. Copies available from IFCC; Thomas, J., & Jeppson, E. (1997) *Words of advice: A training guide on families as advisors.* Bethesda, Md.: IFCC; and *Zero to Three* (1995, February/March) Theme issue: Newborn intensive care and (1999, June/July) Theme issue: Relationships between newborns and parents begin before birth. Available from Zero-to-Three, 734 15th Street, Suite 1000, Washington, DC 20005.

3. More complete survey instruments are available from IFCC. For information on survey tools and other print and audiovisual resources, visit the institute's Web site at www.familycenteredcare.org or call (301) 652–0281.

PART III

Parenthood in Society

When we think of parents, we usually think of childrearing homes. When we think of parenting, we usually think of childrearing activities. We usually do not think of parenthood as a lifelong lifestyle. We seldom think of parenthood as the foundation of society. But without parents who provide children, no society can survive. Without parents who rear children, no society can thrive. Because it is vital to society, parenthood is the most important job anyone can have. Our growing knowledge of child development offers guidance in designing systems and policies to support parents in their jobs of rearing society's children.

Visitors from other nations marvel at the way in which children and parents are regarded in the United States. In their countries, they take for granted that children are protected and that parents are supported by society. These priorities are relatively absent in our marketplace society that exploits the young and seduces parents into valuing material things more than family relationships. Visitors from northern Europe and Asia are concerned that individualistic and materialistic values and behaviors are infiltrating their own societies.

Although the wide variety of childrearing styles in other cultures is interesting, far more relevant insight into our contemporary childrearing practices can be gained from looking at the history of parenthood in America. Stephanie Coontz calls attention to the fact that today's dual-earner family represents a return to older patterns, after a short interlude during the middle of this century mistakenly identified as "traditional." In the 1950s, wives began their rapid movement into the labor force. After 1970, mothers, especially of young children, became the fastest-growing group of female workers. History also demonstrates that men have both the ability and the motivation to care for children on their own initiative. Many English and American fathers in the seventeenth and eighteenth centuries were active in all aspects of domestic life, from overseeing their wives' pregnancies to taking responsibility for the daily socialization of children. Today we are experiencing a rearrangement of the links between families and the wider economy, along with reorganization of employment, gender roles, race relations, family structures, intergenerational expectations, personal rights, and even our experience of time and space. In this context of change, we need to see that in economic and political terms children, like the environment, are a public good.

Urie Bronfenbrenner documents the growing chaos in the lives of children and families and the consequent decline in the competence and character of successive generations as we move into the twenty-first century. He describes a biopsychosocial theory of development. In order to fully develop, a human being requires participation in progressively more complex, reciprocal interactions with persons, objects, and symbols on a regular basis over extended periods of time. Such enduring forms of interaction are referred to as *proximal processes,* which cannot sustain themselves. Their form, power, content, and direction vary with the characteristics of the developing person and the environment—both immediate and remote—in which the processes are taking place; the time through the life course and the historical period during which the person has lived; and the nature of the developmental outcome under consideration. Bronfenbrenner points to the need for transforming changes in our society, such as the GI Bill, which gave new hope and a new life to a generation of World War II veterans and their families. A shift in our society toward valuing parenthood as a vocation worthy of substantive support would be a major step in creating a humanistic society conducive to the healthy development of children.

Larry Bumpass documents the shift toward families with unmarried and single parents in recent decades. If these trends continue, the future holds more instability in the lives of children. There are indications that the trend may be reversing. For example, the percentage of twelfth-grade students who reported ever having sex decreased from 71 percent in 1990 to 61 percent in 1997, according to a report by the Annie E. Casey Foundation.[1] The trend watcher Daniel Yankelovich believes that the "me generation" is winding down. His data reveals that people are increasingly realizing that there is more to life than fulfilling their personal needs. Yankelovich describes the "lurch and learn" cycle: "Mature adults who encounter new circumstances will usually adjust to them in a slow and moderate fashion. But for a variety of reasons, societies react far less cautiously. They tend to lurch suddenly and abruptly from one extreme to another."[2] These trends suggest that a societal shift toward greater commitment to personal relationships may create more stable lives for children in the future.

James Garbarino details the toxic factors for children in the social and ecological climate in the United States and other nations. He notes that the same issues we face today were prominent at the turn of the last century: the costs and benefits of industrialization and a global economy, multiculturalism, "big government," human rights and racism, militarism and empire, the power of the mass media, and a search for the "American family." He views the welfare of children as a public concern and specifies ways in which society could do more to support parents.

Joanne Cantor and Amy Nathanson deal with the media as one aspect of our socially toxic society. They summarize the research showing the adverse short- and long-term physical and emotional effects of television and motion picture violence on children. They describe the largely ineffective efforts made by the industry to rate television shows and the more reliable means available to parents to screen television watching by their children.

Although the federal government took the lead in reforming "welfare as we know it" through the Personal Responsibility and Work Opportunity Reconciliation Act of 1996, the implementation of the act varies from state to state. Wisconsin's experience is relevant to the national scene because it has pioneered a number of reforms and invests heavily in the implementation of Wisconsin Works (W-2). Jean Rogers and Heidi Hammes describe the aims and operations of W-2 and the results of surveys of its effects. Because the changes involved have complicated effects on the lives of parents and children, only time will reveal W-2's benefits and shortcomings. One thing is clear. Unless participants shift their orientation from dependence on W-2 as an institution to becoming active members of their neighborhoods and communities, the likelihood of achieving W-2's long-range goals will be compromised. The aim of welfare reform should not be simply reducing welfare rolls. It should be removing families from poverty. That can only be done by dealing effectively with alcohol and drug abuse, mental disorders, learning and physical disabilities, and access to health care and affordable housing.

Sylvia Ann Hewlett alerts parents to the fact that their interests and the interests of children are not being recognized in our governmental and workplace policies. She casts a "war against parents" in economic and social terms. For thirty years big business, government, and the wider culture have waged a silent war against parents, undermining the work that they do. We live in a nation where marketplace work, centered on competition, profits, and greed, increasingly crowds out nonmarketplace work, centered on sacrifice, caring, and commitment. Hewlett proposes a *Parents' Bill of Rights* as a rallying point for the collective action of the some sixty-two million parents in America. If mothers and fathers were to join together and speak with one voice, we could produce new clout for parents in legislatures and boardrooms throughout the country. Children are 100 percent of our collective future, and it behooves us as a nation to make sure that mothers and fathers handle their parenthood jobs well.

Lisbeth Schorr points out that children need supportive families and parents need supportive neighborhoods and communities. She distinguishes between *didactive* and *interactive* parent education. Her research on failed and successful models shows that successful parent education deals with parents and children in the context of their families and neighborhoods. It has long-term preventive orientations and evolves over time in response to changing circumstances and lessons learned. Most important, successful parent education focuses on results and involves cross-system partnerships. Too many successful models fail in replication attempts because they are bogged down by rules and do not have broad community support. Organizational and individual partnerships increase the chances that neighbors will help neighbors so that families become less isolated. Schorr calls for ways of building transferable knowledge about programs that work to bridge the gulf of mistrust between public agencies and communities.

NOTES

1. *Kids Count Special Report* (1998) When teens have sex: Issues and trends. New York: Annie E. Casey Foundation.
2. Yankelovich, D. (1998) How American individualism is evolving. *Public Perspective,* February/March.

16

Parenthood in American History

STEPHANIE COONTZ

Contemporary parents face serious challenges adapting their childrearing practices to the realities of modern life: the lifelong employment of women; the ethnic and racial diversity of America; the aging of their own parents; the prevalence of divorce, cohabitation, and remarriage; and the pressures of a fast-paced, consumerist society marked by a growing gap between rich and poor. The bad news is that many of these challenges cannot be met by individual parents: they require social and political solutions. The good news is that there is no make-or-break family form or parenting practice in the absence of which children are doomed. In this chapter I review the historical evidence that children can adapt to and even thrive within a variety of family forms and childrearing arrangements.

Historical and cross-cultural evidence shows an astonishing variety of family forms and childrearing arrangements. These range from the complex fostering and child-exchange systems of West Africa, the Polynesian Islands, and the Caribbean to the simple, easily dissolved pairing units of many North American Indian groups, from Tibetan homes where the children's mother is married to two or more men to complex, extended-family households, such as those common in eighteenth-century Russia.

If it is hard to find a "natural" parent-child relation in this variety of cultural family arrangements, it is also difficult to make historical judgments about what kind of family is best for children. Talcott Parsons and other sociologists of the 1950s claimed that the nuclear family was best suited to childrearing in a modern industrial society. The Moynihan Report of the 1960s claimed that the lack of a nuclear family with a strong father figure created weak egos among black Americans. But Richard Sennett argues that in nineteenth-century Chicago, it was the nuclear families of the white middle class that were least able to operate successfully in the industrial economy and most likely to produce "weak egos." Tamara

Hareven suggests that "the family type best equipped to interact with the complexities of modern life" is one "enmeshed with extended kin and closely integrated with the community." In contrast, Linda Gordon points out that in late nineteenth-century America, the support offered by kin networks was much less than commonly assumed, while extended families often exerted brutal repression over women and youth.[1]

Colonial Americans believed that it was important to inspire fear in their children. Cotton Mather, for example, described taking his young daughter into his study and explaining that when he died, which might be very soon, she must remember all he had taught her about combating "the sinful and woeful conditions of her nature." After the eighteenth century, by contrast, there was a growing desire to protect children from fear, but parents attempted to instill *guilty gratitude* in its place. For the upper class, parental financial and status considerations still exerted considerable influence over children's educational and marital options. Most working-class families required children to work and contribute financially to the family. Despite our contemporary revulsion at many such practices, there is no evidence that any of them produced widespread pathologies among the children of the time.[2]

A growing "sacralization" of childhood and an increased emphasis on the sexual innocence of children toward the end of the nineteenth century spurred new protections (or exclusions) for children, such as the passage of statutory rape laws and the abolition of child labor. Yet it is by no means clear that such "altruistic" and protective ideals invariably produced better childhood experiences. As historian E. P. Thompson comments, "Feeling may be *more,* rather than less, tender or intense *because* relations are 'economic' and critical to mutual survival." The fact that children have less to offer the middle-class family in modern America and that there are fewer economic reinforcements of parental-child interactions means there are few supports to shore up the bonds of "love." Some authors even argue that the cult of childhood innocence, at least in the context of expanding consumerism, helped produce an eroticization of childhood.[3]

Historian Louise Tilly has demonstrated that family strategies based on economic calculation and even child-sacrificing work patterns can be extremely loving *or* extremely brutal; conversely, families who value love and altruism can often experience bitter disillusion and violence. There are also social class differences in expressed values that lead easily to misunderstanding. Working-class and peasant families, for example, have historically tended to disguise individual, personal feelings in "tough talk," partly in order to ensure that family ties do not threaten larger social solidarities, while middle-class families have tended to wrap material interests and status considerations in a more sentimental language. To assume that one form of verbal expression reveals more "healthy" or "admirable" sentiments toward children is naive.[4]

THE SINGLE-BREADWINNER FAMILY

One of the most common misconceptions about modern parenting is the notion that cobreadwinning families are a new invention in human history, posing unique and threatening challenges to the nurture of children. In fact, today's dual-earner family represents a return to older norms, after a very short interlude mistakenly identified as "traditional."

Wives in seventeenth- and eighteenth-century colonial America were often called "yoke-mates" or "meet-helps," labels that indicated women's economic partnership with men. Until the early nineteenth century, men and women worked together on farms or in small household businesses, alongside other family members. Responsibility for family life and responsibility for breadwinning were not two different jobs. Furthermore, colonial mothers devoted less time to their children than do modern working mothers, typically delegating these tasks to servants or older children.[5]

But in the early 1800s, as capitalist production for the market replaced home-based production for local exchange and as a wage-labor system supplanted widespread self-employment and farming, work was increasingly conducted in centralized workplaces removed from the farm or home. Men (and older children) began to specialize in work outside the home, withdrawing from their traditional childrearing responsibilities. Household work and childcare were delegated to wives, who gave up their traditional roles in production and barter. While female slaves and free black women continued to have high labor-force participation, wives in most other ethnic and racial groups were likely to quit paid work outside the home after marriage.[6]

It is important to remember that this new division of work between husbands and wives came out of a *temporary* stage in the history of industrialization. It corresponded to a transitional period when households could no longer get by primarily on things they made, grew, or bartered but could not yet rely on purchased consumer goods. Somebody had to go out to earn money in order to buy the things the family needed; but somebody else had to stay home and turn the things they bought into things they could actually use. Given the preexisting legal, political, and religious tradition of patriarchal dominance, nineteenth-century husbands (and youth of both sexes) were assigned to work outside the home. Wives assumed exclusive responsibility for domestic matters they had formerly shared with husbands, older children, and apprentices. Many women supplemented their household labor with income-generating work that could be done at or around home–taking in boarders, doing extra sewing or laundering, keeping a few animals, or selling garden products–but a new ideal began to emerge, identifying masculinity with economic activities and femininity with nurturing care.

Even as an ideal, then, the male-breadwinner family was a comparatively late arrival on the historical scene. As a reality, it has an even shorter history. It was not until the 1920s that a bare majority of American children lived in a home where the children did not have to work and where they had a father who was the sole wage-earner and a mother who was a full-time homemaker. Yet no sooner was the male-breadwinner family established as a norm for children than it began to erode as a norm for wives.

During the 1920s, an expansion of office jobs drew thousands of women into the workforce. In the unstable economic and political climate of the 1930s and 1940s, married women found themselves pulled into work for economic or political emergencies and shoved out when pressures to reemploy men mounted. The result was that more and more women gained work experience. Wives, even with young children, were increasingly seen as a legitimate reserve labor pool, available for use in a pinch. In World War II, women were exhorted to join the workforce. When the war ended, they were bumped to make room for returning veterans.[7]

Yet despite the glorification of full-time domesticity in 1950s sitcoms, it was during this decade that wives began their most rapid movement into the labor force. Mothers of young children still tended to withdraw from the labor force until their children were well established in school. In an expanding consumerist society, however, the need of both families and businesses for female labor soon outstripped the supply of childless married women. After 1970, mothers, especially mothers of young children, became the fastest-growing group of female workers.[8]

THE DUAL-EARNER FAMILY AND CHILDREARING

Today, two thirds of all married women with children, and a much higher proportion of divorced or never-married mothers, are in the labor force, and there is every indication that this is an irreversible change in family life. Wives bring in, on average, more than 41 percent of family income; in 23 percent of families they contribute more than their husbands. While polls consistently show that many women would like to cut back on work hours, most do not want to quit entirely, even if they could afford to.[9]

Through most of this century, even though labor participation rates for women rose steadily, they dropped significantly when women were in their twenties and thirties. By 1990, however, labor-force participation rates no longer dipped for women in their childrearing years. Today, fewer and fewer women leave their jobs while their children are very young.[10]

The conditions of cobreadwinner families are different today than in the past, when much of the work that men and women did took place at the same location, often at home. Neither fathers nor mothers in such families spent the bulk of their time on childcare, but either could more easily keep an eye on a child while working. Many children were gradually initiated into adult roles by participating in some of their parents' work. There also was what might be called on-the-job childcare provided by older siblings or servants in the household. Alternatively, many working families sent their children away from home at a relatively early age—almost certainly before the mid-teens—to work in another household. Either way, working parents in older coprovider marriages did not see supervision and socialization of children as a significant problem.

Today's cobreadwinner family does not offer the same opportunity for combining productive and reproductive tasks. Men and women both work outside the home, at different locations. Rarely is on-the-job childcare available for either parent, as it was in colonial days. The apprenticeship and child-exchange customs that used to provide nonparental adult mentoring and supervision for children no longer exist. Prolongation of schooling has partly substituted for these traditional nonfamilial sources of care and education, but schools cannot cope with ill children, and school schedules do not match parents' work schedules, leaving gaps during critical hours of the day.[11]

Nevertheless, it is important to realize that in the past women successfully combined childrearing with uninterrupted, lifelong participation in the wider economy. Mothers traditionally engaged in production and exchange of goods throughout their lives, sharing childcare with both kin and nonkin, without producing generations of dysfunctional children. Even though today's coprovider families will have to coordinate work, parenting, and childcare differently than those of the past, history shows that it can be done successfully.[12]

FATHERS AND CHILDREARING

History also demonstrates that men can take a much larger role in the nurture of children than they currently do. English and American fathers in the seventeenth and eighteenth centuries, historian John Gillis reports, were active in all aspects of domestic life, from overseeing their wives' pregnancies to taking responsibility for the daily socialization of children. In many contemporary families, the wife keeps track of all significant occasions, even reminding her husband of his parents' birthdays. But prior to the nineteenth century, fathers, not mothers, carried on the bulk of family correspondence and were the masters of ceremonies for baptisms, weddings, and funerals. The idea that fathers are "junior partners" in domestic matters and that women have unique, irreplaceable roles in nurturing infants has no precedent in earlier notions of parenthood.[13]

The memoirs of Cotton Mather, the most famous Puritan clergyman in colonial America, reveal that when he or his siblings got sick during the night, they went to their father, not their mother, for comfort and relief. "Thomas Jefferson's earliest recollections," history professor Mary Frances Berry reports, "included being physically cared for by slaves and nurtured by his father." Being a stepfather did not preclude such involvement. When James Madison married the widow Dolley Payne Todd, he took personal responsibility for tutoring her son by her first marriage until they sent the youngster away to school at age eleven.[14]

These historical observations suggest that there are tremendous opportunities as well as challenges in the task of developing new norms to replace the parenting values and gender roles we learned in the 1950s. Ironically, the main barrier to realizing the opportunities and overcoming the challenges is not that we have changed too much but that we have not changed enough. Therapist Betty Carter argues that pronouncements about the "revolution" in traditional marriage and the rise of "unprecedented" parenting arrangements actually work to *hold back* needed change. Because couples believe that their stresses come from how much gender roles have already changed, they don't realize how much more they still need to change.[15]

MARITAL DISSATISFACTION AND DIVORCE

The failure of men to share housework and childcare with their partners is a primary source of overload for working mothers and a major cause of marital conflict. Yet outdated expectations about marriage continue to prevail among young men. In 1994, a national survey reported that 86 percent of thirteen- to seventeen-year-old girls expected to work after marriage, but only 58 percent of boys in the same age group expected to have an employed wife.[16]

Over and over again, we find that it is this *lag* in adjusting values, behaviors, and institutions to new realities that poses problems for contemporary families. Research psychologists Philip and Carolyn Cowan have found that parenthood frequently triggers a decline in marital satisfaction when couples revert to a male-breadwinner/female-nurturer mode after the birth of a child. Women resent the backsliding in equality, while men are either stressed by their heightened breadwinning responsibilities or frustrated by their wives' seeming lack of appreciation. The more different men and women become in their experiences and attitudes after childbirth, the Cowans found, the more dissatisfied they are likely to be in their marital relationship. When couples work to *decrease* the divergence between husband and wife that has become "traditional" over the past 180 years, the partners are less likely to experience conflict and disenchantment with the marriage.[17]

When disenchantment does occur, men who accept the Victorian notion of separate spheres for men and women have an especially hard time. Having viewed their wives as the main link to their children, they lack the incentive or ability to maintain connections with their kids without the mother at their side, or they easily switch allegiances when they find a new spouse. Another area of lag may be seen in the many battering incidents that seem to be triggered when traditional masculine notions of entitlement are resisted or evaded by wives or children. But the solution is hardly for wives to retreat from demands for equality: a recent state-by-state study of assaults against wives and cohabiting partners found that the more social, economic, and educational status women had gained in a state, the lower was the probability of that state having a high rate of wife assault.[18]

STAGES OF SOCIAL TRANSFORMATION

Family sociologist Arlene Skolnick suggests that adjustment to social transformation typically goes through a series of stages: *personal and family distress, social conflict,* and *restabilization.* From the vantage point of history, we can see that all these stages accompanied the previous major shift in gender roles and family life, when the emergence of the male-breadwinner family in the early nineteenth century disrupted older domestic arrangements between women and men, and between the old and the young.[19]

The first stage is a period of *personal and family distress* that occurs because old understandings and practices are disrupted long before new ones have taken shape. In this stage, most people do not recognize that they are facing new structural dilemmas that may be forcing them or others to behave in new ways. If we would just try harder, people think, we could get back to the way things used to be. Growing numbers of individuals then show signs of psychological stress: personality disturbances; drinking and drug problems. People experiment with ways of coping that may appear irrational or self-destructive, because there simply is *no right way* to behave.

Thus in the early nineteenth century, the old household economy and its childrearing arrangements were transformed by the rise of a cash economy, the loss of independence for small farmers and artisans, new relations among men in increasingly impersonal work settings, the new isolation (or dominion, in the views of some) for wives inside the home, and changing roles for young people. Historians believe that the anxiety evoked by these changes in gender, age, and work relations provided much of the energy behind the religious revivals that swept the country during the period. While some people sought comfort in nostalgia for the old family economy, others showed those signs of personal distress that Skolnick noted. Per capita alcohol consumption reached an all-time high between 1800 and 1830.[20]

In poverty-stricken sections of the growing cities, gangs sprang up. From the 1830s to the 1860s, writes one specialist on gang violence, "hardly a week passed" without a clash between the Bowery Boys and the Dead Rabbits of New York City. Sometimes their battles "lasted two or three days, [with] endless melees of beating, maiming and murder. . . . Regiments of soldiers in full battle dress, marching through the streets to the scene of a gang melee, were not an uncommon sight."[21]

Male-female relations were especially strained during this period of transition. As wives became more economically dependent on their husbands yet took more control over daily domestic matters and childrearing, an undercurrent of antiwoman and antifamily sentiment found expression in stories such as the original Davy Crockett yarns, which were a far cry from the later G-rated Disney movies. Davy Crockett ran away from his father, rejected education and steady work, drank heavily, provoked fights, committed cannibalism on Indians he killed, was obsessed with sexual imagery, and made fun of the emerging etiquette of refined womanhood. For their part, as women accepted a more secluded role at home, they increasingly viewed all men as potential Davy Crocketts: wild, brutish, and fundamentally "licentious." There is evidence that young women regarded marriage with new misgivings.[22]

These personal anxieties soon gave way to the second stage in Skolnick's scenario: *social conflict.* Competing definitions of the problem were raised, spawning political and social movements that attempted to hold back the changes, push them in new directions, or shift the blame to someone else: if we could just bring those individuals or groups under control, people hoped, the old patterns would fall back into place. In mid-nineteenth-century America, several cultural and political movements offered alternative explanations and cure-alls for the anxieties and problems. Many involved scapegoating. Middle-class individuals channeled their gender hostilities into racial stereotypes. Conspiracy theories were rife, with favorite targets including Catholics, Masons, bankers, slave owners, abolitionists, and foreigners. Nativist rallies attacked Catholics; antiblack mobs burned down African Americans' houses. There were sixteen urban riots in America in 1834 and thirty-seven the following year.[23]

Only after the two stages of personal and family distress and social conflict have been worked through, Skolnick argues, does society reach a period of *restabilization.* When people gain a realistic understanding of why change is occurring and what parts of it cannot be reversed, they begin to adapt their institutions, values, and cultural norms to the new realities. Most of the turmoil associated with the transitional period recedes.

After the mid-nineteenth century, such restabilization began to occur. The laws, political institutions, economic practices, workplace norms, and cultural values of an agrarian economy based on household production and intense neighborly involvement in each other's affairs gave way to new institutions that supported individual property development over community norms, established new privacy zones for the nuclear family, and created professional police forces and other institutions to hold personal rivalries and popular demonstrations in check. Family law and customs changed to reflect women's lessened involvement in the public economy. New images of masculinity evolved, defining men by their breadwinning rather than their control over the daily life of the household.

Historian John Gillis reports that one of the ways nineteenth-century families coped with the growing division between home and work was to develop new family rituals and holidays, asserting a symbolic unity of family production and consumption that had ceased to prevail in daily life. When men had worked out of the home, mealtimes had seldom been private, or even very regular. Holidays had revolved around community festivals and visiting rather than home-cooked meals and nuclear family togetherness. Leisurely dinner hours, Sunday "family time," and elaborate family meals on holidays such as Thanksgiving and Christmas were invented in the mid-nineteenth century. These rituals alleviated women's anxiety that men's new involvement in market work made them strangers to the family and reassured men that their domestic authority was not being undercut by their absence.[24]

CONTEMPORARY SOCIAL TRANSFORMATION

Today we are experiencing a socioeconomic transformation every bit as wrenching and far-reaching as that of the early nineteenth century—a total rearrangement of the links between families and the wider economy, along with a reorganization of work, gender roles, race relations, family structures, intergenerational expectations, zones of privacy, and even our experience of time and space. The male-breadwinner nuclear-family package that was put together in the mid-nineteenth century to resolve that particular crisis of transition no longer meets the needs of individuals and families experiencing these changes. Now as then, clinging to old values and behaviors merely prolongs the period of transition and stress, preventing us from making needed adjustments in our lives and institutions.

For example, the new family rituals that developed in the mid-nineteenth century had tremendous emotional appeal because they served to compensate for the daily departure of the man and the normal segregation of male and female activities. But these rituals depended on a situation in which wives were not employed outside the household and were thus able to devote vast quantities of time to preparing the meals and setting out the symbols of each occasion. Under today's very different conditions, holidays sometimes create more stress than they relieve, as working mothers struggle to reproduce nineteenth-century ceremonies that developed when wives had fewer obligations outside the home and more other women around to share the labor. No wonder some women now settle for watching wistfully as Martha Stewart performs the rituals for them on television—and how ironic that her loving attention to these meals and other homemaking activities has been severed from the original point of such labors, to reconnect a wife with husband and children at the end of a day and emphasize her service to the family.[25]

Clearly, parents need to develop new rituals, gender roles, and child-rearing practices to cope with today's family realities. There are some signs that they are doing so. In the 1980s, sociologist Kathleen Gerson conducted in-depth interviews with 138 men to explore their responses to changing gender roles in their own personal lives. She found that some men had welcomed women's greater autonomy for the selfish reason that it seemed to absolve them of obligations. A second group had tried to reestablish the breadwinner role. But a third group had chosen a new path, combining autonomy with commitment in ways that led to the sharing of work and parenting between partners and an increase in the resources available to children. Their restructured relationships "stress[ed] mutual responsibilities as well as individual rights, and they also allow[ed] a more equal exchange than one based on 'complementary' roles." More recently, Gerson's interviews with adolescents and young adults whose mothers worked while they were growing up reveal that most believe they benefited from this arrangement.[26]

Another encouraging finding is that men whose wives have worked for the longest periods of time are the ones who tend to do the most housework, suggesting that, as couples get habituated to women's paid work, men do improve their participation at home. Economist Elaine McCrate points out that the high point of divorce came in the 1970s, just when mothers had begun to work in massive numbers and before any new institutions or guidelines for working parents had developed. She suggests that part of the slowdown in divorce after 1979 may be explained by women's improved bargaining position in many marriages. It is unlikely, however, in light of women's economic independence, that divorce will recede to 1950s levels, so we must also work to increase the already growing number of parents who are learning to minimize conflict after divorce and remain involved in their children's lives.[27]

Although most individuals are doing their best to cope with the changes in family realities, our social and economic institutions have been less responsive. America's employment policies are forty years out of date, constructed for a time when the majority of mothers did not work outside the home and the majority of fathers were happy to leave childrearing entirely in the hands of their wives. Our school vacation schedules are a hundred years out of date, designed for a time when most families needed their children's labor on farms during the summer and only a minority of students finished high school anyway. Our school hours are out of synchrony both with new medical knowledge and new economic realities: school begins much too early for teenagers' body clocks and gets out much too early for parents' time clocks. Social programs are equally out of touch. Of 152 nations recently surveyed by the United Nations, the United States was one of only six that did not have a policy mandating paid parental leaves. Our childcare centers are also far less well funded and regulated than those of Europe and the Nordic countries.

CONCLUSION

We have good reason to believe that innovations in gender roles and construction of more supportive social institutions for families will ease many of the stresses that plague contemporary parenting partnerships. But another lesson of history is that marriage has steadily come to organize less and less of the life course, either for adults or children. The divorce rate has been rising steadily since 1899, and our current divorce rate is exactly where one would predict from its rate of increase in the first fifty years of the century. We may be able to lower it slightly, but we must assume that (as in the more distant past) substantial numbers of single-parent and blended families will continue to raise children. On top of this, the age of marriage is at an all-time high, putting more and more women at risk—or at choice—for an unwed birth. New reproductive technologies and the growing acceptance of gay and lesbian households create still other parenting and childrearing relationships. Like it or not, diversity of parenting arrangements is here to stay. This means that we must adjust our childrearing values and support systems accordingly.[28]

Over the past hundred years, the organization of the nuclear family as an exchange between breadwinning husband and homemaking wife fostered the notion that obligations to children were a "package deal," contingent on blood ties, residence in the same household, and access to the services or support of the other spouse. For some children, the "package deal" was never anything more than an empty box whose attractive wrapper allowed outsiders to assume the children were well cared for even when they were not. For others, the deal worked well when the marriage was strong, but it contained a dangerous trap: if the marriage ended or blood tests revealed incompatibility, too many men (and some women) felt justified in walking away from their childrearing obligations.

Our society urgently needs to create a larger, more inclusive "package deal," where obligations to children (and the benefits of access to children) are not determined by strict biological relatedness, coresidence, the marital status of the parents, or notions of exclusive "rights" to a child. The new package has to start from recognition that every adult has a stake in every child. Of course, parents have special responsibilities for their children, but those responsibilities exist independently of the relationship between the parents.

In many cases, such values will encourage parents, married or unmarried, to stay together for the sake of their children. But in other cases, they will mean that adults continue to meet their responsibilities to their children even after they split up or if they have always lived in separate households. For this reason, we need to acknowledge and encourage the strong, enduring relationships that we know from history often exist between children and individuals *outside* the household.

Many legal scholars suggest that we recognize the variety of actors in children's lives and think about children's rights to an ongoing relationship with such individuals, rather than starting from the standpoint of competing adult rights to the child. At the same time, as several child abuse and pediatrics researchers from the University of Maryland argue, we must reverse the usual pattern of indifference to helping families until a horrendous abuse case leads us to turn on the parents. They suggest replacing the after-the-fact notion of "parental culpability" with a before-the-fact notion of "shared responsibility, including parents, families, communities, and society." Nancy Folbre points out that "children, like the environment, are a public good." So are adults who are willing to parent children. We need to build a network of supports for childrearing that range from parental leave policies to high-quality childcare networks, from workplace reforms to better school funding. Recent debates over whether two parents are better than one or whether working mothers are hurting their children (the issue of working fathers never comes up) distract us from the main point. Every family needs help in today's "winner take all, dependents be damned" culture and economy. No parents should be expected to go it alone.[29]

NOTES

1. Parsons, T., & Bales, R. (1955) *Family socialization and interaction process.* Glencoe, Ill.: Free Press; Moynihan, D. (1965) *The Negro family: The case for national action.* Washington, D.C.: USGPO; Sennett, R. (1984) *Families against the city: Middle-class homes of industrial Chicago, 1872–1890.* Cambridge: Harvard University Press; Hareven, T. (1983) Review essay: Origins of the modern family in the United States *Journal of Social History* 17: 343; Gordon, L. (1988) *Heroes of their own lives: The politics and history of family violence.* New York: Viking, p. 110; and Coontz, S. (ed.) with Parson, M., & Raley, G. (1999) *American families: A multicultural reader.* New York: Routledge.

2. Demos, J. (1982) The changing faces of fatherhood: A new exploration in American family history. In S. Cath, A. Gurwitt, & J. Ross (eds.), *Father and child: Developmental and clinical perspectives.* Boston: Little, Brown, p. 426; Stearns, P., & Haggerty, T. (1991) The role of fear: Transitions in American emotional standards for children, 1850–1950. *American Historical Review* 96; and Lewis, J. (1983) *The pursuit of happiness: Family and values in Jefferson's Virginia.* New York: Cambridge University Press, p. 179.

3. Zeliger, V. (1985) *Pricing the priceless child: The changing social value of children.* New York: Basic Books; Thompson, "Happy Families," p. 501; Schnaiberg, A., & Goldenberg, S. (1975) Closing the circle: The impact of children on parental status. *Journal of Marriage and the Family* (November); and Kincaid, J. (1998) *Erotic innocence: The culture of child molesting.* Durham, N.C.: Duke University Press.

4. Tilly, L. (1979) Individual lives and family strategies in the French proletariat. *Journal of Family History* 4.

5. Coontz, S. (1988) *The social origins of private life: A history of American families, 1600–1900.* London: Verso; Ulrich, L. T. (1983) *Good wives: Image and reality in the lives of women in northern New England, 1650–1750.* New York:

Knopf; Boydston, J. (1990) *Home and work: Housework, wages, and the ideology of labor in the early republic.* New York: Oxford University Press; and Calvert, K. (1992) *Children in the house.* Boston: Northeastern University Press.

6. Coontz, S. (1988) *The social origins of private life: A history of American families, 1600–1900.* London: Verso; and Glenn, E. N., Chang, G., & Forcey, L. R. (eds.) (1994) *Mothering: Ideology, experience, and agency.* New York: Routledge, pp. 211–233.

7. Goldin, C. (1990) *Understanding the gender gap: An economic history of American women.* New York: Oxford University Press. See also chapters 2 and 7 of Coontz, S. (1992) *The way we never were: American families and the nostalgia trap.* New York: Basic Books.

8. Kain, E. (1990) *Myth of family decline: Understanding families in a world of rapid social change.* Lexington, Mass.: Heath, pp. 85–88, 98; Weiner, L. (1985) *From working girl to working mother: The female labor force in the United States.* Chapel Hill: University of North Carolina Press, p. 84; and Hernandez, D. (1993) *America's children: Resources from family, government, and the economy.* New York: Russell Sage Foundation, pp. 98–142.

9. Lewin, T. (1995) More women earn half their household income. *New York Times,* May 11; and Spain, D., & Bianchi, S. (1996) *Balancing act: Motherhood, marriage, and employment among American women.* New York: Sage.

10. Spain, D., & Bianchi, S. (1996) *Balancing act: Motherhood, marriage, and employment among American women.* New York: Sage, pp. 193, xv, 82.

11. Curfews and common sense. (1996) *New York Times,* June 11, p. A14.

12. Glenn, E. N., Chang, G., & Forcey, L. R. (eds.) (1994) *Mothering: Ideology, experience, and agency.* New York: Routledge; Zinn, M. B., & Dill, B. T. (eds.) (1994) *Women of color in U.S. society.* Philadelphia: Temple University Press; Coontz, S., & Henderson, P. (eds.) (1986) *Women's work, men's property: The origins of gender and class.* London: Verso; Boydston, J. (1990) *Home and work: Housework, wages, and the ideology of labor in the early republic.* New York: Oxford University Press; Ulrich, L. T. (1983) *Good wives: Image and reality in the lives of women in northern New England, 1650–1750.* New York: Knopf; and Calvert, K. (1992) *Children in the house.* Boston: Northeastern University Press.

13. Gillis, J. (1995) Bringing up father: British paternal identities, 1700 to present, *Masculinities* 3: 6, 16.

14. Berry, M. F. (1993) *The politics of parenthood: Child care, women's rights, and the myth of the good mother.* New York: Viking, pp. 46–50.

15. Carter, B., & Peters, J. (1996) *Love, honor, and negotiate: Making your marriage work.* New York: Pocket Books, pp. 55–64.

16. Adelmann, P. (1995) *Why don't men do more housework? A job characteristics exploration of gender and housework satisfaction.* Center for Urban Affairs and Policy Research Working Paper 95–31, pp. 4, 18; Spitze, G. (1988) Women's employment and family relations: A review. *Journal of Marriage and the Family* 50; Lavee, Y., Sharlin, S., & Katz, R. (1996) The effect of parenting stress on marital quality. *Journal of Family Issues* 17: 131–132; South, S., & Spitze, G.

(1994) Housework in marital and nonmarital households *American Sociological Review* 59; and Lewin, T. (1997) Traditional family favored by boys, not girls, poll shows. *New York Times,* July 11, p. A1.

17. Cowan, P. A., Cowan, C. P., & Kerig, P. (1993) Mothers, fathers, sons, and daughters: Gender differences in family formation and parenting style. In P. A. Cowan et al. (eds.), *Family, self, and society: Toward a new agenda for family research.* Hillsdale, N.J.: Erlbaum; Nannis, E. D., & Cowan, P. A. (eds.) (1988) *Developmental psychopathology and its treatment.* San Francisco: Jossey-Bass; Cowan, C. P., & Cowan, P. A. (1992) *When partners become parents: The big life change for couples.* New York: Basic Books; and Carter, B., & Peters, J. (1996) *Love, honor, and negotiate: Making your marriage work.* New York: Pocket Books, pp. 4, 9, 15.

18. Arendell, T. (1995) *Fathers and divorce.* Thousand Oaks, Calif.: Sage; and Straus, M. (1994) State-to-state differences in social inequality and social bonds in relation to assaults on wives. *Journal of Comparative Family Studies* 15: 18.

On the connection of traditional values to many pathologies see: Wash, G., & Knudson-Martin, C. (1994) Gender identity and family relationships: Perspectives from incestuous fathers. *Contemporary Family Therapy* 16; Luepnitz, D. (1988) *The family interpreted: Feminist theory in clinical practice.* New York: Basic Books, p. 225; McGrath, C. (1979) The crisis of domestic order. *Socialist Review* 43: 11.

19. Skolnick, A. (1993) Changes of heart: Family dynamics in historical perspective, in P. A. Cowan et al. (eds.) *Family, self, and society: Toward a new agenda for family research.* Hillsdale, N.J.: Erlbaum, pp. 52–56.

20. Johnson, P. (1978) *A shopkeeper's millennium: Society and revivals in Rochester, New York, 1815–1837.* New York: Hill & Wang; Lender, M., & Martin, J. (1987) *Drinking in America: A history.* New York: Free Press; and Rorubagh, W. J. (1979) *The alcoholic republic: An American tradition.* New York: Oxford University Press.

21. Spergel, I. (1995) *The youth gang problem.* New York: Oxford University Press, p. 7.

22. Coontz, S. (1988) *The social origins of private life: A history of American families, 1600–1900.* London: Verso, pp. 234, 219; Cott, N. (1977) *The bonds of womanhood: 'Woman's sphere' in New England, 1780–1835.* New Haven: Yale University Press; and Rosenberg, C. S. (1985) (1) Davy Crockett as trickster: Pornography, liminality, and symbolic inversion in Victorian America. (2) Beauty, the beast, and the militant woman: A case study in sex roles and social stress in Jacksonian America. Both in Rosenberg, C. S. (ed.), *Disorderly conduct: Visions of gender in Victorian America.* New York: Oxford University Press.

23. Ignatiev, N. (1995) *How the Irish became white.* New York: Routledge, pp. 109, 131; Roediger, D. (1991) *The wages of whiteness: Race and the making of the American working class.* London: Verso; Coontz, S. (1988) *The social origins of private life: A history of American families, 1600–1900.* London: Verso, ch. 6; and D'Emilio, J., & Freedman, E. (1988) *Intimate matters: A history of sexuality in America.* New York: Harper & Row.

24. Gillis, J. (1996) Making time for family: The invention of family time(s) and the reinvention of family history. *Journal of Family History* 21; and Gillis, J. (1996) *A world of their own making: Myth, ritual, and the quest for family values.* New York: Basic Books, 1996.

25. Gillis, J. (1996) Making time for family: The invention of family time(s) and the reinvention of family history. *Journal of Family History* 21: 17; and Imber-Black, E., & Roberts, J. (1992) *Rituals for our times: Celebrating, healing, and changing our lives and our relationships.* New York: HarperCollins.

26. Gerson, K. (1993) *No man's land: Men's changing commitments to family and work.* New York: Basic Books, p. 164; and Gerson, K. (2000) Children of the gender revolution. In V. Marshall et al. (eds.), *Restructuring work and the life course.* Toronto: University of Toronto Press.

27. Pittman, J., & Blanchard, D. (1996) The effects of work history and timing of marriage on the division of household labor: A life-course perspective. *Journal of Marriage and the Family* 58: 88; McCrate, E. (1992) Accounting for the slowdown in the divorce rate in the 1980s: A bargaining perspective. *Review of Social Economics* 50; Arbuthnot, J., & Gordon, D. (1996) Does mandatory divorce education work? *Family and Conciliation Courts Review* 34; Blau, M. (1993) *Families apart: Ten keys to successful co-parenting.* New York: G. P. Putnam's Sons; and Ahrons, C. (1994) *The good divorce: Keeping your family together when your marriage comes apart.* New York: HarperCollins.

28. Coontz, S. (1997) *The way we really are: Coming to terms with America's changing families.* New York: Basic Books; and Edwards, J. (1991) New conceptions: Biosocial innovations and the family. *Journal of Marriage and the Family* 53.

29. Bumpass, L., & Raley, R. K. (1995) Redefining single-parent families: Cohabitation and changing family reality. *Demography* 32: 102; Dubowitz, H., Black, M., Starr, R., Jr., & Zuravin, S. (1993) A conceptual definition of child neglect. *Criminal Justice and Behavior* 20: 23; Folbre, N. (1994) *Who pays for the kids? Gender and the structures of constraint.* New York: Routledge, p. 254; and Dowd, N. (1990) Work and family: Restructuring the workplace. *Arizona Law Review* 32.

17

Growing Chaos in the Lives of Children, Youth, and Families

How Can We Turn It Around?

URIE BRONFENBRENNER

This chapter consists of three parts that lay the foundation for understanding and improving the present state of parenthood in America.

The first part draws on demographic data to identify the principal manifestations and sources of chaos in the lives of families living in economically developed societies. Most of the data and most of the chaos come from the United States. The chaos is contagious and is spreading to other societies, although as yet in much less violent form.

In addition to analyzing the developmental disarray of children, youth, and families, today's researchers need to pay more attention to the scientific bases and strategies for turning it around and thereby draw upon untapped constructive potentials. To this end, the second part of this chapter describes the state of developmental science and introduces the *bioecological model* of human development. The third part moves from the theory and the bioecological model to experimental programs designed to counteract the chaos.

THE GROWING CHAOS

Before we can try to turn the chaos around, we need to know what it is. In 1996 my Cornell colleagues and I published a volume documenting the marked changes that have taken place over the past four decades in the lives of children and youth growing up in economically developed nations, particularly in the United States.[1]

Two main trends reinforce each other over time. The first trend reveals growing chaos in the lives of children, youth, and families. The second trend is the progressive decline in the competence and character of successive generations as they move into the twenty-first century.

Among the most prominent developmental trends are the following:

- Over the past two decades, systematic studies based on nationally representative samples document increasing cynicism and disillusionment among American adolescents and youth manifested in a loss of faith in others, in the basic institutions of their society, and in themselves. For example, over a twelve-year period beginning in the 1980s the percentage of U.S. high school seniors agreeing with the statement "Most people can be trusted" fell from 35 to 15 percent.
- A complementary theme is increasing self-centeredness and disregard for the needs of others. Consider the change over time in response to the following questionnaire item: "A man and a woman who decide to have and raise a child out-of-wedlock are 'doing their own thing and not affecting anyone else.'" One wonders what the picture is now.
- Ever greater numbers of American youth are becoming perpetrators and victims of crime. The levels for Canada, Germany, England, and Japan are minimal or nonexistent. The homicide rates for males aged fifteen to twenty-four in the United States tripled from 12 per 100,000 in 1965 to 35 per 100,000 in 1990.
- More and more youth are spending their formative years in prison.
- Although declining somewhat since 1994, rates of teenage births remain higher than ten years ago.
- Standardized measures of school achievement have been falling, even for students in the top 10 percent of the distribution.

These findings also indicate that the rising developmental disarray in the lives of children, youth, and families is the product of marked and continuing changes, taking place over the same time period, in the social institutions and informal structures that have greatest impact on the development of competence and character in the next generation. Among the most consequential of these social changes are the following:

- There has been a dramatic growth of single-parent families, whether through divorce or having a child without ever being married. For example, the percent of American children under six who are being raised by a single parent has more than doubled from 10 percent in 1970 to over 20 percent in the middle 1990s. As a result, the United States leads the developed world in the percentage of children growing

up in single-parent families and in teenage births. The critical problem here is whether there is a second parent figure present on a regular basis who not only cares for and engages in activities with the child but who also provides support, both material and emotional, to the single-parent mother.
- With more and more parents working full-time, there has been a decline in the involvement of parents as active participants in and mentors of activities with children and youth. There is growing conflict between the demands of employment and family.
- At the same time, the teenage and adult models widely watched by children and youth on the media (TV, films, video games, CDs, and the Internet) continue to emphasize commercialism, sexuality, substance abuse, and violence. The end results are (1) a lack of positive adult models for internalizing standards of behavior and long-term goals of achievement and (2) an increasing number of autonomous peer groups bereft of adult guidance.
- Neighborhood ties among families have been eroding.
- A marked increase continues in the percentage of children and youth living in poverty, producing a widening gap between the rich and the poor.
- More and more of these trends are occurring at the same time, thereby increasing the pace, the scope, and the power of their developmentally disruptive effects.

Cross-cultural comparisons are revealing. English-speaking countries lead the economically developed world in teenage births, single-parent families, and divorce in the following order: United States, United Kingdom, Canada, Australia, Sweden, France, Germany, Japan. An explanation for this can be found in observations made by Alexis de Tocqueville in the 1830s. He noted that the young United States of America had two distinctive national characteristics. First, it was the most individualistic society in human history; second, it also was the most "volunteeristic." As I wrote some years ago: "We Americans are all the descendants of those who couldn't stand authority, and of those whom authority couldn't stand."

In his classic *Democracy in America,* de Tocqueville pointed out that individualism had its roots in England. Hence, the "de Tocqueville hypothesis" for our own times: namely that, after the United States, the economically developed societies showing the highest levels of social and developmental disarray will be other English-speaking countries.

DEVELOPMENTAL SCIENCE

There are many ways of knowing: philosophy, literature, art, history. How does science differ from these fields? Science is the only way of knowing in which you are obligated to try to prove yourself wrong. Furthermore, as Albert Einstein noted: "In science, more important than finding the right answers is asking the right questions." How does one find the right questions about how we develop as human beings?

Developmental Science in the Discovery Mode

Human development—or, as some now prefer to call it, developmental science—is the scientific study of the conditions and processes shaping the biopsychological characteristics of human beings through the life course and across successive generations.

Here the principal aim is not the customary one of verifying hypotheses already formulated. It is a more extended process involving a series of progressively more differentiated formulations, with the results at each successive step setting the stage for the next round. The corresponding research designs, therefore, must be primarily generative rather than confirming versus disconfirming. Thus, the procedure is not the usual one of testing for statistical significance. Rather, the research designs must provide for carrying out an equally essential prior stage of the scientific process: that of developing hypotheses of sufficient explanatory power and precision to warrant being subjected to empirical test. In short, we are dealing with science in the *discovery* mode rather than in the *verification* mode.

At the same time, as in any scientific endeavor, it is essential that the successive formulations and the corresponding research designs be made explicit. It is necessary to have a systematic conceptual framework within which evolving formulations and designs can be classified and ordered in terms of their stage of scientific development in the discovery process.

For this dual purpose, I have proposed the Process-Person-Context-Time framework (PPCT). Each of these four terms stands for a feature that has been used as a basis for investigating human development. These four points of emphasis have emerged in the following order. (1) One of the earliest elements employed in developmental research was a person characteristic: age. (2) Environmental contexts such as social class and family structure did not enter the developmental research scene until the early 1900s. (3) The implications for human development of processes—exchanges of energy, such as conditioning and reinforcement—were the forerunners of today's parent-child interaction research and were first recognized during the 1930s. (4) Investigations of developmental change through time over the life course and across successive generations are mainly a phenomenon of the last quarter century.

The PPCT framework is not a specific theoretical model or a corresponding research design. Rather, it is a system for classifying natural phenomena, a taxonomy (from the Greek word *taxis* meaning "order"). It is a system for defining the properties of a particular theoretical system and its operational model.

With an appropriate taxonomy at our disposal, we are now in a position to examine the most recent formulation in the discovery mode.

The Bioecological Model of Human Development

The basic structure and content of the bioecological model are defined in two propositions.[2]

Proposition 1. In order to develop—intellectually, emotionally, socially, and morally—a human being, whether child or adult, requires active participation in progressively more complex, reciprocal interactions with persons, objects, and symbols in the individual's immediate environment. To be effective, the interactions must occur on a fairly regular basis over extended periods of time. Such enduring forms of interaction in the immediate environment are referred to as *proximal processes.* Proximal processes are posited as the primary engines of development.

Proposition 2. Proximal processes cannot structure, steer, or sustain themselves. Their form, power, content, and direction vary systematically as a joint function of (1) the characteristics of the developing person and of the environment, both proximal and more remote, in which the processes are taking place, (2) the time through the life course and the historical period during which the person has lived, and (3) the characteristics of the person in the developmental outcome under consideration.

Note that the characteristics of the person appear twice in the bioecological model: first as one of the four principal elements (process, person, environment, and time) influencing the form, power, content, and direction of the proximal processes; and then again as the "developmental outcome," that is, a quality of the developing person that emerges at a later point in time as the result of the mutually influencing effects of the four principal elements of the bioecological model. In sum, the characteristics of the person function both as an indirect producer and as a product of development.

Examples of Bioecological Research

How does the bioecological model fare when analyzed in a PPCT framework? Which elements are present, and how are they presumed to relate to each other? Two studies conducted some years ago, when analyzed in

PPCT terms, come close to meeting the requirements of this theoretical model and its corresponding research design.

Drillien's Study. The first example dates from the late 1950s and early 1960s. At that time, Cecil Mary Drillien, a physician and professor of child life and health at the University of Edinburgh in Scotland, carried out a seven-year longitudinal investigation of psychological development in two groups: 360 children of low birth weight, and a control group selected by taking the next mature birth from the hospital admission list.[3]

Drillien's interest was twofold: (1) to analyze the impact of the quality of mother-infant interaction at age two on the frequency of problem behaviors observed in the infant at age two and again at age four; and (2) to examine how this relationship varied as a joint function of the family's social class and three levels of infant birth weight—underweight by a pound or more, underweight by up to one pound, and normal weight. Assessments of maternal interactions were based on observations in the home and interviews with the mother.

Drillien's measure of social class took into account not only parental income and education but also the socioeconomic level of the neighborhood in which the family lived. The quality of interactions was assessed in terms of the extent to which the mother was responsive to changes in the state and behavior of the infant. Finally, the measure of the developmental outcome was based on the frequency of reported behavior disturbances, such as hyperactivity, overdependence, timidity, and negativism.

This research design includes all four elements of the bioecological model. Drillien's measure of maternal responsiveness closely approximates the definition of proximal process as the mechanism driving human development on a fairly regular basis over extended periods of time. To complete the picture, the remaining two elements of the characteristics of the person and of the environmental context appear respectively in the form of the infant's birth weight and of social class. Finally, as previously noted, a characteristic of the person appears again, but now in the role of a developmental outcome: in this instance, the average number of problem behaviors exhibited at age two and then again at age four.

With theory and design in place, we turn to the results. In all three social class levels, the infants who had experienced low levels of maternal responsiveness at age two showed higher levels of problem behavior two years later, especially those youngsters growing up in the poorest environments. The proximal process (maternal responsiveness) markedly reduced the frequency of later problem behaviors, but the moderating factor was in a different quarter. Whereas maternal responsiveness made its greatest impact on those children growing up in the most disadvantaged environment, within that environment youngsters with normal birth weights benefited most from the developmental process.

Maternal responsiveness across time still emerged as an exceptionally powerful predictor of developmental outcome. In all instances, responsive maternal interactions reduced significantly the degree of behavioral disturbance exhibited by the child.

Herein lies the main justification for distinguishing between proximal process, on the one hand, and the environments in which the processes occur, on the other hand. In accord with Proposition 1, the former turn out to be an especially potent force influencing the developmental outcome (in this case, the frequency of problem behaviors two years later, when the children were four years old). Furthermore, as stipulated in Proposition 2, the power of the process varies systematically as a function of the environmental context (i.e., social class) and of the characteristics of the person (i.e., weight at birth).

However, one other key element of the bioecological model still remains to be considered. Proposition 2 stipulates that the "form, power, content, and direction of proximal processes effecting development" also "vary systematically as a function of . . . the nature of the developmental outcomes under consideration." Our next research example speaks to this issue. It also illustrates a "next stage" of developmental science in the discovery mode.

Small and Luster's Study. Specifically, we anticipate on theoretical grounds that the greater developmental impact of proximal processes on children growing up in poorer environments is to be expected only for outcomes reflecting developmental dysfunction.

In this context, the term *developmental dysfunction* refers to the manifestation of difficulties in maintaining control and integration of behavior across a variety of situations. In contrast, *competence* refers to knowledge and skills—whether intellectual, physical, emotional, or a combination of them (for example, learning how to care for an infant involves all three).

The theoretical expectation that proximal processes will differ in their developmental effects depending on the quality of the environment rests on the following basis. In deprived and disorganized environments, manifestations of dysfunction in children are likely to be both more frequent and more severe, with the result that they attract more attention and involvement from parents, whereas in advantaged and more stable environments, such manifestations are less intense, and parents are more likely to be attracted by and respond to gratifying signs, such as competence, of their children's developmental progress.

In addition, most parents have the capacity and the motivation to respond to the immediate physical and psychological needs of their children. The situation is rather different, however, with respect to enabling their children to acquire new knowledge and skill. In this domain, either the parents must themselves possess the desired knowledge and skill, or they must have access to resources outside the family that can provide their children with the experiences needed to develop competence.

Taken together, the foregoing considerations lead to a working hypothesis regarding the differential impact of proximal processes as a joint function of the quality of the environment in terms of available resources, on the one hand, and, on the other, the nature of the outcome in terms of dysfunction versus competence.

Some indication of the validity of this hypothesis is provided by the results of an analysis by Stephen Small and Thomas Luster of the University of Wisconsin Department of Child and Family Studies depicting the differential effects of parental monitoring on the school achievement of high school students living in the three most common family structures found in a total sample of more than four thousand cases.[4] The sample is further stratified by two levels of mother's education, with completion of high school as the dividing point. *Parental monitoring* refers to the effort by parents to keep informed about and set limits on their children's activities outside the home.

Once again, the results reveal that the effects of proximal processes are more powerful than those of the environmental contexts in which they occur. In this instance, however, the impact of the proximal process is greatest in what emerges as the most advantaged ecological niche: families with two biological parents in which the mother has had some education beyond high school. In single-parent and stepfamilies, the same degree of active effort yields a somewhat smaller result. Thus, in this case, for pupils who are not doing so well in school, parental monitoring can apparently accomplish a great deal by ensuring stability of time and place so that some learning can occur. In addition, however, superior school achievement would clearly require high levels of motivation, focused attention, prior knowledge, and, especially, actually working with the material to be learned, all qualities that stability of time and place by themselves cannot provide.

In the Small and Luster study, within each family structure, parental monitoring exerted a more powerful effect on the school achievement of girls than of boys, a result that is paralleled by corresponding differences in average GPA for the two sexes. In each of the three family structures, girls received higher grades than boys, with the difference being most pronounced in two-parent households and lowest in single-mother families.

A distinctive feature of the pattern for girls is a marked flattening of the curve of scholastic achievement, especially for daughters of single-parent mothers. This result suggests that, in each of the three family structures, better educated mothers may push their already successful daughters too hard, to the point where conformity to maternal control no longer brings educational returns, particularly when the mother is the only parent.

An analysis of data on students whose mothers had no more than a high school education showed a similar general pattern, but the effects were less pronounced. The influence of monitoring was appreciably weaker, and its greater benefit to girls also was reduced. Nevertheless, girls with less educated mothers both in single-parent and in stepfamilies still had higher GPA scores than boys.

NATURE-NURTURE FROM THE BIOECOLOGICAL PERSPECTIVE

A growing body of research claims strong evidence for the view that individual and group differences in a wide range of developmental outcomes are mainly driven by genetic endowment.[5]

In response, my colleagues and I have proposed an empirically testable theoretical model that (1) goes beyond the established behavioral genetics paradigm by allowing for nonadditive synergistic effects, direct measures of the environment, and mechanisms of organism-environment interaction (namely, proximal processes) through which genotypes are transformed into phenotypes; (2) hypothesizes that estimates of heritability increase markedly with the magnitude of proximal processes; (3) demonstrates that heritability measures the proportion of variation in individual differences attributable only to *actualized* potential, with the degree of *nonactualized* potential remaining unknown; and (4) proposes that, by enhancing proximal processes, it is possible to increase the extent of actualized potentials for reducing developmental dysfunction and for increasing developmental competence. This formulation awaits a rigorous test.[6]

Bioecological Model Experiments

The examples considered thus far are essentially "experiments of nature." That is, they show how development is influenced by variation in the elements of the bioecological model occurring in already existing social conditions. But they tell us nothing about whether, to what extent, or how these elements and their combinations can be changed. This limitation applies particularly to the most consequential component of the bioecological model, proximal processes. The most effective way to answer this question would be to conduct an experiment, with subjects randomly assigned to different experimental conditions, including a control group. Such an experiment has been carried out.

Riksen-Walraven's Experiment. In 1978, Marianne Riksen-Walraven, a developmental psychologist in the Dutch city of Nijmegen, conducted an experiment with a sample of one hundred nine-month-old infants and their mothers.[7] All subjects came from working-class families because this was seen as the group in greatest need. In the research design, mother-infant pairs were randomly assigned to one of three groups. Those who ended up in what Riksen-Walraven called the "stimulation group" were given a "Workbook for Parents," with drawings to match, emphasizing the importance of mothers providing their infants with a variety of experiences that captured the baby's attention, such as pointing to and naming objects and persons and speaking a lot to their infants.

By contrast, the workbook for mothers in the "responsiveness" group stressed the idea that "the infant learns most from the effects of its own behavior."[8] Accordingly, caregivers were advised not to direct the children's activities too much but to give the children opportunities to find out things for themselves and then to respond to the child's initiatives.

Finally, mothers in the third experimental group were given pages from both workbooks, in effect recommending that the mothers use both strategies.

How did the three groups come out in the follow-up conducted three months later? Which group did the best, and which did the worst?

All three experimental groups were influenced by the workbooks they were given. However, it was the children in the responsiveness group who showed the strongest and most pervasive effects on laboratory measures of young children's cognitive development that were administered at the end of the experiment. Specifically, they exhibited the highest gains on measures of exploratory behavior, were more likely to prefer a novel object to one that was already familiar, and obtained higher scores on a learning task. The stimulation group placed second; and the one relying on both stimulation and responsiveness did least well.

Why? What can be inferred from the results when both strategies were used together? The researcher did not address this question, but one possible explanation is that the mothers were faced with having to make a decision about what to do when, thus interrupting a free flow of interaction.

The final analysis revealed marked differences in maternal behavior corresponding to the advice and examples presented in the "Workbook for Parents." This set of results suggests the possibility of designing home-based intervention programs that could operate effectively at much lower cost and reach many more families in need than those requiring on-site professional staff on a regular basis.

A key question, however, is how long the effects can last. Fortunately, the original investigator, together with a colleague, provided an answer in a longitudinal follow-up study of the same families when the children were seven, ten, and twelve years of age, using measures based on teachers' ratings.[9] At these later ages only the girls from the original responsiveness group showed any effects of the original experimental intervention. Specifically, at all three later ages they were rated by teachers as more "competent and skillful," "curious and exploring," "resourceful in initiating activities," "better able to handle stressful situations," "less dependent on adults for help," and "less anxious." In addition, by age twelve, these girls were described by their teachers as more "attractive, interesting and energetic children."

The authors offer the following speculations about why the responsiveness program was particularly effective for girls and not for boys:

> We suggest that different parental attitudes towards competence striving in boys and girls may have contributed to this finding. Striving for competence, independence, and self-reliance are part of the traditional masculine stereotype, which was still current in the early seventies when our intervention started. . . . This means that initially competent boys will have more opportunities to experience themselves as effective agents than initially competent girls. . . . It thus seems possible that competence motivation can maintain itself in young girls only when it is at an "extra" high level and only when the parents are "extra" willing to accept their daughters' autonomy and independent exploration.[10]

In sum, from the perspective of the bioecological model, we have evidence for the power of an experimentally induced proximal process in furthering young girls' psychological development. This result was accomplished by changing the belief systems of mothers, thereby leading them to provide a different kind of experience for their young daughters over an extended period of time. Thus, taken as a whole, the findings encompass all four defining properties of the bioecological model and its corresponding PPCT design, with developmental context deliberately limited to working-class families as the group most in need of assistance. The fact that the long-range effects of the intervention were limited to girls poses an unanswered question regarding the nature of proximal processes that might achieve similar developmental gains for boys.

Vygotsky's Experiment. Is there a known strategy that can reverse disruptive changes that are powerful and widespread in a society? Yes, there is, and it has a long history. But I know of only one instance in which such a strategy was conceived and carried out by developmental scientists. The strategy was based on theory, refined in an "experiment of nature," and applied in an "experiment by design." The central figure in this remarkable achievement was the developmental psychologist Lev Semyonovitch Vygotsky. The central idea underlying the entire enterprise was Vygotsky's concept of the "transforming experiment." By this he meant an experiment that restructures the environment to produce a new configuration that activates the previously unrealized developmental potential of the persons living in that environment.

Alexander Romanovich Luria, one of Vygotsky's best known students, tells the story of Vygotsky's experiment in his autobiography. The time was the early 1930s in the Soviet Union.

> We conceived the idea of carrying out the first far-reaching study of intellectual functions. . . . By taking advantage of the rapid cultural changes that were then in progress in remote parts of our country, we hoped to trace the changes in thought processes that are brought about by technological change. . . . At that time, many of our rural areas were undergoing rapid change with the advent of collectivization and the mechanization of agriculture.

The basic research design took advantage of the fact that the process of modernization had not been introduced in all areas of the Soviet Union at the same time. As a result, it became possible to carry out a comparison of cognitive functioning in communities differing in their degree of exposure to social change. Vygotsky died of tuberculosis before this extraordinary investigation was completed. The following is Luria's summary of the findings:

> Our data indicate that decisive changes can occur in going from graphic and functional—concrete and practical—methods of thinking to much more theoretical modes of thought brought about by changes in social conditions, in this instance by the socialist transformation of an entire culture.[11]

The publication of the study in the Soviet Union was held up for more than three decades. The reasons for the delay are perceptively described by Michael Cole in his preface to the American edition of Luria's book: "The status of national minorities has long been a sensitive issue in the USSR (not unlike the issue of ethnic minorities in the United States). It was all well and good to show that uneducated, traditional peasants quickly learned the modes of thought characteristics of industrialized socialist peoples, but it was definitely not acceptable to say anything that could be interpreted as negative about these people at a time when their participation in national life was still so tenuous."[12]

CONCLUSION

America has yet to confront the reality that the growing chaos in the lives of our children, youth, and families pervades too many of the principal settings in which we live our daily lives: our homes, health care systems, childcare arrangements, peer groups, schools, neighborhoods, workplaces, means of transportation—and communication among all of them.

These are the settings in which our society has concentrated fragmented resources and efforts to reverse the mounting developmental disarray. Even though the United States experienced an economic upswing in the late 1990s, the sparse bits of recent demographic data give little indication of a true and lasting turnaround. The rising trend of chaos and its consequences also extends to other spheres of our society.

Not long ago, one of our nation's leading corporate executives gave a major lecture at Cornell's Graduate School of Management. His title was "Growing Chaos in America's Corporate Enterprises." He said that no sooner is a new production policy implemented after weeks of planning and testing than an order comes down from above "to scrap the whole thing" because the policy has been changed.

Transforming experiments have been carried out in the United States, but their developmental effects have never been investigated systematically. Perhaps one of the most successful was the GI Bill, which gave educational and housing benefits and hope to a whole generation of World War II veterans and their families. The same deserved legacy was not bestowed on their comrades-in-arms in the wars that followed.

A second example is Head Start. But from what I know both from looking at its budgets and its mounting bureaucratic controls, and from personal experience as an external member of a Head Start Parents' Policy Committee, the prospects for the future are hardly rosy. Head Start parents are today drawing on their own meager resources to continue some of the programs that are needed most, and they take time off from jobs (when they have them) to help fellow families in emergencies because of illness or the desperate need for childcare.

Such heroic acts are signals to the rest of American society. They sound a call for a transforming experiment in strengthening parenthood, one that can draw on the deepest sources of our national strength. As yet, this call is not being heard, either by our scientists or by our citizens. We do not heed the immortal words of John Donne: "Do not ask for whom the bell tolls; it tolls for thee."

NOTES

1. Bronfenbrenner, U., McClelland, P., Wethington, E., Moen, P., & Ceci, S. J. (1996) *The state of Americans: This generation and the next.* New York: Free Press.

2. Bronfenbrenner, U., & Morris, P. (1998) The ecology of developmental processes. In R. M. Lerner (ed.), W. Damon (series ed.), *Handbook of child psychology* (5e). *Volume I: Theory,* pp. 993–1028. Propositions, p. 996.

3. Drillien, C. M. (1957) The social and economic factors affecting the incidence of premature birth. *Journal of Obstetrical Gynaecology, British Empire* 64: 161–184; and Drillien, C. M. (1964). *Growth and development of the prematurely born infant.* Edinburgh and London: E. & S. Livingston.

4. Small, S., & Luster, T. (1990) Youth at risk for parenthood. Paper presented at the Creating Caring Communities Conference, Michigan State University, East Lansing, November 27.

5. Plomin, R. (1993) Nature and nurture: Perspective and prospect. In R. Plomin & G. E. McClearn (eds.), *Nature, nurture, and psychology.* Washington, D.C.: American Psychological Association, pp. 459–486; and Scarr, S. (1992) Developmental theories for the 1990s: Development and individual differences. *Child Development* 63: 1–19.

6. Bronfenbrenner, U., McClelland, P., Wethington, E., Moen, P., & Ceci, S. J. (1996) *The state of Americans: This generation and the next.* New York: Free Press.

7. Riksen-Walraven, J. M. (1978) Effects of caregiver behavior on habituation rate and self-efficacy in infants. *International Journal of Behavioral Development* 1: 105–130. Quoted, p. 111.

8. Ibid., p. 113.

9. Van Aken, M. A., & Riksen-Walraven, J. M. (1992) Parental support and the development of competence in children. *International Journal of Behavioral Development* 15(1): 101–123.

10. Ibid.

11. Luria, A. R. (1976) *Cognitive development: Its cultural and social foundations.* Cambridge: Harvard University Press, p. vi.

12. Ibid, p. xiv.

18

The Changing Contexts of Parenting in the United States

LARRY BUMPASS

This chapter brings a sociological perspective to the increasing instability in the lives of children in the United States. My starting point is that the family is a major factor in the well-being of adults, children, and society. I will emphasize the social context in which parenting interactions and child development take place. That social context structures the decisions made by individual parents.

I will describe the nature and strength of the social developments that affect the stability of children's family lives. Then I will summarize my conclusions about changes in family structures: these changes are (1) anchored in the social systems and economies of Western industrial societies reaching back into the last century, and (2) influenced by feedback loops between these trends and the behaviors of parents.

DECREASING STABILITY IN THE LIVES OF CHILDREN

The stability of family life is clearly decreasing. Multiple families during childhood is an inescapable fact of American life. We are on a trajectory in which movement in and out of single-parent status is likely to continue. One half of all children will spend some time in a single-parent family.

From 1960 to 1992, the proportion of children in single-parent families more than doubled among both whites and blacks. Of particular interest from a policy perspective is that the level for whites reached the level for blacks at the time Patrick Moynihan was writing about the instability of families among black children.[1] An array of correlated outcomes results from the parent-child interactions as family structures change: psychological effects on parents and children, educational attainment of parents and children, teen sex, teen pregnancy, substance abuse, and unmarried childbearing, all of which the literature associates with family structure. But it is a complicated task for scientists to sort out the factors that cause these outcomes. Certainly income plays an important mediating role, especially in educational attainment.

Concern for the future productivity of the economy is dire indeed when a quarter of all children are spending at least part of their childhood in poverty. This has serious implications for investments in children now and the nature of the labor force in the next generation. Conservatives and liberals ought to be able to reach common ground over this. Parenthetically, much of the research in this area focuses on the false dichotomy of being "in poverty" or "out of poverty." Economic stress is a variable that extends well across the income continuum. A sharp drop in income following divorce may leave a family above the poverty line and still have dramatic consequences in terms of stress on the family and the lives of the children involved.

With the exception of orphanhood, children's experience with family instability now often results from decisions made by parents. How has this happened to us? Do we really value stable relationships and parenthood?

THE SOCIOLOGICAL CONTEXT OF FAMILY CHANGE

The sociological evidence for the process of change in families grows out of European as well as American data. The underlying dynamics are the atomizing effects of the culture of *individualism* on the one hand and of the *market economy* on the other. In that context *relative value* and *revealed preferences* actually determine the behavior of individual parents.

Individualism and the Market Economy

I believe that the family changes occurring in the Western world result from the interplay between individualism and market economies. They are not the consequences of policies, such as welfare or no-fault divorce or even the increased employment of women.

The seeds of individualism were brought to America from Europe, where individualism plays an important role in family changes as well. Individualism creates a climate in which responsibility to others and the attractiveness of childrearing are diminished. These changes are also increasingly occurring in Eastern Asian societies. I hear my Japanese colleagues bemoan the increase in individualism among the young people in the Confucian context of duty to others. Their individualism grows out of the young people's interface with the market economy and their ability to produce and to consume for themselves. I believe that these changes are due to the increasing legitimacy of self-interest as a criterion for decisions as opposed to the interests of a larger collectivity. This need not be interpreted in the narrowest sense of selfishness but rather in the context of competing values, such as personal freedom, development, and empowerment values that we hold as important as our family roles.

The needs of our market economy define individuals as producers. As a result occupational roles take priority over family roles. We see the consequences of this priority. The father who works extra hours at the office, rather than the one who knocks off at four to take his boy to softball practice, is the one who will get a pay raise the next time around. There is a symbiosis between our market economy's need for us to behave as if we were not tied in obligatory ways to others and our cultural emphasis on individualism.

Relative Value and Revealed Preferences

The perspectives of relative value and revealed preferences are helpful in understanding how decisions are made by parents. *Revealed preferences* is an economic term for which there are fancy equations, which basically mean "actions speak louder than words." If we were interested in whether Americans preferred to invest in home remodeling over taking vacations, holding prices constant, we would quite simply look at whether over time they invested more of their available resources in home remodeling than in vacations. Simple enough, and it is that perspective that I bring to much of my analysis.

How can it then be that Americans truly value family relationships and yet act to the contrary? The notion of relative value offers real insight from at least some economists' perspectives on these matters. We can value something very much. We can even value it more than we used to—and still value it less relative to another competing good—if our value on that other competing good has increased more rapidly.

This is where perceived consumption needs enter the picture. If young people "can't afford" to marry these days, does that mean that their lifestyles would be worse than those of young people with the same resources who married in the 1950s? No. It means that they think that they need more now than young people did then in order to marry.

The values of independence and the realization of individual goals and self-definition are relevant as well. It is in relation to these values that parenting roles are becoming less important, even while they remain important.

A consequence of these competing values noted by many European as well as American observers is the decreased willingness to make long-term commitments. An intergenerational example is that children from unstable families are less likely to form and maintain stable families of their own. This decreased willingness to make long-term commitments has historical and economic roots that go much deeper than one's own family context. The higher values of personal freedom, development, and empowerment compete with and reduce the relative attractiveness of the obligatory nature of family roles.

FEEDBACK LOOPS

From the sociologist's viewpoint divorce, cohabitation, single parenthood by choice, the separation of sexual activity from marriage, and delayed marriage have interacted to increase the instability of family life for children.

Divorce

The accelerating curve that has led to 40 percent of all first marriages ending in divorce reaches well back into the last century, to about 1860. There are fluctuations around this trend line, but we have been at a plateau for about the last twenty years.[2]

Now one third of the children of married parents will see their parents' marriage disrupted. While the current levels of divorce are a continuation of the long-term trend, they also signal a turning point in the economic terms of a contract of marriage until death. That contract has become a weak guarantee of stable family environments for either women or children.

Cohabitation

Marriage no longer signifies a solid commitment to a lifetime relationship. It no longer signifies the point at which sexual activity is expected to begin. It no longer clearly delimits the necessary context for childbirth. It no longer signifies that a couple is likely to begin living together. Once referred to as "shacking up" or "living in sin," cohabitation has evolved from a strongly disapproved behavior to the majority behavior in our society. If we live in a society in which we take for granted that young people are sexually active, then the stigma associated with unmarried childbearing or cohabitation is gone.

One of the most important factors in the present plateau of divorce is cohabitation, which is pruning off a fair number of divorces that would have occurred. My colleague, sociologist James Sweet, calls these "premarital divorces."

In 1995 half of all women in their thirties had lived in a cohabiting relationship. The proportion of women ages forty to forty-four who had ever lived in a cohabiting relationship had increased by more than one third from 1987, as younger cohorts aged into this category. This is a process demographers refer to as *succession* or *demographic metabolism*. As younger generations with high levels of cohabitation grow older, they carry their experience with them in to the next age category. We are facing a day, I would guess, when as many as 60 percent of sixty-five-year-olds will have lived in a cohabiting relationship at some time.

Single Parenthood by Choice

Single-parent families are not new. A qualitative change did occur sometime in the 1960s, however. Single-parent families over the latter part of the last century and the first part of this century were largely the consequence of orphanhood. Somewhere in the 1960s the majority of single-parent families followed divorce. Parental choice became the primary mechanism by which single-parent families were formed, and public attitudes accommodated that choice. In the early 1960s 80 percent of the public agreed that "a couple should stay together." By the 1980s agreement with that statement dropped to 50 percent. A decreased sense that parents were obliged to stay together for the sake of the children occurred.[3]

Thus, as the significance of marriage has declined, single parenthood by choice has become common. This is one of the important feedback loops. With the high levels of divorce since the late 1960s, the increasing number of single-parent families, and the changes in public attitudes about a couple staying together, single parenthood in itself no longer is stigmatizing. Given that change, a young woman who finds herself pregnant and does not want to marry the father is in a different environment.

Half of all single-parent families now begin with an unmarried birth. One third of all children in the United States are now born to an unmarried mother. These are not just first births and certainly not just teen births. Half are second or higher-order births, and only a third of unmarried childbearing occurs among teens.[4]

This trend toward unmarried childbearing in the United States has not occurred primarily among minorities and occurs at all ages. Among white women in the United States at virtually every age, there has been an increase in the rate of unmarried childbearing. There are comparable trends in Europe and Canada, in Australia and New Zealand, and most obviously in Scandinavia. The significance of marriage for childbearing has clearly declined. The roots are in the separation of sex from marriage and in delayed marriage.

Separation of Sexual Activity and Marriage

Unmarried sex probably was accelerated by the availability of oral contraceptives in the 1960s. The point here is that unmarried sex is simply a part of our culture and has continued to increase.[5] The increasing delay of marriage and the resulting increasing proportion of the population that is unmarried and sexually active are having a profound effect on our culture and on the media. The marketplace is addressing a population that is unmarried and sexually active. This increased earlier sexual activity, later ages of marriage, and increased sexual exposure time are resulting in increasing numbers of women who have unintended pregnancies while they are unmarried.

Of all pregnancies in 1987, about 29 percent were unintended and ended in abortion, and 28 percent were unintended and resulted in a birth; only 43 percent of all pregnancies were intended pregnancies that resulted in births. Among the unmarried population 80 percent of all pregnancies are now unintended. Half of the pregnancies to unmarried women end in abortion, accounting for 80 percent of our abortions each year. Yet two-thirds of the births that occur to unmarried women are the result of unintended pregnancy.[6] I emphasize this because unintended pregnancy is the primary route by which these single-parent families are created. This conclusion draws us into a different policy arena than is usually thought about in terms of affecting children's lives. Reducing the levels of unintended pregnancy among unmarried women would restructure the family context of many children.

Delayed Marriage

Delayed marriage plays three roles in this process. First, much of the increase in unmarried childbearing has been due to the demise of "shotgun" marriages; that is to say, pregnancies before marriage followed by a hasty marriage to the father of the child have essentially disappeared. In the past sex was much more likely to occur in a committed relationship that could plausibly result in marriage. As sex is occurring in more casual relationships, the decision to ever marry the father is decreasing as well. There are dramatic declines in marriage following unmarried births beyond the "shotgun" marriage stage. This change has profound implications. The cumulative proportion of women who have married within a given number of years after the birth of a child before marrying has decreased markedly.

In the 1960s, two thirds of white women who gave birth while unmarried had married within five years of that birth, and this proportion has dropped to only about half. On the other hand, the proportion marrying after ten years has fluctuated around 80 percent. Among African American women, only two fifths marry within ten years after having their first birth while unmarried. Thus a substantial proportion of white women and the majority of African American women who have a child while unmarried are simply not marrying for the remainder of their reproductive careers.[7] Some related work we are doing on sterilization is corroborating this fact: there are increasing levels of sterilization among unmarried women because they have had all the children they want: one third of recent sterilizations were to unmarried women.

Finally, delay in marriage produces an increased duration of exposure to risk of pregnancy. The proportion of women who are unmarried in their late twenties has more than doubled over the last couple of decades. So there is increased exposure time when one is unmarried and sexually active. That is a product not only of delayed marriage but also of earlier ages of first sexual experiences.

IMPACT ON CHILDREN

Let us review the impact all of this has on the lives of children. There is a complex set of relationships between cohabitation and the family trends I have been reviewing. One third of all births in the United States are to unmarried mothers. We think of those births as creating single-parent families. It turns out that 40 percent of the births to unmarried mothers occur in two-parent families in which the partners simply are not married. They are cohabiting, so that cohabitation overlays this unmarried childbearing process in a complex way.[8]

Further, the increases in unmarried childbearing over the last decade occurred almost completely in cohabiting two-parent families. Almost half of children will spend some time in a cohabiting family, but the probability that the parents in that family will marry each other in the 1980s was 57 percent; now it has declined to 44 percent. The stability of children's relationships is declining in ways that we do not see in marriage statistics.

About half of all children will spend time in a single-parent family. The probability that a child will experience family disruption has increased because of the experience of living in cohabiting families. The proportion of children living in married families has declined, and the proportion living in cohabiting families has increased. Children living outside married families spend about a third of their time in cohabiting families moving in and out of different family arrangements.

The forces affecting family transitions do not stop at the boundaries of married families. They affect two-parent families in terms of stepfamilies, half-siblings, and the like. One of the most dramatic trends is the increase in the employment of mothers of infants, which is now over 50 percent. This is occurring in spite of the enormous difficulties of arranging childcare for infants. I see this as driven heavily by market forces. Aside from those in real poverty, "economic need" is defined primarily by *relative preference* placed on competing values in our society relating to vocations and consumption relative to family priorities.

In 1994 two thirds of the respondents under the age of thirty to the National Survey of Families and Households felt that unmarried sex, cohabitation, and unmarried births were socially acceptable.[9] These attitudes are relevant to family structures. Unmarried sex is okay if a person is over eighteen years of age. It is okay to cohabit. It is okay to have an unmarried birth. Issues that the older generation opposes strongly have little opposition among younger generations. The demographer sees that, as the younger generation ages through the population, we will move more in the direction that I have described.

Although efforts to turn things in the opposite direction are increasingly visible, these are strong currents against which one must swim if one wishes to increase the stability of families for children.

CONCLUSION

In our policies and in our own personal lives, there is a very strong current that is increasing the instability of children's lives. It is possible to swim upstream, but only for those who feel we must do so and only for those who recognize the strength of the currents against which we must swim.

My view of the dynamic rooted in competitive market economies makes it seem impossible to turn back the clock. Rather we must find creative ways to invest in children more heavily in the new family contexts. Perhaps the Scandinavian countries have led the way, just as they led the way in creating the family changes we have been describing. In Norway a mother receives full-time pay for a year to parent her infant; in Sweden she receives 80 percent. Can we conceive of valuing parenting as much as market roles so that we would actually pay parents to carry out that role?

By shifting priorities in adult decision making toward the interests of children and by reducing unintended pregnancies among unmarried women, we could make a real difference in our own lives and in the lives of those around us.

NOTES

1. Rainwater, L., & Yancey, W. (1967) *The Moynihan report and the politics of controversy.* Cambridge: Massachusetts Institute of Technology Press.

2. Bumpass, L., & Lu, H. H. (1999) Trends in cohabitation and implications for children's family contexts in the U.S. *Population Studies* (forthcoming).

3. Thornton, A. (1989) Changing attitudes towards family issues in the United States. *Journal of Marriage and the Family* 51: 873–895.

4. Driscol, A., Hearn, G. K., Evans, V. J., Moore, K., Sugland, B., & Call, V. (1999) Nonmarital childbearing among adult women. *Journal of Marriage and the Family* 6(2): 178–187.

5. Hogan, D., Sun, R., & Cornwell, G. (1999) The sexual and fertility behaviors of American females 15–19: 1985, 1990, 1995. Paper presented at the Conference on the 1995 National Survey of Family Growth, Hyattsville, Maryland, October 1999.

6. Brown, S., & Eisenberg, L. (1995) *The best intentions.* Washington, D.C.: National Academy Press.

7. Bumpass, L., & Lu, H. H. (1999) Trends in cohabitation and implications for children's family contexts in the U.S. *Population Studies* (forthcoming).

8. Bumpass, L., & Raley, R. K. (1995) Redefining single-parent families: and changing family reality. *Demography* 32(1): 97–109.

9. Bumpass, L. (1998) The changing significance of marriage in the United States. In K. O. Mason, N. Tsuya, & M. Choe (eds.), *The changing family in comparative perspective: Asia and the United States.* Honolulu: University of Hawaii Press.

19

Supporting Parents in a Socially Toxic Environment

JAMES GARBARINO

The quality and character of parenting result in part from the social context in which families operate. One important feature of this social context is public policy. This chapter examines several public policy issues that affect parenthood and highlights the role of "social toxicity" in challenging parental competence as America enters the twenty-first century.

I use the phrase *socially toxic environment* to call attention to the fact that the social world of children has become poisonous to their development. I offer this term as a parallel to the environmental movement's analysis regarding physical toxicity as a threat to human well-being and survival.

THE ECOLOGICAL PERSPECTIVE

An ecological perspective forces us to consider the concept of risk beyond the narrow confines of individual personality and family dynamics. Both are "causes" of parenting patterns and "reflections" of broader sociocultural forces. Viewing parents only in terms of individual and interpersonal dynamics precludes an understanding of the many other avenues of influence that might be open to policy or program interventions, or that might be topics of study for us as scientists.

Risks to parenting can come both from direct threats and from the absence of normal, expectable opportunities. The experience of homelessness is one example of a sociocultural risk factor that has profound implications for parenting. "Home" implies permanence. As a young homeless child wrote, "A home is where you can grow flowers if you want."[1]

Social policy operates through *macrosystems,* the broad ideological, demographic, and institutional patterns of a particular culture or subculture.[2] These macrosystems serve as the master "blueprints" for the ecology of human development. These blueprints reflect a people's shared assumptions about how things should be done, as well as the institutions that represent those assumptions. Religion provides a classic example of the macrosystem concept because it involves both a definition of the world and a set of institutions reflecting that definition—both a theology and a set of roles, rules, buildings, and programs. *Macrosystem* refers to the general organization of the world as it is and as it might be. Macrosystems are ideology incarnate.

An ecological perspective aids us in seeing the full range of alternative conceptualizations of problems affecting children and points us in the direction of multiple strategies for intervention, including macrosystems. Consider the case of child abuse. We need to look to the community that establishes laws and policies about child abuse, as well as to the families that offer a powerful definition of reality for the next generation. And we also should look to the culture that defines physical force as an appropriate form of discipline in early childhood. But we must also look within the individual, as a psychological system affected by conscious and changing roles, unconscious needs, and motives, to know why and how each adjusts in ways that generate conflict.

Social biology is a facet of the ecological perspective. In contrast to sociobiology, which emphasizes a genetic origin for social behavior, social biology concentrates on the social origins of biological phenomena, including the impact of economic conditions and social policy on brain growth and physical development. These social biological effects are often negative, e.g., the impact of poverty and famine on mental retardation and the mutagenic influence of industrial carcinogens. But they may be positive as well, e.g., intrauterine surgery and nutritional therapy for a fetus with a genetic disorder.

Social biology has profound implications for understanding issues of social policy as they affect parenting. For example, psychologist Arnold Sameroff and his colleagues report that the average IQ scores of four-year-old children are related to the number of psychological and social risk factors present in their lives.[3] These risk factors are manifest in or mediated by parenting, e.g., a rigid and punitive childrearing style, parental substance abuse, low parental educational attainment, father absence, and poverty.

But this research reveals that the relationship is not simply additive. The average IQ for children with none, one, or two of the factors is above 113. With the addition of a third and fourth risk factor the average IQ score drops precipitously to nearly 93, with relatively little further decrease as there is further accumulation of the fifth through eighth risk factors (average IQ score at 85). And, as the work of psychologists Carl Dunst and Carol Trivette reveals, the existence of special developmental opportunities helps to explain the variance in outcomes that are not accounted for when models simply address "risk."[4]

Research by child psychiatrist Michael Rutter and others shows that the stress of urban life associated with "family adversity" (Rutter's term) is most negative and potent for the development of young children (while it even stimulates some adolescents who have had a positive childhood).[5] Research that seeks to illuminate the impact of public policy on parenting should focus on the circumstances and conditions constituting adversity that are "growth-inducing," in contrast to those that are debilitating.

A HISTORICAL PERSPECTIVE

A focus on the too distant future is hardly the stuff of which politics—and thus policy—is made. In thinking about a vision for the twenty-first century we might well recall the issues of family policy at the start of the twentieth.[6]

The policy issues relevant to parenthood at the start of the twentieth century were these, among others:

- The problem of substance abuse and addiction was recognized as an insidious and powerful destructive force in family life.
- There was evidence of a widening gap between rich and poor, and already many voices called for action to improve the conditions of the poor, particularly the "worthy" poor.
- Traditional American values and institutions were being challenged by the influx of immigrants who did not speak English and who were perceived as making disproportionate demands on the human service systems and as suppressing wages by accepting low pay, long hours, and inferior working conditions.
- The legacy of slavery and the reality of racism lurked behind the public facade of democracy and broke out in dramatic incidents from time to time.
- To their contemporaries, growing numbers of girls and women appeared to be in moral jeopardy due to the frequency of premarital sex and pregnancy. The sex industry flourished.
- Child abuse was entering the public consciousness, and there was a sense that juvenile crime was escalating.

- Significant numbers of families were not "intact," as mothers frequently died in childbirth, and fathers often abandoned families.

Does this sound familiar?

Reading contemporary analyses of parenting issues, we see that there have been changes in the past hundred years: divorce and unmarried teen births have replaced maternal death and paternal separation in the dynamic of "incomplete" families; overtly homosexual adults now assert claims on parental roles publicly; efforts intended to integrate employment and maternity have become common; and a structural analysis of child abuse as a social problem has arisen.

As America approached the twentieth century some of the major ongoing themes of the national policy agenda were laid down: the costs and benefits of industrialization and a global economy; multiculturalism; "big government"; a human rights perspective on racism; militarism and empire; the emergence of "mass" media; and a search for the "American family."

At the beginning of the twentieth century the United States was being transformed by the seemingly unstoppable social logic of industrialism, and the country was fast becoming a major player in the global economy. Throughout this transformation, the look of America changed dramatically as we started full-scale the process of moving activities from the "nonmonetarized" to the "monetarized" economy and from an agrarian to an urban social model of society.[7]

A hundred years ago the progressive elements in American society began to believe that "big government" was required as a counterforce to "big business" if the best of America's commitment to human rights were to be preserved. This conflict came to a head during the New Deal of the 1930s, when the Roosevelt administration sought to throw the weight of the national government behind efforts to end the Great Depression. That conflict has continued to this very day.

The 1890s saw the initial creation of Imperial America: the America of the military-industrial complex, which projected power globally and imposed a market focus upon foreign policy. At the same time, America was challenged to refine the meaning of its core identity as an Anglo culture. De facto bilingualism in schools and neighborhoods contested with a strong "nativist" streak, an ironic term given the fact that truly *Native* Americans were completely excluded from this culture.

Finally, the rise of the "mass" media created a mechanism for a truly national consciousness and perhaps a *collective unconscious* formed by the implicit images that permeate the shared experience of those who read, listen to, and watch the same material.

THE RELATIONSHIP BETWEEN PARENTHOOD AND SOCIETY

At the heart of many parenthood policy issues is the matter of how and when families are private and how and when they are public. This issue arises in the context of child maltreatment as "the price of privacy," as well as in other situations in which children are understood to be (1) *citizens* with a primary relationship with the state, or (2) *members of families* with no direct link to the state under ordinary circumstances, or (3) the *private property* of parents.

A person who conceives a child can be seen as entering into a contract with the community. This "social contract" model provides a strong moral imperative for public efforts to ensure the safety and "quality" of the resulting child because a contract implies mutual obligations and rights. Contemporary policy debates reflect this fundamental issue when they focus on topics such as child welfare (is it an entitlement? a privilege? a tool for social control?), teen pregnancy (who has authority over a girl who gets pregnant?), and divorce and child support (is financial responsibility for a child purely a private contract issue between divorced adults or a public responsibility?).

Community mental health pioneer Gerald Caplan developed the concept of a social support system in the context of community mental health as *combining* evaluation and nurturance, that is, expecting the same professional to evaluate an individual's behavior on behalf of society and to offer psychological resources to that individual as a matter of that individual's human rights.[8]

But is social support a public matter? On one side of this debate are those who argue that families are essentially private, so the role of government in their care and feeding must be minimal, limited perhaps to the very most basic matters of child protection. They hold that the government should stand outside the family essentially as a bystander, perhaps intervening *in extremis* when there is no other last resort in the "private sector." Is there an authentically American alternative to this viewpoint?

The Declaration of Independence is the original "Contract with America," the touchstone for American public policy debate. In this document is found the essential (and for the time in which it was written, innovative) premise of American political ideology. The premise is not simply the assertion that "We hold these truths to be self-evident, that all men are created equal, that they are endowed by their creator with certain unalienable rights, that among these are life, liberty, and the pursuit of happiness."

The most important ideological innovation of the Declaration was its assertion "That to secure these rights governments are instituted." Here is the fundamental contract with America, the truly revolutionary principle that governments exist to secure basic human rights. The best of American history has been the refinement and the application of this contract—including efforts to rectify the original omissions in the Founders' language of the nonwhite and female and to translate this basic commitment in light of changing social conditions and technology.

This revolutionary concept of government as the guarantor of human rights is the appropriate starting point for our discussions of parenthood policy. The American idea is that government exists not to protect the rich or any other elite, nor to make the world safe for big business, nor to facilitate greed or self-interest, nor to promote a religious group's narrow agenda. Rather, the founders of the nation envisioned that the basic purpose of government is to secure basic human rights, unalienable rights. This is the appeal for those who insist that public policy should support the parental aspirations of homosexuals and teenage mothers. But it also appeals to those who insist that dangerous neighborhoods be restored to safety so children can escape trauma and abuse and that as economic structures change the needs of children remain paramount.

Today we wrestle with the complexities of translating the original "Contract with America" into the realm of contemporary parenthood policy. We face a bewildering patchwork of contradictory evidence. We must conduct policy analysis in a time of great public skepticism: whereas in 1975, 35 percent of American youth agreed with the statement "Most people can be trusted," by 1992 that figure had dropped to 19 percent. In the early 1960s, 77 percent of American adults in one poll agreed with the statement "You can count on the government to do the right thing most of the time." In 1998 only 22 percent did so. In addition, we are dealing with a plethora of well-financed, ideologically driven, and often self-interested groups advocating for privatization and "small government."[9]

The state plays an important role in setting the parameters for parental responsibility, and thus for the realms in which variations in parenting skill will affect child development. For example, most governments in the United States accept responsibility for providing basic services such as potable water and waste disposal. Borrowing a term commonly used in injury control, this is "passive prevention" in the sense that it requires no action on the part of parents to protect their children. In contrast, immunization programs require more active efforts of parents: to bring the young child to a facility that provides the immunization.

Passive prevention efforts in the form of community water and sewage systems absolve individual parents of the responsibility to provide clean water and to dispose of sewage. Making immunization an entrance requirement for mandatory schooling reduces the role of parental initiative.

Of course, the fact that less than 100 percent of young children are immunized is evidence of the "costs" of anything less than fully passive prevention. The deregulation of television programming aimed at children is a prime example of how public policy can affect the individual responsibility of parents.[10] Deregulating television programming aimed at children has increased the individual responsibility of parents to monitor and regulate the television viewing of their children.

If government did not assume responsibility for providing potable water and for sewage treatment, we would expect to find substantial variation in child health due to differences in parental skill, motivation, and resources, as we do in the areas of childhood television viewing and, to a lesser degree, immunization against childhood illnesses.

The conceptual issues involved emerge from the following personal account. When I moved to Illinois in 1985 I brought with me a three-year-old child and a three-year-old automobile. The State of Illinois sent clear messages regarding its conception of responsibility. The state required that the *car* be registered, that it be inspected on a regular basis, that I have liability insurance, and that I be licensed to operate the vehicle. The message was clear: cars are a public matter. With respect to my daughter, however, I received no messages of public interest. She was invisible to the state.

The basic understanding that children are public matters is the foundation for social policy that supports parenting. The conceptual framework for the qualitative issues in parenting policy that harmonize with our human rights legacy and our contemporary understanding of the human ecology of childhood lies in the concept of "social toxicity."[11]

THE CONCEPT OF SOCIAL TOXICITY

Fordham University's Institute for Social Policy produces an Index of Social Health for the United States, based upon sixteen measures including infant mortality, teenage suicide, school dropout rates, drug abuse, homicide, food stamp use, unemployment, traffic deaths, and poverty among the elderly. The index ranges between 0 and 100 (with 100 being defined as the most socially healthy). From 1970 to 1992 the index reported a decline from 74 to 41, and it remains at this level.[12] This means that the overall well-being of our society has decreased significantly.

The Index of Social Health tells an important story validated by other measures.[13] Young people *are* in trouble today. Evidence of this is found in research using the Child Behavior Checklist to assess the emotional and behavioral problems among American children. Parents, or other adults who know the child well, indicate the presence (or absence) and intensity of each of 118 specific behaviors or feelings in words such as "can't sit still, restless, or hyperactive," "lying or cheating," "feels worthless or inferior," "cruelty, bullying, or meanness to others," and "nervous, high-strung, or tense."

Since 1974, 45 of the 118 problems have become significantly worse for American children in general.[14] Negative feelings such as apathy, sadness, and various forms of distress have increased. Moreover, children report disliking school more. To some extent, this difference may result from greater awareness on the part of parents and teachers (the ones likely to fill out the survey). But it is more than just that.

In 1976, 3 percent of a representative sample of American children were seeing therapists. By 1989, that had grown to 8 percent. Greater awareness of problems may play a partial role in this, too, but there is more to it. In 1976, 10 percent of all children studied were judged to be doing so poorly that they could be *candidates* for therapy, even though only a third of these children actually received such therapy. By 1989, more than 18 percent of the children were doing badly enough in their behavior and development to warrant needing therapy, and about half were getting it.[15]

As ever larger numbers of our children display signs of experiencing serious problems we have to ask, "Why?" My own answer to this question is that children are most vulnerable to the negative influence of an increasingly *socially toxic environment*. Unless we do something about it now, the situation for children will only continue to deteriorate.[16]

In the last twenty years, some communities have improved the quality of their physical environment as enhanced public and professional awareness has led to changes. In the matter of recognizing, understanding, and reversing *social* toxicity, however, we lag far behind.

But what are the social equivalents to lead and smoke in the air, PCBs in the water, and pesticides in the food chain? Some social equivalents include violence, poverty, and other economic pressures on parents and their children. They include disruption of family relationships and other trauma, despair, depression, paranoia, nastiness, and alienation—all contaminants that demoralize families and communities.

Research on early brain development reveals that the elements of social biological toxicity most dangerous to the fetus and infant are those that lead to parental neglect and abuse and those that subject the very young child to other forms of trauma and deprivation. All these threats are related to the degree to which the social environment is supportive and benign as opposed to hostile and toxic.

How is the environment for children more socially toxic now than in the 1950s and even the 1960s? For one thing, no child ever died from a drive-by fist fight, and no mother then was terrorized by the prospect of such an assault to the degree that mothers living in "war zones" today fear that their children will be shot. The proliferation of guns among growing numbers of adolescent peer groups means that conflict and confrontation that once were settled with fists now can be "resolved" by shooting. More generally, children and youth must contend with a constant stream of messages that undermine their sense of security. If it is not the threat of kidnapping, it is the high probability of parental divorce. If it is not weapons at school, it is contemplating a future with dim employment opportunities.

There are many more subtle yet equally serious threats. High on the list is the departure of adults from the lives of children. The lack of adult supervision and of time spent doing constructive, cooperative activities are important toxic aspects of the social environment today. Children "home alone" are more vulnerable to every cultural poison they encounter than are children backed up by adults.

As the social environment becomes more socially toxic, it is the children, particularly the most vulnerable among them, who show the effects first and worst. And who are the children who will show the effects of social toxicity first and most dramatically? They are the children who already have accumulated the most developmental risk factors: poverty, racism, abuse, neglect, and absent or incapacitated parents.[17]

Imagine living in a city plagued by cholera. In this city, the challenge to parents to keep children healthy would be overwhelming. Yes, the most competent parents and those with the most resources would have more success delivering drinkable water to their children than would other parents. But even these "successful" parents would sometimes fail. Would we blame them for their failure or point the finger at the community's failed water purification system?

In a socially toxic environment the same principle holds. What we do on the policy front in support of parenthood in detoxifying the social environment will go a long way toward enhancing the quality of life for children and youth in the decades to come, when we really are facing the transition to the twenty-first century as issues of resiliency and coping become ever more important.

CLEANING UP OUR SOCIALLY TOXIC ENVIRONMENT

Convergent findings from several studies of resiliency and coping with stressful experiences during childhood suggest a series of ameliorating factors that lead to prosocial and healthy adaptability:[18]

- actively trying to cope with stress (rather than just reacting)
- cognitive competence (at least an average level of intelligence)
- experiences of self-efficacy and a corresponding self-confidence and positive self-esteem
- temperamental characteristics that favor active coping attempts and positive relationships with others (e.g., activity, goal orientation, sociability) rather than passive withdrawal
- a stable emotional relationship with at least one parent or guardian
- an open, supportive educational climate and parental model of behavior that encourages constructive coping with problems
- social support from persons outside the family

Of these seven factors identified in research on resilience and coping, several are particularly relevant to policy (and some of the others are indirectly relevant). In these three factors is the beginning of an agenda for policy initiatives to enhance parenting, particularly under conditions of high stress and threat.

The first factor is, of course, at the heart of our concern: "social support from persons outside the family." It tells us that the importance of social support increases inversely with the inner resources of the parent: the poorer need more help. Of course, here as elsewhere, we expect to find a kind of "catch-22" in operation: the more troubled and impoverished a parent, the less effective he or she will be in identifying, soliciting, and making effective use of resources outside the family.

The second resilience factor explicitly targets schools, religious institutions, civic organizations, and other social entities that operationalize the concept of "an open, supportive educational climate." Programs and role models that teach and reward the reflective "processing" of experience are an essential feature of social support at the neighborhood and community levels.

The third resilience factor is "a stable emotional relationship with at least one parent or guardian." In addition to having social support effectively available through friends, neighbors, coworkers, and professionals, parents also need social support in its most intensive form: they need "someone who is absolutely crazy about you." This is clear from research on parenting (children *must* have someone in this role), but it is also important in the functioning and development of youth and adults, including those in parenting roles.

It is important to remember that social support has at least two distinct dimensions. The first is its role in simply making the individual feel connected, which is important in its own right. The second is its role in promoting prosocial behavior (e.g., avoiding child maltreatment even under stressful conditions). In a socially toxic environment, policies designed to encourage social support are crucial.

CONCLUSION

This chapter examined several public policy issues that affect parenting including policies regarding state responsibility for children, economic conditions affecting families, the role of neighborhoods in family support, and the allocation of resources to prevention, intervention, support, and empowerment programs.

The foundation for social policy in support of parenting is the basic understanding that children are public matters and that there are qualitative issues involved in approaching the social environment. I think we can find a conceptual framework for understanding these qualitative issues in parenting policy that harmonize with our human rights legacy and contemporary understanding of the human ecology of childhood in the concept of social toxicity.

NOTES

1. Daly, M. (1990) The true meaning of "Home." *Better Homes Foundation 1989 annual report,* Boston.
2. Bronfenbrenner, U. (1979) *The ecology of human development: Experiments by nature and design.* Cambridge: Harvard University Press; and Bronfenbrenner, U. (1986) Ecology of family as a context for human development. *Developmental Psychology* 22: 723–742.
3. Sameroff, A., Seifer, R., Barocas. R., Zax, M., & Greenspan, S. (1987) Intelligence quotient scores of 4-year-old children: Social-environmental risk factors. *Pediatrics* 79: 343–350.
4. Dunst, C., & Trivette, C. (1992) Risk and opportunity factors influencing parent and child functioning. Paper based upon presentations made at the Ninth Annual Smoky Mountain Winter Institute, Asheville, North Carolina.
5. Garbarino, J. (1992) *Towards a sustainable society: An economic, social and environmental agenda for our children's future.* Chicago: Noble Press.
6. Garbarino, J. (1996) A vision of family policy for the 21st century. *Journal of Social Issues* 52: 197–203.
7. Garbarino, J. (1995) *Raising children in a socially toxic environment.* San Francisco: Jossey-Bass; and Garbarino, J., Stocking, H., et al. (1980) *Protecting children from abuse and neglect: Developing and maintaining effective support systems for families.* San Francisco: Jossey-Bass.

8. Caplan, G., & Killilea, M. (eds.) (1976) *Support systems and mutual help: Multidisciplinary explorations.* New York: Grune & Stratton.

9. Garbarino, J. (1995) *Raising children in a socially toxic environment.* San Francisco: Jossey-Bass.

10. Carlsson-Paige, N., & Levin, D. (1990) *Who's calling the shots? How to respond effectively to children's fascination with war play and war toys.* Philadelphia: New Society Publishers.

11. Garbarino, J. (1995) *Raising children in a socially toxic environment.* San Francisco: Jossey-Bass.

12. Miringhoff, M. (1996, May) A very different country. *The Fordham Institute for Innovation in Social Policy social report,* pp. 1–4.

13. Bronfenbrenner, U., McClelland, P., Wetherington, E., Moen, P., & Ceci, S. (1996) *The state of Americans.* New York: Free Press.

14. Achenbach, T., & Howell, C. (1993) Are American children's problems getting worse? A thirteen-year comparison. *Journal of American Academy of Child and Adolescent Psychiatry* 32: 1145–1154.

15. Ibid.

16. Garbarino, J. (1995) *Raising children in a socially toxic environment.* San Francisco: Jossey-Bass.

17. Dunst, C., & Trivette, C. (1992) Risk and opportunity factors influencing parent and child functioning. Paper based upon presentations made at the Ninth Annual Smoky Mountain Winter Institute, Asheville, North Carolina; and Sameroff, A., Seifer, R., Barocas. R., Zax, M., & Greenspan, S. (1987) Intelligence quotient scores of 4-year-old children: Social-environmental risk factors. *Pediatrics* 79: 343–350.

18. Losel, F., & Bliesner, T. (1990) Resilience in adolescence: A study on the generalizability of protective factors. In K. Hurrelmann & F. Losel (eds.), *Health hazards in adolescence.* Berlin: Walter de Gruyter.

20

The Media and Parents

Protecting Children from Harm

JOANNE CANTOR
and AMY I. NATHANSON

Concern about the impact of the mass media on children has surged in recent years—and rightly so. As more evidence of the harm that TV, movies, and videos can do accumulates, and as the media are becoming more pervasive, more intrusive, and more disturbing in content, many parents are at a loss as to what to do to protect their children.

Television seems to be an especially threatening presence because it brings into our homes so many things most parents would never *choose* for their children. No one delivers books or videos to our homes unordered, but television provides an outrageous array of disturbing content that is readily available throughout the day or night.

A lot of what television has to offer involves violence or the threat of harm in some way.[1] More important, the way violence is most frequently presented on television tends to promote children's learning that aggression is the first—not the last—resort and that it is an effective, easy, and even fun way to solve problems.

A review of the hundreds of studies of the effects of witnessed violence on behavior noted three particularly important harmful effects of viewing violence in the media.[2] First, it promotes the *adoption of aggressive attitudes and behaviors*. Second, it leads to *desensitization,* making children less sympathetic to the victims of violence. And third, exposure to violent depictions can cause an *increase in children's fears*. Much research suggests that television viewing is related to a host of negative outcomes in children.

This chapter focuses on the third area, the mass media and children's fears, because it is an important problem that has received much less attention than it deserves.[3] The book *Mommy, I'm Scared: How TV and Movies Frighten Children and What We Can Do to Protect Them* summarizes research findings in this area and makes recommendations to parents, childcare providers, and mental health professionals.[4]

OUR STUDIES OF MEDIA VIOLENCE

One way in which the long-term effects of the mass media on children's fears has been studied is by offering extra credit to first-year college students for saying yes or no to the question of whether they had ever been so frightened by a TV show or movie that the effect had lingered beyond the time of viewing.[5] If the students answered no, that is all they had to do, but if they said yes, they had to write a one-page paper about their reaction and then fill out a three-page questionnaire. Either way, they would get the same amount of extra credit. The results were astonishing. Out of 153 students given this opportunity to receive extra credit, 90 percent chose the yes response. Many of them wrote vivid, detailed descriptions of a program or movie that had frightened them years earlier, including heart-wrenching details of the repeated nightmares, obsessive thoughts, and long-term aversions that their exposure had brought on.

What Were the Residual Effects?

Of the 138 people who reported a lingering fright reaction, 22 percent reported mental preoccupation with what they had seen. In their words, they "couldn't get the movie off their mind" or "couldn't get those disturbing images out of their head." Thirty-five percent avoided or dreaded the situation depicted in the movie or program. For example, students reported effects like refusing to swim in the ocean after seeing *Jaws,* being apprehensive about taking a shower after seeing *Psycho,* dreading cats after seeing *Alice in Wonderland* or spiders after any number of arachnid-infested horror films. Eighteen percent generalized these aversions to related situations—for example, giving up swimming in lakes or even swimming pools after seeing *Jaws.* The most frequent residual effects involved disturbances in eating or sleeping; 52 percent reported these effects. Stomach aches and even vomiting were reported, but the more common effects were nightmares, the inability to get to sleep, and the refusal to sleep alone. In fact, the phrase "I slept with my parents for two whole weeks" is so common in such retrospective reports that the first chapter of *Mommy, I'm Scared* was named "The Suddenly Crowded Queen-Size Bed."[6]

How Long Did the Residual Effects Last?

The most remarkable data to emerge from this study relates to the duration of these residual effects. Only one sixth of these students said the effects lasted less than a day, and only a third said the effects endured less than a week. An astonishing 35 percent said the effects lasted more than a year. Finally, more than one fourth of these students said that the effects of what they had seen (an average of six years earlier) were still ongoing.

These same symptoms are frequently noticed by parents. In a random phone survey we conducted of parents of elementary school children in Madison, Wisconsin, sleep disturbances and stomach ailments were frequently reported as resulting from a child's viewing something frightening on TV.[7] A report from a mother recounts a typical scenario. She and her seven-year-old son were watching a program they both agreed was appropriate when she left the room briefly to answer the phone. By the time she returned, the program her child had been watching had ended, and she found her son staring at gory and grisly images from an episode of *The X-Files*. She made him turn off the program, but it was too late: her son woke up "in a fit" in the middle of the night and insisted on sleeping in his parents' bed, something that happened repeatedly over the course of several weeks. A month later, he was still worried that the horrible, totally unrealistic thing he had seen in the show would come and get him.

PREDICTING WHAT WILL FRIGHTEN CHILDREN

The bulk of *Mommy, I'm Scared* is not about chronicling the problem. It is about helping parents, caregivers, and mental health professionals predict the types of images and events in the mass media that frighten children of different ages and about describing the intervention and coping strategies that work with different-aged children. The book's conclusions and recommendations are based on more than fifteen years of research, using theories and findings in child development to make predictions and provide explanations.

There are two major things to remember when predicting what will frighten children between the ages of two and seven years. (The term *preschoolers* is used here, even though this age group extends into the early elementary school years.) Because preschoolers are most sensitive to appearances, *how things look* is of paramount importance. Several of our studies show that younger children are more likely to be frightened by something that *looks* scary but is actually harmless—a friendly mutant or a benevolent monster, for example—than by something threatening with a benign exterior, such as a handsome villain or a beautiful yet evil witch.[8] The second point is that because this age group has not fully grasped the fantasy-reality distinction, they are just as likely to be frightened by something that is totally impossible—a sorcerer casting an evil spell—as by something that is realistic and could actually harm them, such as a kidnapper or burglar.[9]

By the latter elementary school years, children become more sensitive to media stories about things that are dangerous but may not look scary and things that are realistic as opposed to fantastic or impossible. Children in this age group become increasingly sensitive to threats conveyed by the news; they understand that these events actually happened and could well happen to them.[10]

Younger children are not immune to the news, however. Younger children respond most strongly to real threats that are conveyed visually; for example, vivid footage of tornadoes, earthquakes, and floods especially terrifies preschoolers. Older children are more frightened by stories of kidnapping, murder, and molestation, especially if the victim is a child. These stories are usually less visual than stories of natural disasters because, fortunately for child viewers at least, these crimes are rarely caught on camera.

Even though teenagers have more resources to cope with their fears, they often have long-term fright responses to mass media presentations, whether fictional (in drama) or real (in the news). The two themes that emerge as the most terrifying to this age group are sexual assault and stories involving the supernatural and the occult.[11]

WHAT CAN PARENTS DO?

Mommy, I'm Scared also has chapters on how to reassure a child who has been frightened by something in the media. Again, two- to seven-year-olds are treated differently from older children. For preschoolers, as a chapter title suggests, "Words Won't Work."[12] It is especially ineffective to try to calm children in this age group by telling them that what they have seen is not real.[13] This technique does work for children eight and over. Of course, the remedy works only if the threat being witnessed is impossible as in a fairy tale, that is, it could never really happen to anyone. For preschool children, the fear-reducing techniques that work are nonverbal: a hug, a glass of water, or a distracting activity might help. This age group often requests and responds well to magical or mystical remedies, such as an Indian dream-catcher or a ritual check for creatures in the closet.

Older children are more responsive to reasoning, especially information on why the horrible thing cannot happen to them or how they can prevent it from happening. For all ages, the sympathetic attention of a concerned adult is probably the best medicine. Certainly the worst thing to do is to ignore, belittle, ridicule, or criticize a child for being frightened.

Research shows that the fears induced by exposure to television and films can be remarkably persistent and hard to undo. Therefore, it is wise to practice prevention whenever possible. But how are we to protect our children from choosing—or even stumbling across—a program or movie that may well cause long-lasting negative effects? The problem is a difficult one, but, in addition to information about what frightens children and which fear-reducing techniques are likely to work for different age groups, parents have some new tools to help them. These tools are certainly not the full answer, but they seem to be a step in the right direction.

TELEVISION RATING SYSTEMS

The Telecommunications Act of 1996 prescribed that, within a specified time, most new televisions would be manufactured with a V-chip. The V-chip, which is now mandatory in all new sets with a screen size of thirteen inches or larger, permits parents to block television programs that they feel are objectionable by working in conjunction with a television rating system. That is, television programs (except news and sports) receive ratings. Parents can use these ratings to block out programs.

The first television-program rating system was developed by the entertainment industry. This system, called the TV Parental Guidelines, went into effect in January of 1997 and was based on the Motion Picture Association of America's (MPAA) rating system for movies. The MPAA ratings suggest the appropriate age for viewing a program but do not indicate the content that is responsible for the age recommendations. MPAA ratings include the following four major levels: G (general audiences), PG (parental guidance suggested), PG-13 (parents strongly cautioned), and R (restricted). Similarly, the original TV Parental Guidelines included the following four ratings: TV-G (general audience), TV-PG (parental guidance suggested), TV-14 (parents strongly cautioned), and TV-MA (mature audiences only). One difference between the two systems is that the TV Parental Guidelines added a separate, two-level rating system for children's programs: TV-Y (all children) and TV-Y7 (directed to older children).

Although the idea of having a television rating system to serve parents' needs was a significant advance, many problems with the television industry's original system were quickly identified. The first major problem was that the system was not what parents wanted. Numerous national surveys were conducted to assess parents' preferences regarding the television rating system. These surveys (with the exception of one conducted by the television industry) reported overwhelming support for a system that indicates the content of programs as opposed to a system that makes age recommendations.[14]

The second major problem with the TV Parental Guidelines was that they were not likely to effectively warn parents about the kind of objectionable content (e.g., violence, sex, coarse language) television programs contained. This conclusion was based on the fact that the rating system that the TV Parental Guidelines were based on—the MPAA rating system—had been shown to be ineffective in communicating what kind of content coincides with particular movie ratings.[15] More recent data from television indicated that a program's TV Parental Guidelines rating was, for the most part, unrelated to the presence of violence.[16] Parents feel they know their own children better than anyone else, and different parents are concerned with different types of content on television.[17]

The third major problem with the TV Parental Guidelines was that they were considered likely to attract children to the very programs that parents want to shield them from. In other words, a child who sees that a program is rated TV-14 is likely to be more interested in seeing the program simply because of its restrictive rating. This expectation was based on two years of research conducted for the National Television Violence Study.[18]

For example, one experiment was conducted with children in Milwaukee who ranged in age from five to fifteen.[19] All of the children received booklets that contained the titles of fictitious movies and brief plot descriptions. All of the children read the same titles and descriptions. However, for one movie, one group of children was told it was rated G, another group was told that the same movie was rated PG, another group was told it was rated PG-13, another group was told it was rated R, and a fifth group did not receive any information about the movie's rating. The children were asked to rate how much they wanted to see each movie and were told that their ratings would influence which movie they would actually watch.

The results indicated that a movie's rating had a profound effect on its desirability, an outcome that has been dubbed the "forbidden fruit" effect. Among older children (ages ten to fifteen), interest in the movie was highest when it was rated either PG-13 or R and lowest when it was rated G. Although these ratings did not affect younger children (ages five to nine) overall, younger children who were more aggressive and those who were the heaviest viewers of television were the most interested in the movie when it was associated with a more restrictive movie rating.

In the same experiment, content-based rating systems were subjected to a similar test. For example, one of the other programs described in the children's booklets was randomly associated with violence designations used by the premium cable channels HBO, Showtime, and Cinemax. One group of children was led to believe that the program was rated "V: Violence," another group believed it was rated "MV: Mild Violence," another group believed it was rated "GV: Graphic Violence," and a fourth group was given no rating information. In contrast to the effects observed with the MPAA ratings, the violent content indicators did not stimulate children's interest in viewing the program. It does not appear, then, that all rating systems necessarily attract children to objectionable content. However, age-based systems like the MPAA ratings and, by extension, the TV Parental Guidelines, seem most likely to entice children to the programs parents want to protect them from.

In summary, the TV Parental Guidelines were problematic in their first version for three primary reasons: they did not reflect the type of television rating system that parents wanted, they were not likely to (and, in the case of violent content, they did not) communicate the kind of content that programs contained, and they were likely to attract children to problematic content rather than to deter them from viewing.

The original TV Parental Guidelines received intense criticism from child advocacy and mental health groups, including the National PTA, the Children's Defense Fund, the American Psychological Association, the American Psychiatric Association, and the American Medical Association. Based on these criticisms and pressure from parents in general and from members of Congress, the television industry agreed to modify the rating system in July of 1997, only six months after its original launching.

The new system was revised to add letters to the age-based ratings to indicate the content that led to the ratings decision. Thus, the letters V, S, L, and D were added to indicate the presence of violence, sex, coarse language, and suggestive dialog, respectively, in programs rated TV-PG, TV-14, or TV-MA. The letters FV (indicating "fantasy violence") were added to the ratings of children's programs to indicate the presence of "more intense" violence in those programs. The revised TV Parental Guidelines went into effect in October of 1997 and (as of the spring of 2000) are being used by all networks with the exception of NBC, which has kept the original age-based system, and BET (Black Entertainment Television), which is not rating its programs at all.

The amended rating system, by providing additional content information for parents, represents a significant improvement. However, problems remain with the new system. First, the revisions to the system did not eliminate the age-based component but merely added content letters to the original guidelines. It is therefore likely that the "forbidden fruit" effect of restrictive ratings will continue.

A second problem with the new system is that it is extremely complicated. Programs are now given such ratings as TV-PG-L, TV-14-DV, and TV-MA-S. Depending on the age-based rating a program receives, a parent needs to determine the level of violence, sex, or language that it contains. For example, a rating of TV-PG-V indicates that the program has "moderate violence," a rating of TV-14-V indicates that the program has "intense violence," and a rating of TV-MA-V suggests that the program has "graphic violence." Not only is this system confusing; little information is available that describes what the content letters mean or how they work in conjunction with the age-based ratings. The television industry has made very little effort to publicize or explain the amended system, and recent national surveys have shown that parents have very little understanding of what the letters mean or how the ratings work.[20] For example, a year and a half after the ratings were implemented, fewer than one third of parents who knew about the TV rating system were aware that producers or distributors rate their own programs. Furthermore, only 8 percent knew that FV stands for fantasy violence, and a mere 3 percent knew that D stands for suggestive dialog.

Beyond the obvious difficulties of the amended TV Parental Guidelines, one little-known loophole of the new system is that a programs that has different kinds of content appearing at different levels of intensity does not receive a rating that reflects the diversity of its content. That is, if a program has strong coarse language (and therefore deserves to be rated TV-14-L) *and* moderate violence (and therefore deserves a rating of TV-PG-V), only the TV-14-L rating is displayed. Therefore, a parent who wants to shield his or her child from programs with any kind of violence, regardless of how frequently or intensely it occurs, will find the revised TV Parental Guidelines misleading. A recent content analysis of the use of the new rating system indicates that most programs do not adequately represent the presence of sex, violence, and coarse language in their ratings.[21]

Theoretically, then, the television ratings provide one way for parents to protect their children from witnessing what parents judge to be potentially harmful television. In practice, however, it seems that the currently existing television rating system has a good deal of room for improvement in both design and implementation. Fortunately, parents need not rely exclusively on the television ratings to block out programs. Some television sets and other devices now permit parents to block unrated as well as rated programs.[22] The technology has already been developed to allow parents to block out programs by a variety of means in addition to ratings. If parents express enough demand, electronics manufacturers are likely to give them the products they need to protect their children.

CONCLUSION

In spite of increased public pressure on the entertainment industry to become more responsible, television and movies seem to be moving in the opposite direction. Violence, sex, and sensationalism seem to be garnering the highest ratings and the biggest profits, and the availability of this type of content is likely to increase rather than decrease in the coming years. But even if the television industry, or certain components of it, were to have a change of heart and become more responsive to parents' concerns, television will never change enough so that parents will be able to ignore its effects on their children. Parent education on the impact of television on children is becoming increasingly crucial, and anyone interested in children's welfare should make media education for parents and media literacy for children a high priority.

NOTES

1. Federman, J. (ed.) (1998) *Executive summary: National television violence study.* Santa Barbara: University of California, Center for Communication and Social Policy, vol. 3.
2. Wilson, B. J., Kunkel, D., Linz, D., Potter, J., Donnerstein, E., Smith, S. L., Blumenthal, E., & Berry, M. (1997) Violence in television programming overall. In Center for Communication and Social Policy (ed.), *National television violence study.* Thousand Oaks, Calif.: Sage, vol. 2, pp. 3–204.
3. Cantor, J. (1994) Fright reactions to mass media. In J. Bryant and D. Zillmann (eds.), *Media effects: Advances in theory and research.* Hillsdale, N.J.: Erlbaum, pp. 213–245; and Cantor, J. (1996) Television and children's fear. In T. MacBeth (ed.), *Tuning in to young viewers: Social science perspectives on television.* Thousand Oaks, Calif.: Sage, pp. 87–115.
4. Cantor, J. (1998) *Mommy, I'm scared! How TV and movies frighten children and what we can do to protect them.* San Diego: Harcourt Brace.
5. Harrison, K. S., & Cantor, J. (1999) Tales from the screen: Enduring fright reactions to scary media. *Media Psychology* 1(2): 97–116.
6. Cantor, J. (1998) *Mommy, I'm scared! How TV and movies frighten children and what we can do to protect them.* San Diego: Harcourt Brace.
7. Ibid.
8. Cantor, J., & Sparks, G. G. (1984) Children's fear responses to mass media: Testing some Piagetian predictions. *Journal of Communication* 34: 90–103; and Hoffner, C., & Cantor, J. (1985) Developmental differences in responses to a television character's appearance and behavior. *Developmental Psychology* 21: 1065–1074.

9. Cantor, J. (1998) *Mommy, I'm scared! How TV and movies frighten children and what we can do to protect them.* San Diego: Harcourt Brace.

10. Cantor, J., & Nathanson, A. I. (1996) Children's fright reactions to television news. *Journal of Communication* 46(4): 139–152.

11. Cantor, J. (1998) *Mommy, I'm scared! How TV and movies frighten children and what we can do to protect them.* San Diego: Harcourt Brace.

12. Cantor, J., & Wilson, B. J. (1988) Helping children cope with frightening media presentations. *Current Psychology: Research & Reviews* 7: 58–75.

13. Cantor, J., & Wilson, B. J. (1984) Modifying fear responses to mass media in preschool and elementary school children. *Journal of Broadcasting* 28: 431–443; and Wilson, B. J., Hoffner, C., & Cantor, J. (1987) Children's perceptions of the effectiveness of techniques to reduce fear from mass media. *Journal of Applied Developmental Psychology* 8: 39–52.

14. Cantor, J. (1998) Ratings for program content: The role of research findings. *Annals of the American Academy of Political and Social Science* 557: 54–69; and Cantor, J., Stutman, S., & Duran, V. (1996, November) *What parents want in a television rating system: Results from a national survey.* Report released by the National PTA, the Institute for Mental Health Initiatives, and the University of Wisconsin–Madison. Available at http://www.pta.org/programs/tvrpttoc.htm.

15. Cantor, J., Harrison, K., & Nathanson, A. (1997) Ratings and advisories for television programming. In Center for Communication and Social Policy (ed.) *National television violence study.* Thousand Oaks, Calif.: Sage, vol. 2, pp. 267–322.

16. Cantor, J., & Nathanson, A. (1998) Ratings and advisories for television programming. In Center for Communication and Social Policy (ed.) *National television violence study.* Thousand Oaks, Calif.: Sage, vol. 3, pp. 285–321.

17. Cantor, J., Stutman, S., & Duran, V. (1996, November) *What parents want in a television rating system: Results from a national survey.* Report released by the National PTA, the Institute for Mental Health Initiatives, and the University of Wisconsin–Madison. Available at http://www.pta.org/programs/tvrpttoc.htm.

18. Cantor, J., & Harrison, K. (1996) Ratings and advisories for television programming. In *National television violence study.* Thousand Oaks, Calif.: Sage, vol. 1, pp. 361–410; and Cantor, J., Harrison, K., & Nathanson, A. (1997) Ratings and advisories for television programming. In Center for Communication and Social Policy (ed.) *National television violence study.* Thousand Oaks, Calif.: Sage, vol. 2, pp. 267–322.

19. Ibid.

20. Kaiser Family Foundation (1999) *Parents and the V-chip.* Menlo Park, Calif.: Henry J. Kaiser Family Foundation.

21. Kunkel, D., Farinola, W. J. M., Cope, K. M., Donnerstein, E., Biely, E., & Zwarun, L. (1998) *Rating the TV ratings: One year out.* Menlo Park, Calif.: Henry J. Kaiser Family Foundation.

22. Cantor, J. (1998) *Mommy, I'm scared! How TV and movies frighten children and what we can do to protect them.* San Diego: Harcourt Brace.

21

The Impact of Welfare Reform on Families

The Wisconsin Experience

J. JEAN ROGERS
and HEIDI HAMMES

For more than sixty years, the Aid to Families with Dependent Children (AFDC) program was the nation's financial safety net for families. AFDC's intent was to assist families in financial crisis. In fact, the monthly benefits and the minimal work requirements contributed to a culture of poverty and dependency. Any income the recipient received—earned or unearned—reduced the AFDC payment and discouraged families from seeking other sources of income.

In August 1996, Congress passed the Personal Responsibility and Work Opportunity Reconciliation Act of 1996 (PRWORA), replacing the AFDC entitlement program with Temporary Assistance for Needy Families (TANF). TANF provides "block grants" to states, allowing them flexibility to implement an AFDC replacement program that serves the low-income families in their state.

Each of the fifty states is now engaged in redesigning its welfare programs for parents and children. This chapter is devoted to the experience of one state that illustrates the issues common to all states and the innovative processes developed by one.

BACKGROUND

During the AFDC era, Wisconsin's AFDC caseload grew steadily through ups and downs in the economy. By 1987, one hundred thousand families

(7 percent of Wisconsin's population) received a monthly AFDC check. Beginning in 1988 and continuing through the following decade prior to the implementation of Wisconsin Works (W-2), Wisconsin secured 227 waivers of federal law for demonstration projects aimed at reforming the welfare system. As the demonstration projects took effect, the caseload trend shifted, bringing the number of cases down to 34,491 by the time W-2 was implemented on September 1, 1997. As of September 2000, only 6,700 cash assistance cases remain. An additional 4,400 cases receive employment support through case management services.

WISCONSIN WORKS DESIGN

The first step in planning for Wisconsin Works (W-2) was to develop a core set of principles. This was based on input from hundreds of educators, service providers, clients, and employers, volumes of research, and the results of Wisconsin's welfare reform demonstration programs. The following principles were adopted:

1. For those who can work, only work should pay.
2. W-2 assumes everybody is able to work, or if not, at least capable of making a contribution to society through work activity within their abilities.
3. Families are society's way of nurturing and protecting children, and all policies must be judged in light of how well these policies strengthen and support the responsibility of both parents to care for their children.
4. The benchmark for determining the new system's fairness is by comparison with low-income families who work for a living, not by comparison with those receiving various government benefit packages.
5. There is no entitlement. The W-2 reward system is designed to reinforce behavior that leads to independence and self-sufficiency.
6. Individuals are part of various communities of people and places. W-2 operates in ways that enhance the way communities support individual efforts to achieve self-sufficiency.
7. The W-2 system provides only as much service as an eligible individual asks for or needs. Many individuals do much better with just a "light touch."
8. W-2's objectives are best achieved by working with the most effective providers and by relying on market and performance mechanisms.

W-2 Employment Ladder

The goal for all W-2 participants is self-sufficiency. For most individuals this requires full-time employment. Participants are placed on an employment ladder with four rungs according to their skills and circumstances. They are moved up the ladder as soon as possible:

1. *Unsubsidized employment.* Every job is a good start toward financial independence. The best way to prepare for a higher-paying position is to have a strong work history. Individuals entering W-2 who are ready for full-time employment do not receive payment but receive help finding a job to support their families. Participants may receive case management and other supportive services, such as food stamps, Medicaid, and childcare subsidies. There is no time limit associated with these services.

2. *Subsidized employment (Trial Jobs).* In certain circumstances (for instance, when an individual approaches W-2 with a willing attitude but without a work background), transition to employment is facilitated through a wage-subsidized trial job. Employers receive a maximum subsidy of $300 per month to cover the initial costs of new employee training and supervision. In exchange for the subsidy, the employer is expected to make a good-faith effort to hire the participant when the subsidy ends after three months.

3. *Community Service Jobs (CSJs).* CSJs are available for those who need to develop work habits and skills. While they are receiving work experience training up to thirty hours per week, CSJ participants also attend up to ten hours a week of education and training activities, such as basic education, high school equivalency classes, and short-term, employment-focused training. CSJ participants receive a W-2 payment of $673 per month reduced by $5.15 for each hour the individual fails to participate.

4. *Transition (W-2 T).* Individuals who are unable to perform independent, self-sustaining work in a CSJ are placed in W-2 T. They include individuals who have barriers to employment, such as mental or physical disabilities, and those needed at home to care for an ill or disabled family member. W-2 T participants engage in work activities consistent with their capabilities that improve their ability to work, including education and specialized skill training for the developmentally disabled or treatment for substance abuse. W-2 T participants receive a W-2 payment of $628 per month, reduced by $5.15 for each hour the individual fails to participate.

Time Limits

While eligibility for each of the W-2 employment positions (trial jobs, CSJs, and W-2 T) is limited to twenty-four months, total participation in W-2 is limited to sixty months over the participant's lifetime (whether consecutive or not). Extensions are determined on a case-by-case basis by the W-2 agency, subject to Department of Workforce Development review.

The time limits are a key element of W-2 for five reasons:

1. Time limits underscore a sense of urgency. People are procrastinators by nature, and a time limit makes it clear the program is temporary assistance.

2. Forging an attachment to the workforce takes time. A longer work history is insurance when times are tough and competition is stiff.

3. Case managers need to help people quickly. Staff need the push of a time limit as much as the clients do.

4. Employers need workers today, not tomorrow. The job that is there for the client today may be filled by someone else tomorrow.

5. A lifetime limit encourages people to treat government income assistance like an insurance policy or a savings account, to be used sparingly and only when it is the last resource available.

Eligibility

There are four categories of W-2 eligibility:

1. Custodial parents age eighteen or older with minors in their homes may be eligible for W-2 employment positions and case management services if the family has a gross monthly income that is less than 115 percent of poverty (about $1,356 per month for a family of three) and assets under $2,500, excluding the value of one home and up to $10,000 for a car.

2. Single noncustodial parents with child support orders whose children qualify for W-2 do not qualify for W-2 employment positions but have access to the full range of employment and other services available at Job Centers.

3. Pregnant women with no other custodial children meeting eligibility criteria may receive W-2 case management services and job search assistance. Once the child is born, the mother may be eligible for a $673 Caretaker of an Infant Benefit for up to twelve weeks without work requirements.

4. Minor parents qualify for case management and other W-2 related services, such as childcare, transportation, and health care, depending on the income and assets of the minor's parents.

Work Supports

W-2's success is a result of the increased investment in services that support parents' efforts to go to work. Wisconsin is spending an average of 45 percent more per case under W-2 than was spent under AFDC, while spending less overall because of fewer families needing cash assistance.

Once participants are employed, childcare subsidies, family health care coverage called BadgerCare, food stamps, Job Access Loans, education subsidies, federal and state earned income tax credits, and case management provide them with a network of support services that help them stabilize and prosper in their new work environment. Case management helps newly hired participants think through their work-related needs and provides the opportunity for long-term career planning and training targeted at advancement in the workforce.

W-2 is part of Wisconsin's larger employment and training system, which is run within full-service Job Centers throughout the state. The housing of all government employment services under one roof has helped to diminish the stigma placed on low-income families. Instead of going to a welfare office for a check, individuals now go to a Job Center for employment assistance. The unprecedented success with reducing the W-2 caseload has provided an opportunity to shift funding originally intended for cash assistance to new initiatives. These initiatives are enhancing W-2's ability not only to support parents' entry into the workforce but also to more broadly help both parents and children work toward their career and life aspiration. Recent initiatives include:

Workforce Attachment and Advancement. Provides postemployment services to help parents gain stability in their employment and pursue avenues for career development, higher wages, and better benefits.

Literacy Initiative. Establishes workplace and family literacy programs for low-income families to provide job-specific literacy and vocabulary skills to adults in the workplace and to provide child and family tutoring to improve the literacy skills of individual family members.

Community Youth Grants. Funds community programs that improve the social, academic, and employment skills of low-income youth.

SPECIAL NEEDS PROGRAMS

W-2 created two programs to serve individuals who either cannot or should not be required to participate in work training activities.

Children of Parent(s) on SSI. The Supplemental Security Income (SSI) program serves individuals with severe disabilities that prevent them from working. The maximum SSI benefit is $595 per month. If the parent in a single-parent household or both parents in a two-parent household are receiving SSI, the family is not eligible for W-2 but may receive Medicaid and a monthly cash supplement of $250 for the first eligible child and $150 for each additional child.

Kinship Care. Under the AFDC program, benefits were provided for children cared for by a non–legally responsible relative (NLRR). By caring for a child in need, NLRRs provide a public service and should not be required to participate in work training activities. As a result, Wisconsin created a special program, Kinship Care, for NLRRs. Caretaker relatives who are not parents of the child may apply for Kinship Care through their local social service or human service agency. In order to receive a Kinship Care payment, the placement must be because the child is at risk of abuse or neglect. If eligible, the Kinship Care payment is $215 a month, and the child may be eligible for Medicaid.

COMMUNITY INVOLVEMENT IN W-2

W-2 gives local agencies the flexibility to tailor programs to their communities, while providing the necessary safeguards to protect children and families at greatest risk. Some innovative features of W-2 were developed to meet this goal.

Community Steering Committee. Made up of community leaders from business, government, and the nonprofit sector, this group oversees the creation of job opportunities and assists in tailoring training programs to employ W-2 participants while meeting local business needs. The committee also works to find solutions to local childcare and transportation needs.

Children's Services Network. This network provides a link to the comprehensive array of services for children and families, including charitable food and clothing centers, transportation, and housing, regardless of whether the provider is public or private.

Community Reinvestment Funds. W-2 agencies that operate their programs below contract levels can use a portion of their unspent TANF funding to implement innovative projects that benefit low-income families (below 200 percent of poverty level). These Community Reinvestment Funds are to promote job retention, prevent recidivism, strengthen attachment to the workforce, increase participants' basic skills and literacy levels, provide parenting and life skills training, and broaden availability of supportive service such as childcare.

Special Initiatives in Milwaukee. In Milwaukee County, Wisconsin faces the most significant opportunity for using W-2 to improve not only the nature of public assistance but the quality of life within its communities.

Milwaukee agencies have been focusing their efforts on this issue through special initiatives. One of these programs is the Milwaukee Jobs Initiative (MJI) project, which works with employers, central-city residents, community-based organizations, government, and public and private training institutions to connect unemployed and underemployed central-city residents with permanent, family-supporting employment. The program's goal also is to keep them employed and to provide opportunities for advancement. Another is the Job Ride program, which provides a transportation link between disadvantaged unemployed or underemployed persons living in urban Milwaukee County and job opportunities in suburban areas inaccessible by public transportation.

W-2 PERFORMANCE STANDARDS

In order to achieve a high level of performance and results, W-2 eliminated the "entitlement" that counties were given as a sole service provider of assistance and replaced it with a set of performance standards. County agencies that fail to meet these performance standards have to compete with the private sector for the W-2 contract. This competitive process to select the best and most enthusiastic providers is integral to W-2's success.

As part of the biennial competitive Request for Proposal process, organizations that submit a proposal to operate a W-2 agency must describe their plan for staffing the agency, determining staff qualifications, and ensuring staff are appropriately trained. In addition, W-2 agencies must ensure that each W-2 caseworker serve no more than fifty-five cash assistance cases and no more than 125 cases total, including those receiving only case management services. As part of their professional development, caseworkers are required to participate in a continuum of state-provided training sessions on a variety of case management topics.

A combination of public, private for-profit, and nonprofit W-2 agencies operate in each of Wisconsin's seventy-two counties and two Indian tribes. Because of its size, the program operation in Milwaukee County is broken down further, into six regions. Contracts with the state require all eighty W-2 agencies to meet specific performance criteria, including such measures as participants' job skills attainment, job placement and wage rates, job retention rates, and availability of employer health insurance benefits.

W-2 CHALLENGES

While W-2 has successfully moved parents into the workforce and out of poverty, challenges remain for families in the program. Some will need intensive services provided by other community programs and institutions as partners to overcome formidable barriers. Among the more pressing challenges are family member disabilities, substance abuse, domestic violence, teenage pregnancy, school dropouts, and child abuse and neglect.

Family Member Disabilities

Participants with barriers such as physical or cognitive disabilities or mental health problems are assessed to determine their ability to become employed based on the individual circumstances presented. The services provided through W-2 depend on the type and severity of the disability. Agencies such as the Division of Vocational Rehabilitation, and other counseling and treatment facilities, may provide services in coordination with a W-2 agency to assist participants in moving toward employment. A participant with a severe disability will be assisted by the W-2 agency to apply for benefits through the Social Security Administration. Under certain circumstances a participant can be assigned activities related to the care of another family member.

Substance Abuse

Under W-2, no one is excused from participation, resulting in some drug- or alcohol-addicted parents having work requirements for the first time. Substance abuse problems present states and local communities with unique challenges in meeting the goal of moving people from welfare to work and the integration of recovery and employment activities.

Under the direction of Wisconsin's governor, Tommy Thompson, the W-2 & Alcohol and Other Drug Addiction (AODA) Task Force was charged with promoting collaboration and partnerships to more effectively address the needs of W-2 participants. Their recommendations, including early identification, intersystems collaboration, and comprehensive case management, are the primary mechanisms for addressing substance abuse within welfare reform and are the first steps in breaking down this barrier to employment.

Domestic Violence

A November 1998 report to congressional committees by the U.S. General Accounting Office noted that from 33 to 60 percent of the women in five surveys reported that their partner prevented them from working.[1] Under W-2, case managers work closely with victims of domestic abuse and refer them for other needed services to overcome special barriers that might exist.

Teen Pregnancy

W-2 offers no cash assistance to parents under the age of eighteen. Instead, minor parents are expected to live with an adult parent (who may participate in W-2), with an adult relative (who may receive a Kinship Care grant to care for the children), or in another adult-supervised living arrangement (such as a group home or foster care). Under these living arrangements, W-2 case management services and childcare assistance are available so that they can attend school and prepare for a career.

School Truants/Dropouts

The goal of Learnfare is to help children of W-2 participants fulfill their potential in life by providing programs and opportunities that enable them to attend and complete school, obtain employment, and break the cycle of welfare dependency. Learnfare case management is offered to all school-age children in W-2 and is required for those children who are habitual truants, minor parents, or not enrolled in school.

Child Abuse and Neglect

Although W-2 agency staff are not trained to directly respond to child abuse in a family, as public employees they are mandated reporters of abuse and neglect and are required by law to submit a report of suspected child abuse to the local child welfare agency.

W-2 EVALUATION PROJECTS

The W-2 Management Evaluation Project (MEP) is an umbrella organization created to manage and coordinate the state's own evaluation program with the help of outside specialists. It is administered by the Hudson Institute and managed by a steering committee made up of both Department of Workforce Development leadership and evaluation staff and independent academics nationally and locally recognized as experts in public assistance assessment and evaluation.

The W-2 MEP has two evaluation strategies. *Summative* activities address the effects of W-2 on Wisconsin's families, especially those at risk of needing public assistance, the attitudes of the state's taxpayers, and the costs to state government. The *formative* aspects of W-2 implementation recognize the importance of understanding the management issues involved in implementing and administering W-2.

Under the guidance of the MEP in collaboration with the Department of Workforce Development, twenty-five studies focus on the status and program usage of low income persons. Six examples follow.

Survey of Those Leaving AFDC or W-2. This study examines individual efforts to obtain employment and to remain employed, quality of life issues, and supports to self-sufficiency, such as childcare, medical insurance, and transportation. It includes 547 individuals who participated in W-2 and/or AFDC during any part of the three-month period between January 1, 1998, and March 31, 1998, who ended their participation in the program prior to April 1, 1998, and who had not returned to welfare as of the date of their interviews.

Child Support Waiver Demonstration Project (CSWD). This study by the Institute for Research on Poverty (IRP) at the University of Wisconsin–Madison uses a control/experimental design. It compares eight thousand individuals receiving full child support with individuals receiving partial child support.

Survey of Former AFDC Recipients in Milwaukee. This study is a joint effort by the Hudson Institute and Mathematica Policy Research. It tracks three hundred individuals on AFDC from August 1997 to March 1998.

National Survey of America's Families (NSAF). This study consists of three data collection efforts by the Urban Institute's Assessing the New Federalism (ANF) project. A comprehensive survey completed in 1997 and 1999, with a third wave planned for 2001, covers a variety of topics related to work, family well-being, health insurance access, and childcare. The survey also measures the interviewees' participation in job training and other social services programs. The 1999 survey of 42,000 households included representational samples in thirteen states as well as a comparable sample of households in the rest of the nation.

Wisconsin Public Assistance Database (WisPAD). This project explores the feasibility of developing a permanent longitudinal set of linked administrative and survey data.

What Happens to Families under Wisconsin Works. This study examines twelve hundred applicants to the program in Milwaukee during the fall of 1998 when they entered the W-2 Agency and one year later.

RESULTS OF W-2

The statewide average starting wage for W-2 participants is currently $7.60 per hour. But even parents starting out in a minimum wage position are doing much better off financially.

A single mother with two children who is working full-time at minimum wage is eligible for both the state and federal earned income tax credit, food stamps, and a childcare subsidy. After deducting her childcare copays and the Social Security tax, her annual take-home income plus food stamps is $16,070. This is over $6,000 more than she would have received under AFDC. Additionally, the working mother's growing employment experience is the best ticket to higher paying wages.

Public Opinion Poll

A large majority of Wisconsin residents have a positive opinion of W-2, according to the most recent Wisconsin Poll conducted by the Institute for Survey and Policy Research at the University of Wisconsin–Milwaukee. Of those surveyed, 76 percent are in favor of the W-2 program while only 12 percent oppose it, and 83 percent think W-2 has been either somewhat or very effective in getting people off welfare and into work.

Survey of Those Leaving AFDC or W-2

These are some of the key findings of the survey:

Of the 547 participants, 62 percent were employed at the time of the interview, and 21 percent were not but had been in the workforce at some time since leaving welfare, totaling 83 percent. Thus, only 17 percent had never been employed since leaving welfare.

Of leavers with current or prior jobs:

- 12 percent worked at least two jobs, and 4 percent had three or more.
- 57 percent worked 40 or more hours per week, 23 percent worked 30–39 hours, 10 percent 20–29 hours, and 9 percent 20 or fewer hours.
- The average wage was $7.42. The median was $7.00.
- The average was 61 weeks in their current jobs with a median of 34 weeks.

When interviewed, 38 percent of leavers were not currently employed. They gave the following reasons for not working:

- 33 percent responded that they could not find a job or could not find a job that paid enough, or they didn't have the skills or experience necessary to get a job.
- 32 percent had an illness or injury, or they had to care for someone else.
- 21 percent had childcare problems.
- 21 percent wanted to stay with children or were recently or currently pregnant.

- 16 percent had been laid off, had quit, or had been fired.
- 12 percent had transportation problems.
- 7 percent were in full- or part-time education or job training.

Family support was received by 94 percent of nonworking leavers:

- 18 percent lived with a working spouse/coparent.
- 53 percent received some type of cash benefit, such as Social Security, but did not live with a working spouse or coparent.
- 23 percent received noncash benefits but did not live with a working spouse or coparent or receive cash benefits.

Leavers mentioned receiving the following benefits or supports:

- 71 percent—Medicaid
- 49 percent—food stamps
- 47 percent—school lunch program
- 38 percent—WIC Supplemental Nutrition
- 27 percent—child support
- 25 percent—rent subsidy or public housing

The survey also found that 87 percent of leavers had health insurance coverage from some source, usually Medicaid or private insurance; 66 percent of preschool children were in childcare, and 30 percent of school-age children had pre- or after-school care.

The percentage employed at the time of the interview closely mirrors Wisconsin's statewide adult employment rate of 69 percent, among the highest in the United States. The average wage cited by those employed is well over federal minimum wage and comes close to the $7.50 wage often identified by those who favor the "living wage" concept. In general, people are getting jobs that, when combined with food stamps and the state and federal earned income credit, lift them out of poverty. The findings also tell us that for most who are not employed, other types of income or support are helping them meet their day-to-day needs.

The main reasons given for not being on welfare when interviewed were as follows:

- 54 percent said they left welfare for employment related reasons.
- 34 percent said they did not want to be on welfare.
- 16 percent said they left because they did not want to or could not participate in welfare program requirements.
- 11 percent said they were disabled and unable to work.

We expect that individuals will generally fall into one of four categories: (1) those who have found work and no longer need W-2; (2) those for whom the W-2 work requirements were too high a price to pay; (3) those who gained help or resources from other sources; and (4) those who should have stayed in the program. Some of the reasons listed raise concerns. Although the numbers are low, they are a reminder to everyone who works with this program that some families who leave it will still be in need of some type of assistance. One key lesson we have learned is that continued careful attention must be paid to communicating information about the resources that remain available to people, such as food stamps and Medicaid, who leave W-2 for jobs.

What should be emphasized is not that an unusual number of leavers are working but that work levels are normal or better compared to the old program, even as caseloads decrease at a dramatic rate. Thousands of people believed to be hard to employ are off the rolls—and yet work levels are on a par with states that have reformed less radically.

The National Survey of American Families (NSAF)

The following are among the key findings from the Urban Institute's National Survey of American Families:

- Just over two thirds of Wisconsin's children live with two biological or adoptive parents, a percentage significantly higher than that for the country as a whole.
- 80 percent of Wisconsin's low-income single parents (below 200 percent of poverty level) are employed, compared with 67 percent nationally.
- Wisconsin's 9.7 percent poverty rate among nonelderly adults and children is significantly lower than the national rate of 17.5 percent.
- Low-income families in Wisconsin reported fewer problems with assuring adequate access to food and fewer problems paying for shelter than families in the same income group elsewhere in the country.
- Just under 15 percent of children in low-income families in Wisconsin reportedly lack current health insurance coverage, compared to 22 percent nationwide.

RELATED RESEARCH

Research on the impact of welfare reform on individuals and families is being conducted throughout the nation. Some early reports follow.

Deborah Lowe Vandell of the University of Wisconsin–Madison and Janaki Ramanan of the University of Texas at Dallas studied 224 second graders from low-income, high-risk families.[2] Contrary to those who have argued that extensive early employment results in problematic child development, this study finds positive effects of early employment. If the mother worked moderately or extensively during the child's first three years, the family was less likely to be living in poverty four years later. Children scored lower on reading and math tests when their mothers either did not work or worked very little compared to mothers who worked more during the first three years of a child's life.

A recent study by Elizabeth Harvey at the University of Connecticut looked at effects of early parental employment on children in the National Longitudinal Survey of Youth. She found that overall there were no significant effects on young children when parents go to work. However, early parental employment was somewhat more beneficial for children of single mothers and lower-income families, positively affecting children's behavior and academic achievement.[3]

This study, along with another by Sonalde Desai, Robert T. Michael, and P. Lindsay Chase-Lansdale, indicates that "the income and resultant improved environment may outweigh effects on the child that result from mother-child separation or less effective child care."[4]

A multisite project entitled "Welfare Reform and Children: A Three-City Study" will follow 2,800 families for four years as welfare reform evolves in Boston, Chicago, and San Antonio. A preliminary report of fifteen focus groups revealed that the participants were cautiously optimistic. They expressed support for work requirements as long as exceptions were made for parents who could not find adequate childcare or had children with special needs. They suggested that there be more time for transition to work and better provisions for childcare, education, training, medical coverage, and learning English.[5]

These studies are a sample of evidence that mothers who work outside the home, in providing increased income and positive role models, are beneficial to their children's development. Although there are many calls for government to take on direct responsibilities for ensuring the well-being of children, at the end of the day, government cannot raise children; only the parents can.

CONCLUSION

W-2 is addressing the fundamental issues at the heart of welfare dependency using the lessons learned from the failed AFDC system. Unlike AFDC, W-2 seeks to move all families toward self-sufficiency and a better way of life by tailoring employment services to the needs of the participants and their families. Parents once thought to be unemployable because of personal barriers are being offered a legitimate opportunity to address their needs through counseling and treatment, literacy programs, or vocational rehabilitation. After W-2 participants begin a job, they qualify for more support than they could ever have attained without working. W-2 does all it can to keep them working and help them move into better jobs as well.

While W-2's emphasis is on helping parents obtain and maintain employment, it is our expectation that the greater outcome will be improvement in the quality of life of the family. Research indicates that children from low-income working families are better off than their counterparts with welfare-dependent parents.

By breaking the welfare cycle, we can help to overcome the larger problems of the inner city. Welfare dependency is at the center of the web, and if we make it work appropriately, we can hope to untie the Gordian knot of poverty in America.

W-2 represents a public work effort critical to the future of Wisconsin and, indeed, the nation.

NOTES

1. U.S. General Accounting Office (1998*) Domestic violence: Prevalence and implications for employment among welfare recipients.* Washington, D.C.: U.S. General Accounting Office.

2. Vandell, D. L., & Ramanan, J. (1992) Effects of early and recent maternal employment on children from high risk families. *Child Development* 63: 939–949.

3. Harvey, E. (1999) Short-term and long-term effects of early parental employment on children of the National Longitudinal Survey of Youth. *Developmental Psychology* 35: 445–459.

4. Desai, S., Michael, R. T., & Chase-Lansdale, P. L. (1990) The home environment: A mechanism through which maternal employment affects child development. Population Research Center at NORC and University of Chicago: Paper no. 90–9.

5. Angel, L., Burton, L., Chase-Lansdale, P. L., Cherlin, A. J., Moffit, R., & Wilson, W. J. (1998) *Welfare reform and children: A three-city study.* Baltimore: Department of Sociology, Johns Hopkins University.

22

Neighborhoods and Communities That Support Parenthood

LISBETH B. SCHORR

In order to succeed in life, children need supportive families. In order to be successful parents, many parents need support and education. This chapter defines two kinds of parent education and shows why the most effective kind of parent education requires supportive neighborhoods and communities.

I distinguish between two kinds of parent education that raise very different kinds of policy issues: *didactive* and *interactive.*

DIDACTIVE PARENT EDUCATION

Didactive parent education aims to transfer knowledge and information. The person who has knowledge and information tries to transmit it to persons who lack it, usually in a classroom setting.

The didactive form of parent education has been the most popular because it is easier to carry out, is less expensive, and requires less training. When parent education is mandated by a court in a child abuse situation, it is likely to be the didactive form with the hope that a few classes in childrearing will solve the problem. However, didactive parent education has never been shown to influence parenting practices among those at highest risk.

Didactive parent education has analogs in other fields. A physics teacher who teaches simply by lecturing does not really have to understand physics. If you give her the right materials, she can read them or memorize them. She may not be able to figure out why a particular student does not understand a particular concept, because she does not understand enough about the concept herself to be able to diagnose the student's problem. In the same way, a parent educator who tries to teach a parent that a two-year-old's playing with his food is not a punishable offense has to get beyond the curriculum materials if she wants to understand why that information does not change the parent's behavior.

INTERACTIVE PARENT EDUCATION

The second type of parent education is interactive, based on the idea that how one parents depends on one's own experiences as much as it does on information. It is much more individualized and supportive. It most frequently takes place in a setting where other activities are also going on: a Head Start center, a parent support center, or a home.

Interactive parent education is extremely important for parents who did not experience good parenting, who are trying to change not only what they know but how they feel and how that affects their behavior, or who are trying to raise their children in neighborhoods that do not support childrearing.

Some attributes of interactive parent education are important to think about because the very characteristics that make it effective also make it hard to spread and sustain. In my book *Within Our Reach,*[1] I identified the attributes of a variety of effective programs in several domains:

- They are being flexible and responsive. Sister Mary Paul, who runs a family service agency in Brooklyn, reports that nobody in the program ever says, "This may be what you need, but it is not part of my job to help you get it."
- They deal with children in the context of families and families in the context of neighborhoods.
- They are rooted in the community.
- They have a long-term preventive orientation.
- They continue to evolve over time in response to changing circumstances and lessons learned.
- They operate in settings that support high quality standards.
- Their managers are supportive and hold staff accountable for achieving shared purposes.
- They operate with enough intensity and perseverance to achieve agreed upon outcomes.
- They encourage staff to expand the boundaries of their job description and to build strong relationships based on mutual trust and respect.

These are the characteristics that make the best kinds of parent education so difficult to sustain and spread. When I found that almost half of the effective programs described in *Within Our Reach* had gone out of existence within a few years, I tried to understand why they were not sustained even though they had succeeded in achieving their goals. I found that the organizations that fund, regulate, hold accountable, and even mandate specific services are not a good fit with most of what we know works best.

People running successful programs tell you that they are swimming upstream. Whether they are working on school reform, early childhood, family support, child protection, or welfare-to-work, they must surmount obstacles put in their way by the organizations that fund and regulate them. The people and places that were able to implement and sustain responsive and flexible programs adopted new strategies to make systems more hospitable to effective interventions. These strategies had a number of common elements that are the basis of my book *Common Purpose*.[2]

STRATEGIES OF EFFECTIVE EFFORTS TO SPREAD AND SUSTAIN WHAT WORKS

One of the big mistakes we have been making in the social policy arena is to assume that front-line program people can make the necessary changes in systems in order to make them supportive of our best programs. Many of the most promising strategies now require vertical alliances between front-line people who know what works and what is important to sustain and the people who have the clout to change the rules under which the front line operates.

Focus on Results

The first of these strategies is to *focus on results*. Successful programs focus unambiguously on results as a way of taming bureaucracies, to make sure that funders and voters know that they are accomplishing the outcomes the public cares about, and to make sure that every activity they undertake is clearly linked to the outcomes they are trying to achieve. Some of those outcomes are more measurable than others, but, to the extent that we can identify outcomes that show that we are achieving shared purposes, we trade accountability for *outcomes* for accountability for *complying with rules*.

For example, in *Within Our Reach* I described a demonstration home-visiting program in Elmira, New York. That program documented reductions not only in child abuse, which was its primary purpose, but also in the hospitalization of infants and in long-term outcomes of mothers who returned to school or work and who were more effective parents. When the foundation funds ran out, the city of Elmira was so impressed with the outcomes of the demonstration that they took it over and funded it with Medical Assistance funds. Because funds were limited and they wanted to reach more families, the city diluted the program. Oblivious to the effect on outcomes, they doubled the nurses' caseloads. They cut the amount of time that the nurses could spend with families. They stopped the visits to each home when the baby was four months old. Then they were surprised that they did not get the same results.

Attention to outcomes also promises to reduce some of the long-standing confusion between the means and ends of intervention. There always is a temptation to fall back on process measures as evidence of progress. When you count the number of people who are attending a class, you at least can show that something is happening. This is what you have to do when you are woefully underfunded, as so many of these programs are. You get the grant with the promise of reducing child abuse and teenage pregnancy, and after a year the evaluators come and want to document reductions in child abuse and teen pregnancy rates. The program people say, "But it's absurd to think that we could reduce child abuse and teenage pregnancy with twenty thousand dollars in this community of fifty thousand families." The evaluator replies, "You are right. Let's figure out what we can count that will show that something is happening, such as counting the number of people attending parent education classes."

A focus on results forces funders and evaluators and program people to be much more realistic about what they can accomplish. It forces a discussion of whether we really want to continue to fund some of the most important family support programs "on the cheap"—or do we want to invest enough so that we can change outcomes? Inner-city neighborhoods and other places that are seriously depleted require a critical mass of intensive and interactive intervention to change outcomes. Especially for them, a focus on results can help funders and program people resist temptations to hide the limitations of so many of their current efforts. Such a focus clarifies the fact that single circumscribed interventions often are not sufficient to change outcomes.

Adapt Models to Local Circumstances

A second strategy of effective programs is that they do not try to use a cookie-cutter method of replication. They *do not expect a single model to be effective* everywhere in exactly the same form that made it succeed in another time and place. They try to sort out essential principles from the attributes of the program that can be shaped to fit a community's needs and strengths and desires. When people say, "We really should not have to reinvent the wheel," I say to them that parts of the wheel often do have to be reinvented. However, time, money, and energy can be saved—

even in reinventing the wheel—when outsiders provide local entrepreneurs with the formula for calculating the circumference of the wheel and with information about the materials that go into sturdy spokes. The local wheels that work smoothly typically involve imported principles together with local construction.

Use Intermediary Organizational Support

A third strategy of successful programs is that they *create or utilize intermediaries.* The scale-up of successful programs rarely occurs without the support of outsiders. Almost uniformly the successful initiatives I have studied received crucial help in developing and sustaining reform from some sort of intermediary organization that offered expertise, outside support, legitimization, opportunities for networking and peer dialogue, and the clout to help change the rules under which the intervention operates. Every one of the systems and institutions in which scale-up efforts try to gain a foothold contains features that eventually exhaust reformers by forcing them back into the status quo. Intermediary organizations can support and strengthen local reformers in countering these pressures.

Cross-System Partnerships

A fourth strategy is *establishing partnerships* between formal systems and community-based organizations. These partnerships often are essential because many prevailing services are removed physically, psychologically, and administratively from the communities they serve. For example, in child welfare we see more child protection agencies partnering with networks of community organizations so that they can make families and neighborhoods, including churches, part of their efforts to strengthen families and protect children. Partnerships do a lot to increase the chances that neighbors will help neighbors. They help families feel less isolated in their childrearing and respond to a family's self-defined needs for help. They bridge the gulf of mistrust between public agencies and the community.

Long-term View

A fifth strategy is taking a *long-term view of change.* Outcomes do not change overnight. Politicians who expect you to be able to change behavior that is rooted in a long personal history and powerful social forces during the two years they hold office are spitting into the wind. We have to convince them that it cannot be done. We need interim indicators to show that we are making progress toward long-term goals. But we cannot promise that most of these life-changing interventions will succeed quickly.

A long-term view of change also means a two-generation focus, recognizing that strong families are the keys to healthy children. Often parents must be nurtured so that they can nurture their own children. A long-term view of change also requires that the interests of children not be sacrificed to short-term efforts to move their parents into the workplace in welfare reform efforts.

When you superimpose the findings of brain research showing the importance of the early years onto new welfare policies, our laissez-faire attitude about childcare during the early years becomes totally untenable. It is untenable for government to say, "We will force you to leave your children"—in Wisconsin at the age of twelve weeks—"and we take no responsibility for what happens to those children." While welfare reform provides some childcare subsidies, we do not have a system that will make certain that childcare is accessible, affordable, and of high quality.

In New York City mothers are told that their benefits will be reduced if they do not use whatever childcare is offered to them. The *New York Times* reported recently that a mother found her fourteen-month-old toddler's "day care" consisted of spending eight hours a day tied to a dirty stroller. She told the welfare office that she was not going to leave her child under those conditions and said, "If I can't find other childcare, I'm not going to work." The welfare worker said, "You will be docked on your welfare check." Since we know how to do this right and since there are plenty of examples showing how to do it right, it is difficult to understand why we allow this scandal to persist. Why do we not have more of a sense of outrage about what is going on?

Perhaps part of the answer is that people do not believe that government can do anything right, and therefore government subsidies and standards will not do it right. Columnist William Raspberry writes, "You don't have to be mean-spirited to walk away from social problems, you just have to believe that nothing can be done to solve them." This pervasive distrust of government in our country today is getting in the way of acting on so much of what we know.

Safe Neighborhoods

The sixth strategy involves *making neighborhoods safe and protective places* in which to bring up children. The influence of neighborhoods on families and life outcomes has long been apparent to people working on the front lines, although research in this area was almost nonexistent for many years. But the influence of neighborhoods on individual outcomes now has become a hot topic again. We owe so much to Urie Bronfenbrenner (see chapter 17) for pointing out long ago how crucial it was to understand the ecology of childhood. The latest research shows that even the best parents have a hard time rearing their children well in violent, chaotic neighborhoods.

Children who are blessed with extraordinary resiliency or unflagging adult support can beat the odds against growing up well in very depleted neighborhoods, but we have to change those odds. Some of the most encouraging things I see around the country are efforts to do just that by putting together what we know works in specific neighborhoods and by addressing directly the challenge to build communities and restore bonds of trust among neighbors.

Not long before he was killed, presidential candidate Robert F. Kennedy called attention to the destruction of the thousand invisible strands of common experience and purpose, affection, and respect that tie people to their fellows. He believed that the world and the neighborhood "had become impersonal and abstract, beyond the reach of individual control and even understanding." In his 1968 presidential campaign he called for the restoration of communities as places "where people can see and know each other, where children can play, and where adults work together and join in the pleasures and responsibilities of the place where they live."

When we think about community as broadly as Robert Kennedy did, we realize how closely a thriving community is connected to the ability to be an effective parent. People who are engaged in community building today recognize that formal services are not enough, that you cannot service people out of poverty. You cannot even service children into school success. It takes more. That is why successful community-building efforts act in more than a single domain, and why many of those community-building efforts are reaching out to people who are working with parents and could become partners in this effort to rebuild community.

Build Knowledge of What Works

The seventh strategy has to do with the responsibility all of us have to continue to *build a sturdy knowledge base about what works*. Those of us involved with community-based interventions have discovered that the old approaches to evaluation are not a good fit with the far-reaching kinds of things we are trying to do.

Parent education and neighborhood rebuilding and family support are not "treatments" like penicillin and cannot be measured that way. They are not like an injection of an antibiotic, whose effectiveness can be assessed if you compare a group of experimental treatment subjects with a group of control subjects. Especially as we try to reach out and change norms in neighborhoods and change how neighborhoods function, we cannot use the kind of evaluation that has been used in the past based on the medical experimental model. It is encouraging that there are people who are thinking about new ways to evaluate those more interactive, more comprehensive, and more community-based trends of intervention.

CONCLUSION

A focus on parenthood in America is an enormously useful reminder of how much better we could do by acting both on our best instincts and on our ample knowledge base.

Successful parent education programs require more than didactive techniques. They provide interaction between parents and professionals in a larger supportive context. They focus on results, adapt models to local circumstances, use intermediary supportive organizations, and draw upon cross-system partnerships in safe neighborhoods. Most important, we need to build transferable knowledge of what works.

As we join with others who are determined to reach all children—such as like Stand for Children, a brand-new, grassroots organizing attempt to leave no child behind—we can work toward the day when every American child grows up with a full stake in the American dream.

NOTES

1. Schorr, L. (1988) *Within our reach: Breaking the cycle of disadvantage.* New York: Doubleday.

2. Schorr, L. (1997) *Common purpose: Strengthening families and neighborhoods to rebuild America.* New York: Doubleday.

23

Parent Power

SYLVIA ANN HEWLETT

In the mid-1990s, the Larry King radio show was one of those hugely popular call-in radio shows that reached vast numbers of people across the country. It aired between 10:00 P.M. and 2:00 A.M. All kinds of people called in to talk to Larry: lonely truck drivers spinning along interstate highways trying to stay awake; security guards and insomniacs killing the dead hours at the middle of the night—and new mothers and fathers struggling to deal with 2:00 A.M. feedings.

One call came from Gary, who was twenty-seven years old and lived in Phoenix, Arizona. Gary wanted to talk about what was going on in his family. He and his wife had just put their three-week-old baby daughter in a kennel.

"A kennel!" Larry was shocked and disbelieving. "You put your baby in a kennel?"

"Hold on," Gary said, becoming defensive. "Let me explain."

Gary and his wife, Brenda, both worked full-time. He was a maintenance person at a local office complex; she worked as a checkout clerk at a convenience store. Together they earned twenty-three thousand dollars a year, a sum of money that "didn't go a whole distance in Phoenix." After taxes their joint take-home pay was just over four hundred dollars a week, half of which went to pay the rent. When their daughter, Jenny, was born, they found themselves dealing with heavy-duty problems. For starters, neither of their jobs carried medical insurance, and consequently Jenny's birth triggered some huge bills: $3,930 to be precise. As Gary put it, "Jenny will be three years old before we have paid off the obstetrician." Another problem they faced was that neither of them was entitled to parenting leave. They worked for small employers and did not qualify for job-protected leave under the terms of the Family and Medical Leave Act, which excludes businesses with fewer than fifty employees. Brenda could not simply quit her job, as Gary's paycheck did not even cover rent and utilities.

They coped with the actual birth by fudging and lying through their teeth. Brenda called in sick for ten days, then used up a week of accumulated vacation. When Jenny was two and a half weeks old they hit the daycare market in Phoenix and found that the only thing they could afford was "informal" family daycare, which in their neighborhood boiled down to a private home where two elderly women—unlicensed and untrained—looked after eighteen babies and toddlers. When Gary dropped Jenny off, he discovered to his horror that the other children were strapped in car seats watching television, dirty and disconsolate. Despite a frantic search Gary and Brenda had so far failed to find anything better. Their budget was forty dollars a week—tops—and this is what it bought you on the private daycare market in Phoenix. In Gary's bitter words, "Dogs and cats have a better deal. At least kennels are tightly regulated in this city and are required to live up to some kind of standard of cleanliness and care."

Gary's parting shot was indignant: "We're not welfare cheats. We're just regular Americans working as hard as we know how in order to do the right thing for our kid. Why is it so difficult? Why is everything stacked against us? We feel such shame that we can't do better by our baby." Gary's voice rose in raw, sharp pain as he faded off the air.

There was a short silence as Larry King struggled to absorb the meaning of Gary's poignant words. He then cleared his throat and offered some tentative sympathy. What a stressful situation. How could any family deal well with such an impossible set of circumstances?

Gary's story is far from being exceptional. In a nation of plummeting blue-collar wages and threadbare social supports, hundreds of thousands of Americans are in precisely the same situation as Gary and Brenda when they embark on the serious business of raising a child. Unlike new parents in other rich nations, American mothers and fathers are expected to do a stellar job without the benefits of a living wage, medical coverage, or paid parenting leave. In 1996 there were six million American families in which two adults held four jobs in order to keep the show on the road. Falling wages and heightened insecurity are forcing more and more parents to work longer hours. Like hamsters on a wheel they are running harder and harder to stay even.

THE WAR AGAINST PARENTS

Despite the importance of parents, we have made it extremely difficult for mothers and fathers to do a good job by their children. For thirty years big business, government, and the wider culture have waged a silent war against parents, undermining the work that they do.

Mothers and fathers have been hurt by falling wages, pounded by tax and housing policy, undercut by divorce laws, and invaded and degraded by the media. Our leaders talk as though they value families but act as though families were a last priority. We live in a nation where market work, centered on competition, profits, and greed, increasingly crowd out nonmarket work, centered on sacrifice, care, and commitment.

What really counts in America is how much you get paid and what you can buy. Small wonder then that parenting is a dying art. Small wonder then that parents have less and less time for their children. And time is, of course, at the heart of the childrearing enterprise. Being a good parent requires providing a child with the gifts of love, attention, energy, and resources, generously and unstintingly over a long period of time. It involves nourishing a small body, but it also involves growing a child's soul—sharing the stories and rituals that awaken a child's spirit and nurturing the spiritual bonds that create meaning and morality in that child's life. None of these tasks is easily undertaken by stressed-out contemporary parents.

A Shared Struggle

One of the greatest surprises of my work with Cornel West, professor of philosophy of religion and Afro-American studies at Harvard University, over the last three years has been the discovery of powerful common ground. Despite our obvious differences—and who could be more different than a black father from a blue-collar neighborhood in Sacramento and a white mother from a working-class community in South Wales—we share the bedrock stuff: we are crazy about our kids. This might not be obvious every hour of every day, because our teenagers are capable of being as exasperating and challenging as any others, but when push comes to shove, we know we would give our lives for them. There is not a whole lot in life that can compete with this commitment.

We also share a load of frustration and guilt. For two decades we have been on the front lines wrestling with the enormous challenge of trying to be a good mother and a good father in this parent-hurting society of ours. We have dealt with the same problems as millions of moms and dads across the country: too much work, too little support or recognition, and never enough time or energy for our children.

For me the most painful crunch came with my second pregnancy, when I discovered I was carrying twins. I gave serious thought to taking a leave of absence from my job, but my place of work had no maternity or parenting leave policy. In fact my boss told me that if I took time off I would lose my job. Twelve years of grinding work had gone into this career of mine, and I just could not toss it aside; my paycheck was too important to my growing family. So I decided to stick by my job and stamp down my worries.

When I was six months pregnant, I was sitting in my office in a state of utter exhaustion after a ten-hour work day, trying to summon up enough energy to go home, when liquid began to trickle down my legs. As the trickle turned into a stream, I realized in horror that my waters had broken and that it was much too early to go into labor. I was rushed to the hospital, and two days later I gave birth to twins. One baby was dead, the other was dying. For a long time afterwards life was truly hard to bear. I mourned my children with an intensity that frightened me. I felt I had failed to protect my babies and, therefore, had no pity on myself.

That dark winter of 1979–80 put me in touch with the significance of social supports. The right to parenting leave would have made an enormous difference to the life chances of my babies. At the time I wondered how other women dealt with hostile work environments. And the fact is they do not. The sad fact is millions of American women are pushed to the edge when they give birth to children. Despite the Family and Medical Leave Act of 1993, 30 percent of working women still have no right to time off for pregnancy or childbirth because they work for a company with fewer than fifty employees.[1] They are in precisely the same position I was in when I lost the twins: they have to choose, either their babies or their jobs.

PARENTS MAKE A DIFFERENCE

Parents are an enormously powerful force in the lives of children. Whether Johnny can read, whether Johnny knows right from wrong, whether Johnny is a happy, well-adjusted kid or sullen and self-destructive: it has a whole lot to do with the kind of parenting Johnny has received. If Johnny's mom and dad have been able to come through with sustained, steadfast, loving attention, the odds are Johnny is on track to become a productive, compassionate citizen. If they have not, Johnny is in trouble—and so is our nation.

Thirty years ago Chicago sociologist James S. Coleman showed that parental involvement mattered far more in determining school success than any attribute of the formal education system. Across a wide range of subject areas, in literature, science, and reading, Coleman estimated that the parent was twice as powerful as the school in determining achievement at age fourteen.[2]

Psychologist Lawrence Steinberg recently completed a six-year study of twenty thousand teenagers in nine different communities and confirms the importance of parents. Steinberg shows that one out of three parents is "seriously disengaged" from his or her adolescent's education, and this is the primary reason why so many American students perform below their potential—and below students in other wealthy countries.[3]

A weight of evidence now demonstrates ominous links between absentee parents and a wide range of behavioral and emotional problems in children. A 1997 study of ninety thousand teenagers, the Add Health Project undertaken by the Carolina Population Center and the Adolescent Health Program at the University of Minnesota, found that youngsters are less likely get pregnant, use drugs, or become involved in crime when they spend significant time with their parents. This study found that the mere physical presence of a parent in the home after school, at dinner, and at bedtime significantly reduces the incidence of risky behavior among teenagers.[4]

Parents Strive to Do the Right Thing

Parents are not less well-intentioned than they used to be. They do not love their children less. They are as passionately attached to their children as they have ever been. In their gut they understand that they are indispensable—that three-week-old infants should not be in "kennels," that eleven-year-olds should not be home alone—and they strain and stretch to buck the trends and come through for their children.

"You have to work more than one job just to keep up with where you were three, four, five years ago," said Ed Gagnon, a New York City police sergeant who moonlights at two other jobs because of mortgage payments and tax bills.

Ed has spent sixteen years on the force and now earns sixty-five thousand dollars a year, but that only brings in three thousand a month in terms of take-home pay. Of this Ed shells out twenty-one hundred dollars a month in carrying charges for the modest home he bought five years ago. "We don't have a huge mortgage by New York City standards, but the rate is high (8 percent) and our property taxes are crazy—they just hit seven hundred dollars a month. I reckon I spend close to seventy percent of my sergeant's pay on housing. With a wife and two kids there is just no way that I can make the nine hundred dollars left over stretch an entire month. So four years ago I took on a second job working nights as a security guard at a shopping mall. Then that wasn't enough, so last year I took on this third job on the weekends. I load passengers and luggage for the Royal Caribbean Cruise Lines. I try real hard to see my kids in the afternoons. I just got my police shift changed to the six A.M. to two P.M. slot so I can pick up my eleven-year-old from the bus stop. Now that's made a difference. You should see his eyes light up when he sees me waiting there. He's handicapped and goes to this special school, and he kind of relies on his dad to be his buddy. It would be great to have more time for him at the weekends."

WHAT CAN PARENTS DO?

So how do we turn this thing around and give new support to parents? Over the past three years we have gathered testimony from parents in communities across America and constructed a Parents' Bill of Rights—a document imbued with healing and hope for beleaguered mothers and fathers everywhere.[5] Whether you are black, brown, male, or female, whether your family income is twenty-three thousand or eighty-five thousand dollars a year, these measures can help you come through for your children.

The following Parents' Bill of Rights is offered as a blueprint for supporting parents. It is not a top-down directive but presents a list of options—sometimes overlapping, sometimes less than comprehensive—for the serious consideration of parents. We mean for mothers and fathers to try it on for size and then mold and add to it as they see fit.[6]

A Parents' Bill of Rights

Mothers and fathers are entitled to:

I. Time for their children
Grant parents the "gift" of time by providing twenty-four weeks of paid parenting leave at the time of birth. Develop flexible workplaces that give working parents discretion over when and where work is done; create part-time career ladders; and devise special tax breaks for at-home parents.

II. Economic security
Underpin the lives of parents by guaranteeing a living wage for full-time workers. Support school-to-work initiatives; offer help with housing; and provide a family allowance for families with children under six. Eliminate payroll taxes for families with small children; and get rid of sales taxes on children's necessities such as diapers and car seats.

III. A profamily electoral system
Encourage mothers and fathers to participate in our democracy by creating incentives to vote and easing registration procedures. Make election days national holidays; and attach voter registration forms to

the papers parents fill out when they obtain a birth certificate for a child.

IV. A profamily legal structure
Strengthen the institution of marriage by promoting premarital counseling and making it harder for couples to split up. Guarantee generous visitation rights for noncustodial parents; restructure welfare benefits to favor two-parent families; and replace the current emphasis on foster care with an emphasis on adoption.

V. A supportive external environment
Extend the school day and year; encourage the formation of parent patrols to create safe zones around schools; and outlaw the sale of handguns to young people. Increase spending on early childhood education and fund higher salaries for childcare workers. Underwrite drug prevention programs in every school; mandate a Children's Hour on network television; and make it much harder for kids to rent an R-rated movie or buy a CD with a parent advisory label. Create a powerful advocacy voice for parents, like the American Association of Retired Persons (AARP) is for seniors.

VI. Honor and dignity
Establish an Index of Parent Well-Being to provide a counterpoint to the Dow Jones Index. Promote National Parents' Day. Introduce an education credit for at-home parents and offer specially-designed parent privileges. Priority seating on buses and priority parking in shopping malls for pregnant women and parents with small children would make our public places much more welcoming to families with children.

The Power of Collective Action

This brings us to a crucial question. How do we turn this Parents' Bill of Rights into a reality? The answer lies in collective action. There are sixty-three million parents in America, and the vast majority are desperately worried about finding enough time and energy for their children. (According to a survey undertaken by the National Parenting Association in 1996, 91 percent of parents see the time crunch as a huge problem).[7] If mothers and fathers were to join together and speak with one voice, we could produce new clout for parents in Congress and in boardrooms around the country. [8] An AARP for parents could make sure that American parents finally get the support they need and so richly deserve. We are not talking selfish, special interest group politics here. Children are not bit players. They are 100 percent of our collective future, and it behooves us as a nation—parents and nonparents alike—to make sure that mothers and fathers do good jobs as parents.

NOTES

1. The 1993 Family and Medical Leave Act entities eligible employees to take up to twelve weeks of unpaid, job-protected leave for specified family and medical reasons, including childbirth and adoption. More than a third (36.5 percent) of men and slightly less than a third (30.9 percent) of women are not covered by the FMLA. See Commission on Leave, U.S. Department of Labor (1996) *A workable balance: Report to congress on family and medical leave policies.* Washington, D.C.: USGPO, p. xvi.

2. Coleman, J. S. (1973) Effects of school on learning: The IEA findings. Paper presented at the Conference on Educational Achievement, Harvard University, November, p. 40.

3. Steinberg, L. (1996) Failure outside the classroom. *Wall Street Journal,* July 11, p. A14; and Steinberg, L., et al. (1996) *Beyond the classroom: Why school reform has failed and what parents need to do.* New York: Simon & Schuster, p. 119.

4. Resnick, M. D., et al. (1997) Protecting adolescents from harm. *Journal of the American Medical Association* (September): 823–832.

5. National Parenting Association (1996) *What will parents vote for? Findings of the first national survey of parent priorities.* New York: National Parenting Association.

6. Hewlett, S. A., & West, C. (1998) *The war against parents.* Boston: Houghton Mifflin.

7. National Parenting Association (1996) *What will parents vote for? Findings of the first national survey of parent priorities.* New York: National Parenting Association.

8. Contact: National Parenting Association, 444 Park Avenue South, Suite 602, New York, NY 10016, (800) 709-8795, fax (212) 679-3127, info@parentsunite.org, www.parentsunite.org.

Epilog

JACK C. WESTMAN

> The institution of the family is decisive in determining not only if a person has the capacity to love another individual but in the larger sense whether he is capable of loving his fellow men collectively. The whole of society rests on this foundation for stability, understanding and social peace.
>
> Martin Luther King Jr., 1965

Thirty years ago experts assured us that technology would bring more time for leisure and for our families. The opposite has occurred. The more money we have, the more money we want; the more we can do, the more we want to do. Ironically, as we enter the new millennium, most parents are too busy to grow with their children. Yet, whether we are consciously aware of it or not, most of us yearn for deeper levels of fulfillment in life.

One way to find fulfillment is to share the wonders of life with children and to participate in their growth. But too many parents, and other adults, miss this opportunity by doing things for, rather than with, children. Too many parents have limited opportunities to be with their children. Added to this is instability and disadvantage in the family lives of too many children.

We need to shift our focus from shaping children to conform with our desires for them to improving the quality of their family lives and their environments. We need to think about why childrearing is not recognized as the foundation of our society. We need to think about ways in which our society can be more supportive of parenthood.

TURNING TO THEORY FOR HELP

Theories are not facts, but they can help organize our thinking about complicated social problems, such as instability and disadvantage in the lives of children. These problems defy logic and are deeply embedded in human nature and in our society. Rushing to find solutions for them is counterproductive when the name of each problem is unclear, when the causes are uncertain, and when linear, single-cause, single-effect interventions can make matters worse.

Addressing instability and disadvantage in the lives of children calls for sound judgment and wisdom, best generated in deliberative dialog. Factual information is necessary but not sufficient. Looking to experts to tell us what to do is not productive. Instead we need to work through conflicting motives and perceptions. Our challenge is to identify actions that will narrow the gap between what is and what we agree ought to be. In order to find agreement on what ought to be, we need to look at our fundamental beliefs.

The belief that an objectively verifiable universe can be known by human beings with certainty underlies much present-day difficulty in understanding and solving our social problems. It encourages the belief that we can achieve certainty and predictability in our lives. It encourages the belief that everything will be better if we just do one thing—the thing I advocate!

In fact, modern science recognizes that uncertainty and unpredictability are inherent in all living systems. We do not live in a static, unchanging society. We live in evolving social systems in an evolving Universe. General Systems Theory, first proposed by Ludwig von Bertalanffy and elaborated by James G. Miller, holds that understanding living systems requires focusing on the relationships between the components of a system and between that system and its environment.[1] The organization of this book is based on General Systems Theory and recent versions of chaos and complexity theory.

Living systems, whether a human body, family, community, or society, require the continuous inflow of energy to maintain themselves. They are always in a state of flux. The more complex a system is, the more unstable it is. Thus, social systems from the family to society are inherently unstable and vulnerable to break down in to chaos. In fact, being on the edge of chaos provides a strong motivation for constructive change.[2]

The inevitability of uncertainty and change is a difficult fact for most of us to face. It takes work to maintain any system whether it be our bodies, our families, our schools, our communities, or our society. Unless we tend to the needs of our bodies and families, we jeopardize our personal well-being. Unless we vigilantly guard our liberties and maintain social order, we lose our freedom and our safety. Anyone who has lived in a totalitarian state knows how fragile liberty is. Anyone who has experienced a natural disaster or a riot knows how important the police and the national guard are when order breaks down. The same applies when families break down and courts must be brought into the lives of parents and children.

In the political and economic spheres, our civilization appears to be evolving toward increasing stability. As we enter the twenty-first century, democracy and controlled capitalism are the favored choices for technologically advanced societies. However, in the social and moral spheres history appears to be cyclic, with social order ebbing and flowing over the course of generations.

In describing the cyclic phenomenon of social disorder, Émile Durkheim identified "anomie"—valuelessness—as so intensely uncomfortable that societies seek new rules to replace ones that have been undercut.[3] He traced the social disorder of the late eighteenth and nineteenth centuries to the disruptive effects of the so-called industrial revolution. We now are in the similar throes of "anomie"—valuelessness—as we adapt to the information revolution.

More specifically, we now are in a cycle of disorder in our families and schools. This is progress from the cycle of community disorder in the 1960s and 1970s. But instability in the family lives of children is a serious social problem. Childhood poverty has increased. Classroom control and school safety are as important as education, sometimes more important. The extension into middle-class schools of children shooting children exposes the extent to which significant numbers of our young feel hopeless, abandoned, and enraged.

All of this means that instability and disadvantage (being on the edge of chaos) in the lives of our children can offer opportunities for change, if we can identify and agree upon our long-term goals for children. Our implicit goals for childrearing actually have been codified in juvenile and family legislation and iterated in court decisions about family relationships. We expect parents to:

- Rear their children to become productive consumers, who are informed citizens.
- Rear their children to become responsible adults capable of committed attachments to other people and of contributing to the common good.

When we look at these expectations of them, we see that we rely on parents to instill our basic values in children so that they will become productive citizens. The need to explicitly recognize the essential role of parenthood in our society and to support parents in their childrearing efforts becomes obvious. Parents are antidotes to our contemporary "anomie." At the same time, because even small choices we make as individuals and as governments have long-range consequences, we need to base our support of parenthood on our long-term goals for our society, not on the exigencies of the moment.

GOALS FOR OUR SOCIETY

We human beings are social creatures. We develop societies based on shared goals in response to human dilemmas. In America our goals are based on maximizing individual freedom (rights) within the context of the common good (responsibilities).

Our society tries to balance the needs of groups with the needs of individuals, the needs of individuals with the needs of families, the needs of women with the needs of men, and the needs of adults with the needs of children. Our society has created values in the form of laws that balance our rights with our responsibilities.

Values such as honesty, respect for others, keeping commitments, and justice are more than worthwhile virtues. They have tangible economic and humanistic payoffs and inform our laws. They help individuals, groups, and our society achieve their goals. They are learned by children from their parents. But parents need support from the broader society in the face of strong peer, neighborhood, community, and media influences that undermine their efforts.

The following graphic contrasts the present status of parenthood in the United States, where parents bear the full responsibility for nurturing and protecting their children, with a more equitable paradigm that backs up our society's expectations of parents with society's support of parenthood.

PARENTHOOD: PRESENT	**PARENTHOOD: FUTURE**
Parents feel isolated.	Neighborhoods and communities support parents.
Child's future determined by parents' resources.	Every child has an opportunity to succeed.
Parents expected to protect children from risks.	Society helps parents protect children from risks.
Society intervenes only after neglect or abuse.	Society acts to prevent child neglect and abuse.
Tax structure unfavorable for childrearing.	Tax structure favors childrearing.

The first step toward realizing this paradigm of societal support for parenthood is to make our goals for our society explicit. What kind of a society do we want? What kind of persons do we want our children to become?

Our society needs law-abiding citizens. Our economy needs producer-consumers. Without effective parenting that builds respect for others and a work ethic, children will not become the kind of citizens we need. Thus parenthood is the foundation of our society and our economy. Without progeny who become law-abiding citizens, no society can survive. Without productive consumers, our economy will not prosper. In the long run, parenthood is more important to our society than paid vocations.

The second step is to recognize that "work" is defined in our capitalistic economy as a paid activity. Unpaid activity like childrearing is not regarded as work. This conflicts with the fact that childrearing is work and has vital financial value for our economy. Both parenthood and paid vocations are careers.

The third step is to recognize that parenthood truly is the foundation of our society and deserves support at all levels of our society. Our childrearing and societal goals are congruent. These goals and our shared values provide a template for stabilizing the lives of children and for reducing childhood disadvantage.

Social support in return for service has been a characteristic rationale for Americans to combine their deep respect for individual freedom and initiative with due regard for the obligations of all members of society to further the common good.[4] Social Security and the post–World War II GI Bill are prime examples. The broad constituency of parents and child advocates now represented by a wide variety of volunteer organizations at the local, state, and national levels could work toward recognizing the service that parents provide to society through the personal sacrifices they make in rearing our nation's children.

STRATEGY FOR ACHIEVING OUR SOCIETAL AND CHILDREARING GOALS

What can we do to narrow the gap between what is and what we agree ought to be our goals for childrearing and for our society? The most important strategy is to create opportunities for parental dialog at every system level that affects parents and their children. This would permit working through conflicting motives and perceptions so that problem-solving techniques based on attainable goals for supporting parenthood can be applied to the following challenges.

Challenges for Our Society

As Americans, we vigorously assert our individual rights and downplay our responsibilities. In contrast, we expect parents to bear the responsibility for rearing our children without granting them sufficient rights, as outlined in Sylvia Ann Hewlett and Cornel West's "A Parents' Bill of Rights" in chapter 23. The imbalance between rights and responsibilities lies at the core of our society and of our family lives.

The multiple risks that children experience due to social, economic, health, and other factors require community-wide and societal efforts that are comprehensive and interdisciplinary. Such an approach needs to be sensitive to and celebrate the racial and cultural diversity that is the strength of our nation.

We know that children who are not nurtured in their homes fall behind in developing language, physical, social, and learning skills. But our service systems tend to view such children apart from their family and community contexts. The focus is almost exclusively on individual problems and risks, while ignoring assets and liabilities in both families and communities.

Solutions to disadvantage and instability in the lives of children will come from strategies that are strength-based, culturally appropriate, family-focused, and preventive. Top-down approaches must be connected with bottom-up activities so that people can participate in making decisions that affect them. In the process rights and responsibilities must be balanced.

Strategies are needed to address the following formidable challenges that our society faces in according parenthood the status it deserves:

Economic factors.

- Childrearing is not viewed as having economic value.
- Materialistic values place consumerism above personal relationships. ("I am what I own" rather than "I am what I stand for.")
- Parental employment is often seen as a way of obtaining fulfillment in a career and of adding to family income rather than as a financial necessity.
- More hours of work or an additional job are required for the financial security provided by a forty-hour-a-week job a generation ago.
- Employers prefer employees without family responsibilities.
- The frequency of divorce and cohabitation introduces the need to plan for fending for oneself and children after separation.
- A single breadwinner fears unemployment.

Legal factors.

- Giving birth to or conceiving a child often is regarded as the sole determinant of parenthood.
- A child often is viewed as the possession of the persons who conceived or gave birth to that child.

Political factors.

- There is resistance to expecting people to be prepared for marriage and childrearing by both the political left, on the grounds of individual freedom, and the political right, on the grounds of family privacy.
- There is no unified political voice for parents.

All of these obstacles could be overcome if our society recognized parenthood as a career with economic and social value defined by the person committed out of love to lifelong rearing of a child, not solely by the events of conception and childbirth.

Challenges for Parents

Genetic and peer influences on children play important roles in their temperaments, fashions, and interests and can override parental influences. However, overemphasizing these factors takes the focus off the importance of parent-child relationships. When it comes to character, the origins of empathy, persistence, and morality are within the domain of parenthood.

When there are clear boundaries between childhood and parenthood, childrearing is a process of mutual growth for both children and parents. When those boundaries are blurred, the rights of children and parents are not balanced by their respective responsibilities. The specific rights of parents and the rights of children surface when divorce or child abuse and neglect occur. But they also are a part of daily life in families where the question of whose way will prevail arises frequently.

One of the reasons for blurred boundaries in families is that parental and child responsibilities are not clearly defined. Unless parents are in charge of their families, the exploitative tendencies of children can make parenthood stressful. As a result, when a stressed parent has a choice, the inducements are strong to delegate parenting functions to childcare persons and to schools.

Parenthood is a committed, mutual growth-producing relationship between a parent and a child. Parents can delegate caregiving, educational, and protective parenting functions and retain emotional and moral developmental functions. This is what most parents try to do. But they lack support for their efforts in our society because parenthood is not viewed as an economically essential career, and because they do not have an effective political voice. In fact, strong pressures described in this book undermine and devalue parenthood.

Parental efforts to integrate employment away from home with childcare exemplify the dilemma over how many parenting functions can be delegated without undesirable consequences. Israel has a relevant experience. After some sixty years, the Israeli kibbutzim discontinued childcare during early infancy because of the long-term negative effects of even high-quality infant childcare on parent-child relationships.[5] Now during their first three months, kibbutz infants receive exclusive maternal care at home in all but three of the 260 kibbutzim. During the second half of the infants' first year, caregivers gradually assume responsibility for the children as the mothers return to their employment. As it did in Israel, it will take years to assess the long-term effects of current practices of delegated infant and toddler childcare in the United States on parent-child relationships, on child development, and on childrearing patterns.

Parents may founder because they live in stressful environments with limited financial support and inadequate health care; because they lack knowledge of child development; because they have unusually difficult babies; or because they have not received adequate nurturing themselves.

Parents need to find ways of dealing with the following factors that detract from the personal fulfillment of parenthood:

- the decline of committed, sacrificial relationships
- guilt for being an imperfect parent
- self-absorbed individualism that weakens family bonds
- an ethos that encourages parents to please and entertain their children and discourages helping children learn to tolerate frustration and to postpone gratification
- an ethos that deemphasizes the responsibility of children to contribute to the well-being of the family
- competition that pressures children to excel
- reliance on experts for advice about minimum necessary parenting
- childrearing stress that leads parents to prefer employment away from home
- childrearing stress that contributes to marital dissatisfaction
- viewing children as property so that parents do not grow with their children

In a broader sense, although individual parents have little power to influence peer groups, schools, neighborhoods, and communities, parents acting together have a great deal of power.

WHAT CAN BE DONE?

Families are affected at so many system levels that the only effective strategy is to involve or represent parents in all decision making that affects them and their children. Empowering parents and grandparents to represent their own interests would bring the parent and child perspective to each of the childrearing challenges confronting our society and parents. Current conditions in the United States all too often disenfranchise parents, who need to be involved in dialogs about social policies at all levels. However, because we live in a democracy that responds to interest groups, support for parenthood will not be forthcoming unless parents and grandparents seek it.

Parents are realizing that in order to become effective advocates for their children and their families, they need to be well versed in the workings of government and business. The family support movement and parent and child advocacy organizations are giving parents a growing voice in our society.

The Family Support Movement

The Family Support America is a national leader in the family support movement.[6] It is committed to serving constituencies at all levels: government, academia, networks, practitioners, community leaders, and parents. It provides technical assistance and consulting services, which model the roles that parents can play in society and the ways in which parenthood can be respected and honored.

Family support programs act as models for the burgeoning movement to involve parents in the design and governance of human service systems and for efforts to develop parents as leaders. Any effort to provide services and support to families and communities is inappropriate without attention to the unique cultural, ethnic, and linguistic norms that the communities and families value.

Parent training materials are available to enhance the capacity of parents to advocate for themselves, for their families, and for their own parents. These efforts tend to center around a variety of issues that cross generations, such as family-supportive tax policies, quality education for all ages, accessible childcare for employed parents, health care for children and the elderly, and safe neighborhoods.

A National Organization of Parents

If organized, the some sixty-two million parents in the United States would be a powerful force in creating a society that respects and supports parenthood. Such an organization would give parents a unified voice in defining and advocating equitable social, health, and economic policies for families. It would provide information, education, resources, and other benefits to help parents rear their children. It would help to equip parents with the tools they need to empower themselves. It would help to remove barriers to the engagement of parents in decision making at all levels of society.

One strategy for forming a national organization for parents is to involve existing child, parent, and grandparent advocacy organizations in finding ways to further their own missions and the interests of their members through representation in a broadly based national organization.

CONCLUSION

The time has come to give up searching for a single inoculation that will protect against the effects of growing up in unstable families and in disadvantaged families in neighborhoods without decent schools, safe streets, and a sense of community.

This book calls attention to the growing body of knowledge for designing systems and policies to support families and to build a society that values parenthood as the most important job one can have. Supporting parenthood should be a clear priority in our schools, neighborhoods, communities, and society.

We should hold society accountable for recognizing the social and economic value of parenthood and for supporting, rather than undermining, family life. Social policies should not be based on the assumption that full-time employment of both parents will continue without adjustments in workplaces. Already the prediction by futurists that we will become a society of home-based workers is being realized in flexible work locations, job sharing, schedules, and hours that benefit some parents.

We should hold parents accountable for responsibilities that cannot be delegated without undermining parenthood. These responsibilities include reliable availability throughout childhood and adolescence; an unconditional relationship that fosters a child's moral and emotional development; arranging for a child's education and health care; and acting with a child's interests in mind.

We should hold children accountable for cooperating with their parents and contributing to the well-being of their families.

Recognizing society's debt to parents by supporting parenthood is in everyone's interests. Parents banding together across cultures and socioeconomic classes can change our society. If parents had more political clout, we would focus on our goals for childrearing and for our society. We would work to provide children the kinds of family lives and environments they need. We would have less crime, safer streets, more integrity in commerce and politics, and more wholesome environments. We would find more opportunities for personal fulfillment in life beyond producing and consuming goods. Most important, we would articulate and apply our society's basic values.

NOTES

1. Von Bertalanffy, L. (1968) *General systems theory.* New York: Braziller; and Miller, J. G. (1978) *Living systems.* New York: McGraw-Hill.

2. Kossman, M. R., & Bullrich, S. (1997) Systematic chaos: Self-organizing systems and the process of change. In F. Masterpasqua & P. A. Perna (eds.), *The psychological meaning of chaos: Translating theory into practice.* Washington, D.C.: American Psychological Association.

3. Watts Miller, W. (1996) *Durkheim, morals and modernity.* Montreal and Buffalo: McGill-Queens University Press.

4. Skocpol, T. (1997) *Lessons from history: Building a movement for America's children.* Washington, D.C.: Children's Partnership.

5. Aviezer, O., Van Ijzendoorn, M. H., Sagi, A, & Schuengel, C. (1994) "Children of the dream" revisited: 70 years of collective early child care in Israeli kibbutzim. *Psychological Bulletin* 116: 99–116.

6. Family Resource Coalition of America, 20 North Wacker Drive, Suite 1100, Chicago, IL 60606; (312) 338–0900; fax (212) 338–1522; e-mail frca@frca.org.

Contributors

Index

Contributors

Diane B. Adams holds a master's degree from the University of Wisconsin–Madison in continuing and vocational education and has an adjunct joint appointment in the Department of Human Development and Family Studies there. For over twenty years, she was affiliated with Community Coordinated Child Care (4-C), one of the first childcare resource and referral agencies in the United States. Her publications include *Parent Education and Public Policy* (coedited with Ron Haskins), *The Family Child Care Handbook,* and *The Nuts and Bolts of Child Care/Early Education Administration.* She has been a consultant with the statewide Child Care Resource & Referral Network (Wisconsin) and works with colleagues in Kenya and Uganda on early childhood issues. She has just become the project manager with the Wisconsin Child Care Research Partnership, a three-year federal project designed to answer the question: "What is the level of quality of childcare for subsidized children in Wisconsin?"

Benjamin A. Benson holds a B.E. from the University of Wisconsin–Whitewater and an M.S. in education administration from the University of Wisconsin–Madison. He has thirty years of experience as a classroom teacher and twelve years as a member of the Middleton–Cross Plains Area School Board. His publications include *Success in School: Handbook for Students and Parents.* In 1992, he was a finalist for Wisconsin Middle/Junior High Teacher of the Year.

Marc H. Bornstein, Ph.D., is senior investigator and head of Child Family Research at the National Institute of Child Health and Development. Among his numerous publications, he is editor of *Child Development* and of *Parenting: Science and Practice,* of the *Handbook of Parenting* (vols. 1–4), and of *Maternal Responsiveness: Characteristics and Consequences;* a coauthor of *Development in Infancy* and *Perceiving and Comprehending Metaphor;* and a coeditor of *Developmental Psychology: An*

Advanced Textbook and *The Role of Play in the Development of Thought.* He is the author of several children's books and puzzles in the *Child's World* series.

T. Berry Brazelton, M.D. is Professor Emeritus of Pediatrics at Children's Hospital, Harvard Medical School, Boston, Massachusetts. He has written nearly two hundred scientific papers and thirty books, including his most recent ones, *Touchpoints Vol. I, The Irreducible Needs of Children* (with Stanley Greenspan), and *Touchpoints Vol. II* (to be released in 2001).

Urie Bronfenbrenner is the Jacob Gould Sherman Professor of Human Development and Family Studies and of Psychology at Cornell University. He received a B.A. from Cornell, an M.A. from Harvard, and a Ph.D. from the University of Michigan. He has pursued three mutually reinforcing themes: (1) developing theory and corresponding research designs at the frontiers of developmental science; (2) laying out the implications and applications of developmental theory and research for policy and practice; and (3) communicating the findings of developmental research to undergraduate students, the general public, and decision makers. His widely published contributions have won him honors and distinguished awards in the United States and abroad.

Larry Bumpass is a professor of sociology at the University of Wisconsin–Madison and codirector of the National Survey of Families and Households. He is widely known for his extensive research on the social demography of the family, including cohabitation, marriage, the stability of unions, nonmarital and marital fertility, and the implications of these processes for children's living arrangements and subsequent life course development.

Joanne Cantor, Ph.D., is a professor of communication arts at the University of Wisconsin–Madison. In addition to her book, *Mommy, I'm Scared,* she has published numerous articles and chapters on the impact of the media on children and adolescents. Her research has been supported by the National Institute of Mental Health and the National Science Foundation. She consults with many organizations, including the American Medical Association and the National PTA, on issues related to children and television.

Stephanie Coontz teaches history and family studies at Evergreen State College in Olympia, Washington. Her numerous publications and books include *The Way We Never Were: American Families and the Nostalgia*

Trap, The Way We Really Are: Coming to Terms with America's Changing Families, and *American Families: A Multicultural Reader* (with Maya Parson and Gabrielle Raley). She currently is researching how the processes of growing up and the dynamics of parenting have changed in the United States.

James Garbarino, Ph.D., is a professor of human development and codirector of the Family Life Development Center at Cornell University in Ithaca, New York, and former president of the Erikson Institute for Advanced Study in Child Development. He is the author or editor of numerous articles and books, most recently *Raising Children in a Socially Toxic Environment* and *Lost Boys: Why Our Sons Turn Violent and How We Can Save Them.* Currently he is focusing on the developmental pathways that lead to lethal youth violence and the rehabilitation of violent youthful offenders.

M. Elizabeth Graue, Ph.D., is a professor of early childhood education in the Department of Curriculum and Instruction at the University of Wisconsin–Madison. Her research focuses on children's readiness for kindergarten and on interactions between parents and schools. Her publications include the books *Ready for What? Constructing Meanings of Readiness for Kindergarten* and *Studying Children in Context: Theories, Methods, and Ethics* (with Daniel Walsh).

Patricia M. Greenfield holds a Ph.D. from Harvard University. She is a professor in the Psychology Department of the University of California at Los Angeles. Her interests include cognitive and language development, cross-cultural research, developmental and comparative psycholinguistics, and the cognitive and developmental effects of media. Among her numerous articles and books are *Cross-cultural Roots of Minority Child Development* and *Interacting with Video* (both with R. Cocking).

Heidi Hammes has been a program and planning analyst for the Wisconsin Department of Workforce Development since 1994. She is a member of the team that developed and implemented Wisconsin's early welfare reform demonstration projects leading up to the Wisconsin Works program. Prior to her work at the department, she spent four years at the Dane County Department of Human Services as a caseworker for the Aid to Families with Dependent Children, Food Stamps, and Medicaid programs.

Sylvia Ann Hewlett, Ph.D., is widely known as an economist, a public speaker, and the author of several books, including the award-winning

When the Bough Breaks and, most recently, *The War against Parents*. She is the founder and chairman of the National Parenting Association and was awarded a fellowship at the Center for the Study of Values in Public Life at the Harvard Divinity School.

Lois Wladis Hoffman, Ph.D., is Professor Emerita of Psychology at the University of Michigan. She is a developmental psychologist with a particular interest in the socialization of the child. She is widely known for her studies on the effects of mothers' employment. Her books include *The Employed Mother in America* (1963) and *Working Mothers* (1974). Her most recent book, written with Lise Youngblade, is *Mothers at Work: Effects on Children's Well-being* (1999).

Beverley H. Johnson is president and chief executive officer of the Institute for Family-Centered Care in Bethesda, Maryland. She has had clinical and administrative experience in an academic medical center and served as a hospital trustee for other health and educational organizations. She has authored and coauthored many publications on family-centered practice in maternity care, newborn intensive care, and pediatrics. She is currently developing patient- and family-centered materials for adult oncology and geriatrics and additional resources for maternal and child health programs.

Robert E. Larzelere is director of Behavioral Healthcare Research at Boys Town, Nebraska, and an adjunct faculty member of the Psychology Department, Munroe-Meyer Institute, University of Nebraska Medical Center, Omaha, Nebraska. He received his Ph.D. from Pennsylvania State University in 1979. He was an NIMH postdoctoral fellow under Murray Straus at the University of New Hampshire and under Gerald Patterson at the Oregon Social Learning Center. He has published extensively on statistics, research methodology, and parental discipline.

Richard M. Lerner is the Bergstrom Chair in Applied Developmental Science in the Eliot-Pearson Department of Child Development at Tufts University. A developmental psychologist, he received a Ph.D. from the City University of New York. He is the author or editor of numerous books and scholarly publications and is the founding editor of the *Journal of Research on Adolescence* and of *Applied Developmental Science*.

Amy I. Nathanson holds a Ph.D. in communication arts from the University of Wisconsin–Madison and is assistant professor in the School of Journalism and Communication at Ohio State University. She studies the uses and effects of television, especially as they relate to children. Her recent work focuses on the role that parents play in mediating the effects of violent television on children's aggression.

E. Ree Noh is a Ph.D. student in developmental psychology at Boston College. She has a particular interest in the bicultural experience of Korean American college students.

David Popenoe holds a Ph.D. from the University of Pennsylvania. He is a professor of sociology at Rutgers University, where he also is codirector of the National Marriage Project and former social and behavioral sciences dean. He specializes in the study of family and community life in modern societies. In addition to numerous professional publications, he is the author or editor of nine books, including *Life without Father, Disturbing the Nest: Family Change and Decline in Modern Societies,* and *The Suburban Environment.*

J. Jean Rogers holds an M.S. degree in counseling and behavioral studies from the University of Wisconsin–Madison and an undergraduate degree in education from Chicago University. She is the administrator of economic support in the Wisconsin Department of Workforce Development, where she oversees welfare programs for the State of Wisconsin. In 1994, she was selected to attend the Harvard University John F. Kennedy School of Government's Program for Senior Executives in State and Local Government.

Lisbeth B. Schorr is a lecturer in social medicine at Harvard University and director of the Harvard Project on Effective Intervention. She has woven strands of experience with social policy and human service programs together to become a national authority on "what works" to improve the future of disadvantaged children and their families and neighborhoods. Her publications include *Common Purpose: Strengthening Families and Neighborhoods to Rebuild America* (1998) and *Within Our Reach: Breaking the Cycle of Disadvantage* (1988).

Lalita K. Suzuki is a doctoral candidate in the Department of Psychology at the University of California at Los Angeles. Her research interests include cultural psychology, life-span development, and Asian American psychology. She is currently working on her dissertation, comparing Euro-American and Asian American children of different ages, and parents, on their views of filial piety and future parent-child relations.

Judith S. Wallerstein was educated at Hunter College, at Columbia University, at Lund University in Sweden, where she received a Ph.D. in psychology, and at the Topeka Institute for Psychoanalysis in Kansas. She is Senior Lecturer Emerita at the University of California at Berkeley, where she was on the faculty of the School of Social Welfare, and founder of the Judith Wallerstein Center for the Family in Transition. The results of her research have been published in numerous journal articles and in the books *Surviving the Breakup: How Children and Parents Cope with Divorce* (with Joan Kelly), *Second Chances: Men, Women, and Children a Decade after Divorce* (with Sandra Blakeslee), and *The Legacy of Divorce: A Twenty-Five-Year Landmark Study* (with Julia Lewis and Sandra Blakeslee).

Bernice Weissbourd, widely known as an initiator and leader of the family support movement, is founder and president of Family Focus, an agency serving families in the Chicago metropolitan area, and the Family Resource Coalition of America, a national organization representing practitioners, researchers, and policy makers in the family support field. She is a contributing editor to *Parents* magazine and has authored and edited numerous publications on family support policies and practices. She is a lecturer at the University of Chicago School of Social Service Administration.

Jack C. Westman holds an M.D. and M.S. from the University of Michigan. He is Professor Emeritus of Psychiatry at the University of Wisconsin Medical School. He has published extensively on individual differences in children, juvenile delinquency, learning disabilities, child abuse and neglect, child advocacy, family therapy, children's and parents' rights, and public policy. He has been the editor of *Child Psychiatry and Human Development,* president of the American Association of Psychiatric Services for Children, and president of the Multidisciplinary Academy of Clinical Education. He currently is president of Wisconsin Cares.

Roger T. Williams has M.S. and Ph.D. degrees in Continuing and Vocational Education from the University of Wisconsin–Madison and is professor and chairman of the Professional Development and Applied Studies Department there. His teaching, writing, and program coordination interests include stress management, team building, prevention and wellness, self-help/mutual support, farm and rural issues, family issues, and men's issues. His chapter grows out of his interest in men's and family issues and his department's cosponsorship of the 1998 Parenthood in America Conference at the University of Wisconsin.

Clancie Mavello Wilson holds undergraduate degrees from Emory University and Tuskegee University, has an M.A. in early childhood development from Atlanta University, and is a Ph.D. student in developmental psychology at Boston College. She taught in public schools for twenty years and is interested in parental and social support of the achievement of adolescents.

Index